David Duff was born in 1912 and educated at Rugby School. He was a member of the London Scottish Regiment and served with the Royal Artillery from 1939–47. He then joined the Cabinet Office Historical Section.

Mr Duff is an experienced biographer of 'royals' and has written *Eugenie and Napoleon III*, *Elizabeth of Glamis*, *Albert and Victoria* and *Alexandra, Princess and Queen.*

Also by David Duff in Sphere Books:

ALEXANDRA: PRINCESS AND QUEEN

George and Elizabeth

A Royal Marriage

DAVID DUFF

SPHERE BOOKS LIMITED
30–32 Gray's Inn Road, London WC1X 8JL

First published in Great Britain by
William Collins Sons & Co Ltd 1983

Published by Sphere Books Ltd 1984

TRADE
MARK

Reproduced, printed and bound in Great Britain by
Hazell Watson & Viney Limited,
Member of the BPCC Group,
Aylesbury, Bucks

For Doreen

ACKNOWLEDGEMENTS

My thanks are due to many people who have helped me with information and anecdotes. In particular, I owe a deep debt of gratitude to Robin Baird-Smith and Gill Gibbins, of Collins, for unceasing aid from the time of the conception of the book in 1981, through each and every chapter and in the production stages, which coincided with a period of personal loss.

CONTENTS

PREFACE

Since the detailed biography by the late Sir John Wheeler-Bennett, published in 1958, little has been written about King George VI, although a number of works have appeared on his consort, now Queen Elizabeth the Queen Mother. A quarter of a century later there begins to emerge, in clear focus, the vital importance of the reign of King George VI and Queen Elizabeth.

It was said by Mr James Maxton in 1936 that the 'Humpty Dumpty' of royalty had fallen from the wall and no power could put him back again. 'Humpty Dumpty' was put back; in a matter of three short years. Even before war broke out the clear-thinking royal couple discarded, in a modern way, those trappings of royalty which had dated, introduced a fresh approach, a 'walk about' image, which has continued ever since and gained strength on the way.

Intense courage was called for in those few critical weeks before the Abdication of Edward VIII. George could not bring himself to believe that he would be King until he heard the words pronounced. The task of succeeding was made even more difficult by the knowledge that there were many people who doubted if he were up to the task and who were considering the possibility of his place being taken by his younger brother, the Duke of Kent. It was not a legal necessity, as was generally thought, that the brother next in age should become King, and in any case George could have opted out had he chosen to do so. He waited for three days, cut off from the King and his advisers, and from senior statesmen, while the decision was made. Thereafter, within hours, he was King. Even so, in the early months of 1937 he had to endure a bitter attack on his capabilities: a 'rubber-stamp' King he was dubbed, a sovereign in name alone. The fact and effect of the Coronation turned the scale, yet strangely it was not his own country which first realized the immense potential of King George and Queen Elizabeth. As war began to seem more certain, the couple visited France. Their impact on this vital ally was immense, Queen Elizabeth playing a star role which is recalled today. There followed a tour of Canada from coast to coast and back, a tour the success of which exceeded all expectations. Then came their visit to the United States. Never have Washington and New York responded so warmly and vociferously to prominent visitors, yet the deep importance of this tour lay in their private stay with the President and Mrs Roosevelt. Britain and United States had drifted apart in sympathy and understanding, due to the insular attitude of George V and later the Mrs Simpson affair. As guests in the family home of the Roosevelts George and Elizabeth closed that gap within a few days: a friendship was forged which was to prove a great asset during the Second World War.

George VI sacrificed any hope of a long and peaceful old age by the part that he played in that war. He slaved at his task, for ever visiting troops and factories and using his power as King to influence the trend of affairs with the world's leaders. When, with the termination of hostilities, there should have come a time to rest, there was no rest. Instead came a change in Government, a change in the attitude of the people as to what a democracy should be. He had not the strength left to adjust to that change; he had given his all. As his elder daughter has said, he never faltered. The uninterrupted royal role played by Queen Elizabeth the Queen Mother has kept alive her husband's memory, yet only those now close to middle-age recall him. Since his death even greater changes have taken place in all spheres and ways of life, but their joint ground work in building national and international ententes contributed greatly to comparative peace since 1945.

This book, having introduced the two main characters in their childhood, deals in the main with the married life of George and Elizabeth. It ends with the death of the King in 1952. Although only five years separated their respective births, those five years had brought as much change to Britain as had the previous fifty. George VI was born into the Victorian age and the stamp of the great Queen was put firmly upon him: her way of life and her thinking ruled his nursery, her descendants peopled the palaces of Europe. In his early years motor cars, aeroplanes and radio played no part – even the bicycle was a novelty. Elizabeth, although in her cradle when Queen Victoria died, was an Edwardian: the inventions of the opening of the twentieth century were taken for granted by the time that she reached the schoolroom.

George was unfortunate in that his parents, King George V and Queen Mary, lacked much understanding of him. He was bullied and over-disciplined. Left-handed by nature, he was forced to use his right; he had an impediment in his speech; suffering from knock-knees, he had to undergo the agony of splints; a victim of gastritis, he was provided with the wrong diet; not clever, he was over-taxed mentally; unprepared, he was thrown into the tough dormitories of the naval colleges. Elizabeth, on the other hand, enjoyed a normal, happy life in a Hertfordshire garden and in the hills of Scotland. She had a brilliant mother and a sympathetic father.

To understand George and Elizabeth we must, therefore, look first at their antecedents.

1

Background

George V was a grandson of Queen Victoria, the second son of Albert Edward, Prince of Wales, and his wife Alexandra. In 1892, following the death of his elder brother, Albert Victor, Duke of Clarence, George was created Duke of York. He was a naval officer and did not relish the thought of being second in line to the throne. In 1893 he married his late brother's fiancée, Princess Mary of Teck, widely known as 'May' after the month in which she was born, in 1867. Their first child was born in 1894 and was christened Edward Albert Christian George Andrew Patrick David, known in the family as David. He was destined to make his mark in the British story by abdicating the throne in 1936.

Their second child was due in mid-December 1895. For a number of reasons the timing was unfortunate. The 13th, the expected arrival date, was a Friday and the superstitious prayed that the baby would be spared this omen of ill luck. But the parents and the royal family in general were more concerned that the event should not take place on the 14th, known to them as 'Mausoleum Day'. Then Queen Victoria moved slowly through the hours, cocooned in a black cloud of gloom and prayer, for on that day in 1861 her husband, Prince Albert the Consort, had died; on the same date in 1871 her eldest son, the Prince of Wales, had all but died of typhoid; and on 14 December 1878 her second daughter, Alice, Grand Duchess of Hesse, had slipped away in her sleep, a victim of diphtheria caught from kissing her young son who was suffering from the dread disease. But for George, 'Mausoleum Day' it was fated to be. In the early morning of Saturday, 14 December 1895, he was born at York Cottage, Sandringham, the Norfolk estate of the Prince and Princess of Wales.

Although the birth was easy and the eight-pound baby normal, the night was one of chaos. Firstly, the Home Secretary was not there, as it was his bounden duty to be. A carriage had met the last train to reach Wolferton station, but Sir Matthew White Ridley was not among its passengers. Protocol demanded that he be in attendance to ensure no trickery took place and that the child was the true offspring of the mother, a custom dating back to the days of King James II and the 'warming-pan' plot.* But York Cottage was too small and already packed with doctors and nurses, and the Duke of York had made it plain that he did not want the Home Secretary 'hanging about' for days before the event. So Sir Matthew took a risk. He caught a train to Norfolk on the 14th, only to discover that he was too late. A newspaper posed the question: 'Does this remissness involve a penalty and, if so, what?' The second element of chaos and upset concerned the domestic staff. Short of quarters as they were, with some even living out, the evening of the 13th was a nightmare of rush, with every guest room occupied, trains to be met at the station and hardly space for the assembled throng to sit down to dinner. Just as the staff were preparing for bed, the Duchess's pains began. Back on duty they went and four and a half hours later the baby arrived. Demands for hot water were taxed to the limit and, once medical needs were satisfied, the calls began for early morning tea and shaving water. There were endless telegrams to despatch.

The Duke was a man of routine and habit and, come birth, war or coronation, he must have his breakfast. At a quarter to seven he took his place at table, but he was in a state of fear and trepidation about what his revered grandmother would say about the error in timing. To add to his worries, Queen Victoria was in a bad temper anyway. A few days earlier the Imperial Institute Amateur Orchestra had visited Windsor Castle and an artist, whose task it was to depict the scene, had shown the Queen giving her arm to one of her Indian servants. This was a *faux pas* indeed, for the Queen would never take the arm of anyone under the rank of sovereign. (In fact the Indian servant was in the habit of supporting the Queen's elbow when she found difficulty in walking.) An abject apology was called for and the head of the artist must fall.

* When Prince Charles was born in 1948 George VI requested the Home Secretary to waive his historic duty.

The *Illustrated London News*, who published the picture, put such an apology at the head of their column of Court news, giving it precedence over the report of the service at the Mausoleum:

> On Saturday, Dec. 14, the anniversary of the death of the Prince Consort, and that of Princess Alice, Grand Duchess of Hesse, a special memorial service was performed in the Royal Mausoleum Chapel at Frogmore. It was attended by the Queen, the Prince and Princess of Wales and their daughters, the Duke and Duchess of Connaught, Prince and Princess Christian of Schleswig-Holstein, Princess Louise and her husband (the Marquis of Lorne), Princess Beatrice and the Duchess of Albany.[1]

It will be seen that the royal family was present in force, not even the baby's grandparents, the Prince and Princess of Wales, being excused Church Parade. Even after 'Mausoleum Day' was over, Edward and Alexandra were unable to escape from Windsor. The reason for this was that there had been an upset in the domestic life of the Queen and at such times she demanded the presence of her family. The upset in question was that her beloved son-in-law, Prince Henry of Battenberg, had gone to war, sailing with the expeditionary force raised to subdue young King Prempeh of Ashanti who, despite warnings from London, was raiding the Gold Coast and indulging in slave traffic and atrocities such as human sacrifice. The Queen referred to Henry as 'a bright sunbeam in my home'.[2] One of the four handsome and adventure-loving Princes of Battenberg who enriched the life of Europe in the last years of the nineteenth century, he could do as he liked with Victoria. He enticed her on to the dance floor when she was seventy-two and he was even allowed to smoke. His wife, Beatrice, the Queen's youngest daughter, who acted as a second right hand, secretary and nurse, was not an exciting lady and apt to give undue priority to events such as local garden fetes. For the Prince of Wales, the enforced stay at Windsor was no great hardship. He was not enamoured of crooning at babies in cots and was content enough to indulge in his favourite pastime of banging away at the birds in the Great Park, but for Alexandra the absence from Sandringham was a sadness indeed and it was not until the 20th that she was able to hurry back to Norfolk with her daughters.

The absence of the Prince and Princess of Wales from Sandringham was in fact welcomed by the Yorks. As far as May was concerned, the further her mother-in-law was away at times of confinement the better she was pleased. George had no such revolutionary view, being a middle-of-the-road man who sought peace above all, but he was glad his parents were at Windsor for two reasons: he was able to learn at first hand of the mood prevailing there and, in the face of it, he was relying upon them to smoothe matters over. The first communiqué from the Prince of Wales read: 'Grandmama was rather distressed that this happy event should have taken place on a darkly sad anniversary,' adding that the family was trying to convince her that the baby's arrival might 'break the spell' of this unlucky date.[3] George rushed off a letter of apology and regret to his grandmother. Two days later the Prince of Wales, with his gift of diplomacy, came up with the long-term answer. It concerned the baby's name.

When the Duke and Duchess's first son was born Queen Victoria wished his first name to be Albert, but to her annoyance that of Edward was bestowed. Now the Prince suggested that not only should the new baby be called Albert, but also that the Queen should be asked to be godmother. The suggestion worked like a charm. Victoria wrote to George:

> Most gladly do I accept being Godmother to this dear little boy, born on the day his beloved Great Grandfather entered on an even greater life . . . I must end now to save the post. V.R.I.[4]

The baby was due to be christened Albert Frederick Arthur George at the church of St Mary Magdalene at Sandringham on 3 February but the first of many sad and dramatic events to crowd his life caused a postponement. On 22 January there arrived at Osborne a telegram containing the news that Prince Henry of Battenburg was dead of fever. His body was brought home in a warship, in a rough tank fashioned out of biscuit tins and filled with rum.[5] The tragedy crowded the headlines, and the Queen was waiting to lay a wreathe upon the coffin when it reached Cowes in the royal yacht *Alberta*. Apart from her husband's death, these were the saddest moments of Victoria's life. The reports of the funeral in the Isle of Wight swamped the news; and the christening of young Albert, already known as 'Bertie', slipped down the priority list of royal engagements. It took place on the 17th, before a small congregation, although on this occasion Sir Matthew White Ridley made it on time. Also present was Bertie's elder brother. David was intrigued with his new playmate and behaved well until such time as Bertie took exception to being cradled in the arms of the Bishop of Norwich and made a loud vocal remonstrance. In sympathy, David joined in with a yell so penetrating that it was thought best to remove him to the vestry.

The main reason the Duchess of York had been relieved her mother-in-law was not at Sandringham for the confinement was a straightforward one of temperament. The two women reacted against one another as violently as orange does with milk. They were friendly enough when meeting on casual occasions, but their thoughts and reactions were diametrically opposed. Alexandra was fun-loving, forthcoming and made friends within minutes; May kept herself to herself, confided seldom and was incapable of pouring out the stream of small but interested talk which is such a valuable asset to royalty. Alexandra was incurably unpunctual; May stuck to her timetable, considering it bad manners not to do so. Alexandra squandered money, being lavish with her charities and, if she ran short, turned her magnetism on rich business men who surrendered without a fight; May counted her pennies and never dreamed of using her eyes or smile to increase their number. Alexandra held the spotlight at royal festivities, while May was so slow in coming forward that she was labelled a bore. Alexandra was not well read, nor called by culture; May was highly intelligent, with a prodigious memory. Alexandra's face showed clearly her emotions; May hid behind a mask. Alexandra would rush into other people's houses unannounced; May liked to dwell behind a door marked 'Private'. Particularly did she like to be alone during the process of birth; a time which embarrassed and somewhat revolted her. The fact that Alexandra was not in the 'Big House' at the time of young Albert's birth, rushing in and out of York Cottage with her flock of daughters and dogs, was to May an infinite relief.

May's relief stemmed from her experiences as a child of the Duke and Duchess of Teck. They were an extraordinary couple and their odd behaviour embarrassed their children. Before her marriage May's mother had been Princess Mary of Cambridge, a granddaughter of George III, a fact no one was ever allowed to forget. She was a product of the famous 'Royal Marriage Race'. This matrimonial sprint, in which the runners were the middle-aged sons of George III, became necessary when the Prince Regent's* only child, Princess Charlotte, died in childbirth in 1817, leaving the British throne with no direct heir in the third generation. It was a close run thing. Adolphus, Duke of Cambridge, had a son† on 26 March 1819. On the 27th, William, Duke of Clarence, had a daughter and, being an elder brother, took the lead, but tragically the girl died later that day, so the Cambridge colours were once again to the fore. Then, on 24 May, Edward, Duke of Kent, became the father of a bouncing girl and, being older than Adolphus, was thus the winner. The name of his daughter was Victoria.

Adolphus and his wife, despite their marriage of convenience, found connubial happiness. They had a daughter named Augusta‡ in 1822 and, eleven years later when the Duke was in his sixtieth year, another girl, whom they named Mary. This child of elderly parents soon showed signs of becoming a problem. She had a huge appetite and early became fat, her dimensions increasing with the passing years. The famous statesman, Lord Clarendon, forecast that, as regarded the matrimonial field, no Prince would venture upon 'so vast an undertaking';[6] the American Minister estimated her weight at eighteen stone. The sad fate of a girl who collided with Mary during the Lancers was that she was sent spinning across the dance floor and ended up flat on her back.

While her weight was a distinct handicap from the standpoint of marriage, Mary's behaviour with men was even more so. She was a coquette. She flirted in a noisy way interspersed with guffaws of Georgian laughter. If a likely candidate were produced for her she would shower her attention upon others. (The future Queen of Denmark informed her daughter, Alexandra, that, if she behaved like her cousin of Cambridge she would get her face smacked.) Staid German Princes, demanding domestic discipline,

* Afterwards George IV.

† George, afterwards Duke of Cambridge and Commander-in-Chief.

‡ Afterwards Grand Duchess of Mecklenburg-Strelitz.

saw no future with her in the ballroom, the bed or the kitchen. She came to thirty-three years and still there was not a glimmer of hope. Then the miracle happened. After a romance lasting but a few weeks, she married the most 'beautiful' young man in Europe.

Francis, Count of Hohenstein, was a character from Strauss and, as a young man, the darling of Vienna. He was tall and well built with his hair so black that, in the lamplight, it shone dark blue. Below his high forehead were magnetic eyes. Beneath his waxed moustachios was 'a little tuft of an imperial'. He was an officer in the Imperial Gendarmerie and he was four years younger than Mary. His father, Duke Alexander of Wurtemberg, son of the King, had married the beautiful Countess Claudia Rhédey in 1835, she then being created Countess of Hohenstein; but, as it was a morganatic marriage, Duke Alexander forfeited his right to succession. In 1841 the Duke and his wife, both mounted, were watching army manoeuvres. Her horse reared, she lost control, and it ran away with her straight into the path of galloping cavalry. She fell and was trampled to death. In 1863 Francis was given the title of Prince Teck and became a Serene Highness. Emperor Francis Joseph and Empress Elizabeth of Austria liked him and he accompanied the ill Elizabeth to Madeira in 1860. Queen Victoria loaned the royal yacht, *Victoria and Albert*, for the trip and it was during those days that the idea of an opulent Britain took shape in Francis's mind.

In 1864 the Prince and Princess of Wales met him in Vienna. He was just the sort of decorative young man who appealed to them and they conceived the idea that he might do for Mary of Cambridge. They invited him to Sandringham and were satisfied. In March 1866 he came to England to complete his matrimonial mission and within four weeks was engaged to Mary. The attractions, for him, were that she was an HRH, a granddaughter of George III and that her brother, George, was Commander-in-Chief. Later, disillusioned, he was to say that the marriage was pushed upon him by the Cambridges and that he would have preferred to marry the daughter of an industrial magnate. Owing to her size, there were many doubts as to the fate in store for Mary the Mountain when her time came to produce a child, but a daughter arrived safely in May 1867. She was named Mary after her mother but dubbed 'May', a sobriquet which stuck throughout her life. Three brothers made their appearance. In 1871 Francis was created Duke of Teck.

Mary and Francis shared two weaknesses – over-obsession with rank and a complete disregard for the value of money. Despite their small income they attempted to run a set of apartments in Kensington Place and White Lodge, Richmond, entertaining on a lavish scale. The debts piled up, a permanent worry. Francis wished to become an HRH, but his efforts failed. He had dreamed of a sinecure being passed to him by his brother-in-law, George the Commander-in-Chief, but there was no luck there either: all he got was an Honorary Colonelcy of the Post Office Volunteers.[7] He fretted that he was being robbed of his rights in Wurtemberg and ignored in Britain, and occupied his days with interior decoration and gardening. His temper grew worse and worse until it became startling. Arriving at an hotel he would, on principle, complain loudly about the rooms and the meals and, when he left, roar with fury at the bill. His wife did not help matters. She poured money away and at the same time courted popularity with the public and attempted to elevate her status, driving about in a carriage of similar colours to those of Queen Victoria. After the death of Prince Albert the Consort, the Queen was seen seldom in London streets whereas Mary was often on parade. The British public applaud fat royalties who laugh and are in high spirits and forget their shortcomings – they adored Mary. Queen Victoria watched these 'royal progresses' with both annoyance and suspicion.

In 1883 the Tecks' financial disarray could no longer be ignored. Apart from vast amounts owing to relatives and bankers, £18,000 was owed to local tradesmen, and it was this last amount which decided their immediate future: they must leave the country and retrench in Florence. In the late evening of 15 September 1883 the family gathered on the Continental departure platform of Victoria station – the Duke and Duchess, May and her three brothers. To May, standing in the shadows thrown by the station gaslights, pulling her travelling coat high around her as if to avoid recognition, it was like a sentence of deportation. For once the Duchess was silent. A few relatives gathered to see them off. They had feared the Duke would give way to one of his volcanoes of temper and create a scene but he stood like a man in a dream and without fuss took his seat in the saloon. So the sad girl of sixteen who was to become, by the Grace of God, Queen of Great Britain, Ireland and the British Dominions beyond the Seas, Empress of India, went into exile, too ashamed to cry as the boat train took her to the English Channel.

Installed in Italy, the Duchess returned to her old habits of lavish entertaining and the social rounds she so enjoyed, relying on the hospitality of friends and relatives when money ran out. May, on the other hand, made good use of the Florentine interlude, learning about history, art and furniture. The Duke became even more fractious and explosive than before. He suffered a stroke – something the Duchess attributed to the Italian sunshine – which resulted in a paralysed left arm, a useless left leg and a twisted mouth. Although his health gradually improved, Francis was an old man at forty-seven, and never normal again. His family would explain that 'his brains were loose in his head'.

The following year the Tecks returned to England, living at White Lodge, Richmond. They were deflated and clearly in the category of 'poor relations', a tragic classification indeed in the nineteenth century: 'poor relations' did as they were told. Yet May impressed many people by her restraint, culture and efficiency. She was of great help to her parents and there were no signs of flightiness. Such things were noticed.

The eldest son of the Prince of Wales, Albert Victor, was becoming a thorough nuisance to his father – his mother adored him but she was the only one so to do. He was incapable of concentration and his sole interest appeared to be in his clothes. He was involved in a number of nasty incidents, including a visit to a homosexual brothel off Tottenham Court Road. He had shown sparks of interest for certain young ladies, but they were only sparks and the young ladies in question, eligible or not, were not attracted. At last May, the solid poor relation, was produced and the pair became engaged at a dance at Luton Hoo, Bedfordshire in December 1891. May soon realized that she was heading for a strange marriage, the Prince of Wales making it clear to her that her role would be a cross between governess and nurse. May told her mother she did not think she could go through with it. The Duchess, by this time known universally as 'Fat Mary', was both horrified and indignant: when, at long last, she saw the end of her financial difficulties, here was her daughter revolting at the thought of marrying a young man in direct line to the throne. She said, and plainly, that if she could put up with irascible, impoverished Francis for twenty-five years, her daughter could cope with Albert Victor, with all his trimmings. 'Of course you can do it,' she snapped.[8] May was saved by an act of God. In January 1892 her fiancé died of pneumonia. The Tecks were back in 'short street' again.

But Queen Victoria had no intention of losing this paragon of a bride. Albert Victor's younger brother, George, in the Navy, was single and now, distressed by his brother's death, he viewed with trepidation the job which lay ahead of him on his father's death. It was clear that a stable, steadfast companion should be provided for him. He showed little interest in women, except for a rumoured flirtation in Malta, where the sun and gay naval life were guaranteed to raise romantic notions, however deeply buried. In 1893 May and he were propelled into an engagement. At the time they were looking at the frogs in the garden pond of East Sheen Lodge, the home of George's sister, Louise, Duchess of Fife. Throughout their engagement the couple never publicly went near one another, touched hands, exchanged smiles or whispered asides; in the London clubs there was some speculation as to what would happen on their wedding night. But Queen Victoria had a theory that if two young people of the opposite sex were left in a bedroom and the door closed the result would always be the same. She was wrong on a number of occasions, but on this one she was right.

May was cultivated and informed and she knew how to economize but she knew little of people, and never learned more. When it came to the choice of a nurse for her baby boys she relied on references instead of personal observation. If the Duchess of . . . and Lady . . . said the nanny was all right, then she must be. But Nanny turned out to be a terror. She developed an obsession of maternal love for David and had a strange way of showing it. Each evening it was her duty to take her charge into the presence of his parents. On the way there she would pinch David's arm with vigour and, of natural course, the boy screamed. The Duke and Duchess viewed the evening inspection in much the same way as they did their visits to the horses in the stables or the dogs in the kennels – they anticipated, and expected, some sign of appreciation. As their heir bawled his head off and writhed in the nurse's arms, they lost patience and signalled for withdrawal, just what Nanny, consumed with jealousy, wanted. On the arrival of Bertie, Nanny's feelings went into reverse. She disliked the child and showed it in a distinctly unpleasant fashion: not only did she underfeed him, she prescribed the wrong diet. No one would dream of interfering in those days with nursery dictums, so Bertie got away to a bad start. It was some time before Nanny's shortcomings were discovered and she was sent on her way.

She was succeeded by the under-nurse, the children's beloved 'Lala', who was as great a success as her predecessor had been a failure. Soon Lala was in charge of a caravan of three prams which toured the paths of Sandringham, for a baby girl, Mary, was born to the Duchess of York on 25 April 1897. The three children lived a simple life. They had a day nursery where they lived with Lala, and a night nursery; otherwise they had only their airings in the park and the evening parental inspection. Sometimes they travelled to their parents' home in London, York House, St James's, and on rare occasions they visited Queen Victoria. Of the three David was the ebullient star, bouncing, rosy-cheeked Mary the target of affection by baby lovers. Bertie, sandwiched between them, was apt not to be noticed. He was shy, liable to burst into tears and showed some signs of the Teck temper. He suffered from gastric trouble, probably caused by Nanny's maladministration.

Visits to 'Gangan', as Queen Victoria was called, were an ordeal both for her grandchildren and her great-grandchildren. In general she was not attracted to the young and would tolerate none of their infant ways. She once said to Empress Eugenie of the French, 'Children are insufferable creatures.'[9] She was hard on them. Lord Salisbury, the Prime Minister, came across one of her granddaughters tied by the hands to a door in a corridor at Windsor. Queen Victoria believed the only diet for children was roast beef, mutton and rice pudding for lunch and bread and milk at night. They were not allowed to speak at table and, if they dared to do so, were bodily removed by one of the Indian servants. Sometimes she would fire off questions, usually of a religious nature. She asked Princess Ena of Battenberg 'What are the

Epistles?'[10] Terrified, her mind a blank, Ena replied that they were the wives of the apostles. For at least once in her life Queen Victoria was too flabbergasted to comment.

Of the York children, Mary, gurgling happily, was too young to be aware of expectations or solecisms. Predictably it was David who proved the exception among the tribe of obedient young descendants. He started life as he was to continue – he was not impressed. He had to put up with many attacks and attempts to subjugate him but, inside himself, he was never impressed. He was a born star, and it was this quality which appealed to Queen Victoria who in fact respected those who stood up to her. She paid tribute to him in her diary: 'David is a delightful child, so intelligent, nice and friendly. He is a most attractive little boy, and so forward and clever. He always tries at luncheon time to pull me out of my chair, saying, "Get up, Gangan," and then to one of the Indian servants, "Man pull it," which makes us laugh very much.'[11]

Poor little Bertie got no mentions. He demonstrably lacked the star quality and worse, would break into floods of tears at the sight of the squat old lady with steely blue eyes, into whose presence he had reluctantly come. This behaviour upset the old Queen considerably – accustomed to acclamation and subservience, signs of obvious repulsion were a new experience. It was beyond her understanding that little people whose health is below normal, or who suffer from such troubles as gastritis, cling to those who love and care for them (in this case 'Lala') and shrink from the aged, the infirm and the ugly.

Yet for Bertie, as for the others, there was one place where pleasure could safely be anticipated – the 'Big House', as Sandringham House was known. There dwelt Grandpapa and Grannie, the Prince and Princess of Wales. Grandpapa was a man who treated small children as though they were puppies. He would let them crawl round him, over him and have races with pats of butter down the length of his trouser legs. When he became bored, he would good-naturedly brush the litter away. He was generous and liked the sort of food children like – buttered toast and cream cakes. Alexandra was a perfect Grannie. She was beautiful and she spoke the children's language. She loved games and dressing-up and was never bad tempered. With her, lessons took second place to happiness. She had pets galore and pony carriages in which she would race round the park and visit the villages.

The contrast between the bright lights and gay colours of the 'Big House' and the austere, cramped rooms of York Cottage perhaps symbolized the difference in attitude to the children. While the Duke and Duchess of York were deeply attached to their offspring, George was not cut out to be a father and May, in the words of a contemporary, was 'no mother at all'. But in fairness to her it must be said that she faced many problems. One of them was that of playing a very muted second violin to her in-laws. Another was connected with her own relatives, difficulties with them continuing from the time of her marriage to the end of the century. Her second brother, Frank, was a permanent headache as, in fact, he had been since a boy. When a pupil at Wellington College he had thrown the headmaster over a hedge, a feat of strength and insolence which called for his immediate removal. The high marriage of his sister did not impress him one little bit and he was constantly making unseemly jokes about it, but his main drawbacks were that he had inherited his mother's profligacy with money and that he was a devotee of the turf. In 1895 he lost £10,000 on a bet at Punchestown races. By a supreme effort Mary managed to raise the total amount, for Frank had little funds beyond the cash in his pocket. He was despatched to India and there continued on his troublesome way.

A further worry was the Duchess of Teck. Since the days of exile in Florence and the Duke's stroke, 'Fat Mary' had become increasingly dependent on her daughter. May had guided the household, watched the finances, nursed her sick father. After her marriage the old Duchess still clung to her and May did her best to help, but there was a snag. George was irritated by and generally annoyed with his mother-in-law. Her unpunctuality drove him mad and her sudden and unannounced invasions of his privacy upset his ordered timetable. The Yorks were at White Lodge for the birth of their first son and after the stay was over George commented bitterly; 'I would not go through the six weeks I spent at White Lodge for anything . . .'[12] May took the hint and when Bertie was born her mother was not invited to see him until he was a month old, and she was not at his christening; she was abroad.

The Duke was becoming more and more odd as the months passed. His wife never had and still did not fully comprehend his illness. For interest, she increased her efforts to help the many charities with which she was associated and she travelled Europe. There she received the full rècogniton of being an HRH and the red carpets were rolled out for her. She felt more regal, more wanted there. Her last great occasion was the Diamond Jubilee of 1897. She was still a popular figure and the reception which awaited her in the streets of London, especially in the East End, was tumultuous. In October she became ill; an operation was necessary, her heart would not stand the strain and she died. The general upset and ceremonial connected with her death proved too much for her husband. He was despatched to his relations in Wurtemberg, but they could not cope with his incoherent speech and mental wanderings and sent him back. Early in 1898 he was confined at White Lodge in the care of a doctor and male nurses. Visits by his children were rare, for the sight of them upset him further. He died on 27 January 1900; he was only sixty-two.

There were also troubles on the family front for George. Though but thirty-three in 1898 when these difficulties really came to the fore, he had the staid outlook of a much older man and disturbance was anathema to him. In his eyes the family springing from the union of Victoria and Albert was a sacrosanct Trades Union; in addition to which, upsets meant trouble with omnipotent grandmother at Windsor. Still, upsets there were. To begin with, three of his first cousins* were in marital deep waters and heading for divorce. Queen Victoria was dead set against divorce. Whether the judgment went for or against the ladies concerned they were not thereafter received at Court or by any of her Ambassadors abroad. Then there was his cousin Alfred, only son of the Duke of Coburg. Alfred was in the German army and painting Potsdam red. He died in 1899, in circumstances which were hushed up. Empress Frederick, mother of Emperor William II of Germany, wrote to her daughter Sophie: 'You ask about the cause. It is true that he was giddy and wild . . . and that he contracted an illness, of which I know next to nothing . . . one

* Princess Marie Louise, daughter of Prince and Princess Christian, who had married the Prince of Anhalt; and Ernest, Grand Duke of Hesse, and his wife, Victoria Melita, daughter of the Duke of Saxe-Coburg and Gotha.

dislikes thinking about it, and still more speaking or writing about it.'[13]

On 11 October 1899 the Boer War began; Mafeking, Kimberley and Ladysmith were besieged and news of the military reverses shocked Britain. In December came 'Black Week' when three British generals were defeated in turn. All festivities at Sandringham were cancelled, so the general family gloom spread even to the nursery. In troubled Europe public feeling was pro-Boer, anti-British, and anarchists stalked the rulers. In 1898 beautiful Empress Elizabeth of Austria had died at Geneva with a dagger deep in her back. George shared with his cousin, Emperor William of Germany, a constant dread of such attacks, exacerbated by the knowledge that the Prince and Princess of Wales were high on the list of those who organized them. On 4 April 1900 they were sitting in their compartment at the Gare du Nord, Brussels, waiting for the train to leave. A bullet passed between them, missing each only by inches. Alexandra telegraphed home: 'The ball passed between our heads. I felt it whizzing across my eyes.'[14] It was the greatest shock ever to disrupt the peace of Sandringham, impossible that the children should not learn of it. The Duke realized that had the bullet gone but a few inches to either side he would have lost either his father, whom he worshipped, or 'Motherdear', who was a part of his being.

Another sad day came for him in that summer of 1900. His uncle Alfred,* known in the family as 'Affie', died at Coburg. Duke Alfred was a close friend and had been a 'supporter' at his wedding. George had served under him in the Mediterranean and been a frequent visitor to his uncle's home in Malta. On 4 August, the day on which Duke Alfred was buried, Queen Victoria knelt in prayer at a funeral service in Osborne House. She was a very tired old lady, weighed down by the strain of the Boer War and the tragedies which had overtaken her family. HMS *Australia* steamed into the Bay and her guns thundered over the Isle of Wight in salute to the dead Duke, who had been an outstanding sailor. At Sandringham the four children with the nurses took their morning walk. David and Bertie were on foot, Mary and Harry† in prams. The flag was hanging at half mast above the church of St Mary

* Duke of Edinburgh and (1893) of Saxe-Coburg and Gotha.

† Prince Henry, born 31 March 1900, afterwards Duke of Gloucester.

Magdalene in the park. For the four-year-old Bertie that 4th August began a link of strange coincidences between his life and that of the dead Duke Alfred. The Duke died at the age of fifty-six; so did George VI. The Duke died of cancer; so did George VI. The Duke's London home was Clarence House; it was also to be the home of George VI's elder daughter and, later, of his widow. Alfred was Duke of Edinburgh; George VI's daughter was to become the wife of Philip, Duke of Edinburgh.

There was another happening on that fourth day of August, one which would make the day the most important in Bertie's life. At No. 20 St James's Square, London SW1, a girl-child was born. Her name was Elizabeth.

2

Childhood Days

ON 14 DECEMBER 1900 the Duke of York wrote to his second son:

> Now that you are five years old, I hope you will always try and be obedient and do at once what you are told, as you will find it will come much easier to you the sooner you begin. I always tried to do this when I was your age and found it made me much happier.[1]

The last sentence was a direct untruth; it was his habit of gilding his own image and distorting past events to suit his own convenience which was later to irritate his sons, in particular the eldest. As a boy, the Duke had been mischievous, pugnacious and a thorough nuisance. 'Ill bred and ill trained,' Queen Victoria had described him. Sent under the table for bad manners at luncheon, he was rude when he was told that he could return to his place. He played havoc with the game when grown-ups were playing croquet, interrupted conversations and used rude words which he had picked up in the stables. He was for ever fighting his elder brother. When driving out with her sons, Alexandra sat between them. On being asked why, she replied that the occasion demanded a buffer state between two warring elements.

His letter to Bertie was hardly one to bring birthday brightness to a five-year-old boy, looking forward to Christmas. But it might have been a portent of things to come, for the following weeks were a period of misery for the York children. David developed German measles and his sister and brothers were put in quarantine. Then Queen Victoria died at Osborne. The Duke went down with German measles and was confined to bed, nursed by his wife, so that neither was able to attend the funeral, though it is doubtful if the old Queen would have accepted the excuse. But the Yorks were determined that their elder children should witness the historic scene and they were taken to Windsor. Thus, on 2 February David, aged six, Bertie, five, and Mary, three, huddled at the service in the chill of St George's Chapel; two days later they went down the hill for the final interment at the Frogmore mausoleum. It was bitterly cold and the waiting for the next move seemed interminable to the children, lost among the crowd of Kings and Princes, Grand Dukes and Archdukes, and the black figures of the royal ladies sobbing behind their crêpe veils. 'Sleep thy last sleep,' the choir sang.

The funeral was hardly over before a row broke out between Bertie's mother and the new King and Queen, Edward VII and Alexandra. May learned that her husband and herself were to be henceforward known as the Duke and Duchess of Cornwall and York – she, as wife of the Heir Apparent, wished to become the Princess of Wales immediately. The German love for royal preferment flared up and she complained bitterly. The Duke said nothing, as he was not in the habit of crossing swords with his parents. The King's decision, in fact, was based on a minor point of practicality. He and his wife had been Prince and Princess of Wales for nearly forty years and he thought a sudden change of title would inevitably lead to misunderstandings and confusion in the mails. The differences subsided in tears on 16 March when the Duke and Duchess of Cornwall and York sailed from Portsmouth on SS *Ophir* at the start of a forty-five thousand mile tour of the British Dominions, the highlight of which was to be the opening of the first Commonwealth Parliament in Australia. One misgiving they shared regarding their eight months' absence concerned the educational progress and general state of discipline of their brood. Most detailed orders were issued as to the programme of learning and also concerning the regular despatch of letters by David and Bertie. To ensure their compliance the Duke took with him Mr Jones, the schoolmaster at Sandringham, whose task was to check that the incoming mail kept to schedule and to despatch detailed and enlightening reports on the progress of the tour. The children said their goodbyes in London, while their elders headed for Portsmouth and a farewell lunch on board *Ophir*. Tears fell like rain into the last toasts. Of the sailing away George wrote to his mother: 'May and I came down to our cabins and had a good cry . . .'[2]

Bertie, ever a one to follow instructions, rushed off a letter to Gibraltar, expressing the hope that the travellers did not 'have a big wave' in the Bay of Biscay and were not seasick. Neither of his prayers was answered. May was no sailor. 'I *detest* the sea,' she wrote home from the Indian Ocean.[3] All possible efforts were made to lessen her plight. She slept in a swinging-cot and a soft, non-skid appendage to the lavatory seat was devised to prevent accidents should *Ophir* roll at an inconvenient moment. But on land, revelling in the new sights, she was the star, swinging graciously from function to function on her long legs. As bands played 'Rule Britannia' and 'Life on the Ocean Wave', the two bobbed about the places marked red on the map, laying foundation stones, presenting medals, receiving addresses, in Australia and New Zealand, South Africa and Canada.

For the three main parties concerned – the Duke and Duchess; the King and Queen; and the York children – the tour was a blessing. For the first time the Duke and Duchess had to stand on their own feet on a global stage. What a pity it was that the Duchess's parents – 'Fat Mary' and *der schöne Uhlan* – had not lived a few more years to see their dreams become reality. For the King and Queen, for whom the past few years had been blighted by the Boer War and the failing health of Queen Victoria, the best tonic they could have had was a tribe of happy children rushing about the home. As for the children, their parents' absence meant the end of rebuke and solemnity, and these really proved the happiest days of their young lives.

The Duke of Cornwall and York shared with Prince Albert the Consort the belief that education was the corner-stone of Princes. Edward VII was of the mind of Lord Melbourne, who had advised Queen Victoria not to put too much store by learning. In charge of the children's education was Mademoiselle Hélène Bricka, a fat and elderly lady from Alsace who had been governess to their mother. She was completely incapable of coping with the Sovereign power. The King and Queen liked to have their grandchildren with them at luncheon and allowed them to chatter away and romp as much as they liked. At the allotted time Mlle Bricka would appear at the door and intimate that the moment had come for the commencement of afternoon learning. The King would send her away, muttering some excuse, but his wave was an imperial gesture few dared to ignore. He became so bored with the persistence of the Alsatian lady that he left her behind in London when he took the children to Sandringham for a fortnight. In fury, Mlle Bricka reported this misdemeanour to the Duchess who, with a courage founded on distance, protested to the Queen. Alexandra's reply was a hotch-potch of English which made little sense; and the spoiling continued unabated.

David, Bertie, Mary and Harry accompanied the Court as it moved from Marlborough House, London, to Osborne and then to Balmoral. The elder boys were thus able for the first time to explore, and get to know, the royal homes without a restraining hand upon them. With them went an artist, Mrs Gertrude Massey, for the King and Queen planned to give the Duke and Duchess miniatures of their children as a present to mark their return. In her memoirs Mrs Massey gave an intimate and revealing picture of them, for all were attached to her and she was accustomed to dealing with young sitters. Her first glimpse of them was on the summer Osborne shore, learning to swim, 'three pink little figures all mixed up with blue water and white splashes', sometimes their heads above water, sometimes their feet.

It was David – Prince Edward to her – who was outstanding. 'He was the most interesting child I have ever met. He was naturally childish and unspoilt, full of joy and interested in subjects about which most children and many adults never think at all.' As she painted him, he asked: 'Are there kings and queens in heaven? Is everybody equal?' On being told, 'Yes, they are all equal,' he replied: 'Great Granny won't like that!'[4] Mary – called Princess Victoria – was the most mischievous and difficult to pose, sometimes refusing to look at the artist. Bertie was little noticed, but one day he asked if, for a change, he could draw Mrs Massey. 'His face was so expressive that one could almost read his thoughts.' It was always to be the same, right up to the January afternoon in 1952 when he stood on the tarmac at London Airport, waving farewell at the aircraft which was carrying his elder daughter away to Africa. His expression showed that he was well pleased at his effort to construct a likeness of Mrs Massey. But the final touches defeated him. 'Would you mind if I don't give you any arms?' he asked. 'Arms are so difficult to draw.'[5]

King Edward greatly enjoyed pulling the children's legs. He

gravely informed them that, as their parents had been so long in the hot sun of the southern climes, they would be black-skinned on their return. Seeing their astonishment, he enlarged further, until David, Bertie and Mary became convinced that the *Ophir* would bring back to them a version of Cetewayo, King of the Zulus, and a coal black Mammy. It was therefore with relief that, on 1 November 1901, they saw their Papa and Mama in familiar guise as they waved from the liner's deck. In fact, owing to the roughness of the sea, they were even paler than on their departure.

The Duke and Duchess were now created Prince and Princess of Wales and, despite some concern at the changes in behaviour and outlook of their children, an air of bonhomie and general satisfaction pervaded Sandringham, the Prince delighted that he was back in time to bang away at the birds and the Princess purring with pleasure at her elevation. Plans for the Coronation filled everyone's thoughts – there had not been such an occasion for sixty-five years and there were many problems to unravel. In addition there were endless complications to face over changes in residence. The King handed over to the Wales Frogmore House, in Windsor Home Park, and Abergeldie Castle on Deeside. As he intended to move into Buckingham Palace, Marlborough House was allotted to his heir, but this move did not take place until the following year, the Palace being in poor state of repair and cluttered with reminiscences of Queen Victoria. Among these were many reminders of her faithful gillie, John Brown. HM personally disposed of these; finding a collection of statuettes of Brown, he took delight in smashing each one on the stone floor. Then there was Osborne, a real problem. Queen Victoria had determined that it should remain a family residence, but Edward did not want it and George announced that in no circumstances would he live there. So, unwanted, Prince Albert's Italianate villa became the Osborne Royal Naval College, destined to play a painful part in the young life of Bertie of Wales.

The goodwill and excitement at the forthcoming festivities and moves lasted until March. The Princess of Wales' fifth pregnancy was announced. The King was due to be crowned on 26 June, but collapsed on the 24th with appendicitis. It was doubted whether he would survive the operation and the Prince of Wales was near to collapse himself with worry. 'He is not ready to reign yet,' sobbed his wife.[6] But the King pulled through and was ready for Westminster Abbey by 9 August. Bertie and David watched from the Royal Box reserved for the Princess and nudged one another and whispered together incessantly. It was, to them, in the nature of a grand sideshow. When an elderly aunt dropped her Order of Service over the edge of the Box, the strain proved too much for them and they burst out laughing.

The Princess, tired out and six months pregnant, took her children to Abergeldie. The focus was off them for a while and they ran wild about Deeside, exploring the countryside on ponies and bicycles, searching the turrets for the Castle ghost and racing across the narrow, swaying suspension bridge which spanned the river. On 20 December a baby brother arrived at Sandringham; and he was christened George Edward Alexander Edmund.* Once this excitement, and Christmas, were over, life became harder and more serious for Bertie and his elder brother. The birth brought home to the Prince of Wales the truth that he would soon become paternal colonel of what amounted to a royal regiment and he decided that his elder sons should commence their training as junior officers. Accordingly they were moved from the loving care of nurse 'Lala' and entrusted to a stalwart manservant named Finch. Soon afterwards arrived a tutor, Mr Henry Peter Hansell. He was tall, gaunt and decorated with a large and somewhat unkempt moustache. He was solemn and a bachelor. A product of Malvern College and Oxford, he specialized in history and the classics, was a good all-round athlete and was never known to utter a remark of wit or above average intelligence. He might have been taken from the pages of an Ian Hay novel. As he was of Norfolk stock, could sail a boat and was a crack shot, and he was silent, he was considered an ideal man for the job by the Prince of Wales.

Without dramatics, and imparting only a modicum of knowledge, Henry Hansell guided David and Bertie through the next decade. Where his secret heart lay nobody ever found out, but at least he avoided the pitfalls which overcame the first tutors of Prince Albert the Consort and Albert Edward, his son, both of whom developed childish sexual passions for their male mentors. The only sight to bring the light of interest into Hansell's eyes was

* Afterwards Duke of Kent.

that of cathedrals and churches. He worshipped them, dragged his charges round endless precincts; on his annual holiday he would make pilgrimage to some cathedral city which he had selected as his Mecca for that year. There was one strange thing the boys noticed about Mr Hansell. Each morning after breakfast he would trudge away to a nearby rise in the park and stare out over the Norfolk countryside for some minutes. When, at length, he was asked why he did so, he made one of his few revealing utterances: 'Freedom'.[7] This yearning probably had a prosaic basis: breakfast at York Cottage was a claustrophobic experience and a monotonous repetition of exactitude. Each morning the Prince of Wales emerged from his bedroom at exactly the same time, tapped the barometer in the same way, said the same things and ate the same things and lit his cigarette exactly on schedule. He was a man who hated change. When his collar stud broke, he had it soldered together.

To his credit, the tutor did not approve of the Prince's educational programme for his sons. He wanted the boys to go to a good preparatory school where they would learn to mix but the Prince would not listen. As he and his brother had been trained, so now should his sons; in due season the Navy would teach them all they needed for life. Under these conditions the boys fell behind standard and other teachers were brought in to brush up their French, German and mathematics. M. Gabrial Hua, ancient and with a long beard, was selected to polish up the French. Bertie did not favour the language and rebelled. M. Hua reported this, complaining that on being reprimanded Bertie pulled fiercely at his beard. Learning that in his own country M. Hua ate frogs' legs, the children caught some tadpoles and persuaded the cook to broil them and serve them on toast. He sampled the savoury and thereafter made a fast and furious retreat to his bedroom. It required a royal apology from Mama and all her family before he would emerge. Fortunately Papa was away.

Lessons began at 7.30 in the schoolroom on the second floor of York Cottage. It was furnished only with two standard desks with attached wooden seats, a blackboard and textbooks; in winter it was dark and icy cold. A quick breakfast followed the first session, then work until lunch. A brisk walk with Mr Hansell followed that, and then more lessons. There were no organized games with boys of their own background. Cricket instruction was given by Mr Hansell but, as the other participants were such grown-ups as could be pressed in, it was not much fun and neither of the boys made noticeable progress. Bertie's outstanding memory of the game was that he once met the immortal Dr W. G. Grace. In winter there were occasional games of football in which the teams were brought up to strength by recruitment from the local village school. As these boys had obviously been instructed to be on their best behaviour and not to get rough with the Princes, there was little excitement there either.

Mr Hansell made daily reports to the Prince and those on Bertie were often not encouraging. 'Division by two seems to be quite beyond him.' 'Prince Albert has caused two painful scenes in the bedroom this week.' Such reports were followed by a summons to attend his father's study in the evening. The Prince's study was as cheerless as the schoolroom, dominated by a large desk, which was usually covered with stamps. On the walls hung the mottoes which ruled his life; such as 'Teach me neither to cry for the moon nor over spilt milk.' These walls were covered with red fabric, identical with the material used for making trousers for French soldiers. The moths eventually made a meal of it. The Prince, in the manner of the quarter-deck, would snap reprimands, criticisms and threats. He would ask questions, then, before Bertie could reply, supply the answers himself, always in the worst light. In truth, he thought he was a good father, even imagining himself as a playmate and close friend of his children. No doubt he knocked good manners and sound rules of behaviour into them but, generally speaking, his assessment of himself was completely off course.

The result of pressure on Bertie caused a tragedy which was to handicap him his life through. Up to the age of seven his speech had been normal but now he began to stammer. It wasn't just the effect of academic pressure which manifested itself in this way; a variety of health problems took their toll. Bertie had knock-knees. So had his grandfather, King Edward, and his father. Queen Victoria had taken exception to her heir's nether limbs but Lord Clarendon, her Foreign Secretary, had told her that he could not see that it mattered much, 'as people always wear trousers,'[8] But Prince George of Wales thought much as had his grandmother and was determined that Bertie's legs should be straight. Accordingly he was put into splints, to be worn night and day. The pain they caused was severe. So bitterly did the boy cry that one night his manservant left them off. The Prince heard about this, roared with fury and displayed how ugly legs can be by pulling up his trousers. Poor Finch was told that, if Bertie grew up like that, it would be all his fault. Fortunately Mr Hansell pointed out that his pupil could not do justice to his lessons under this torture and the royal doctor agreed that the splints should be removed at bedtime. Then again, Bertie's ill health as a baby, gastritis trouble, continued through the years and added to the strain of concentration. He was left handed but, as his father insisted on standardization in all things, he was forced to write, and do other things, with his right. When, later in life he was able to use his left hand, as he did when playing tennis, he was at ease. Additionally, Bertie was competing with a brother who was not only older but stronger in health and achievement. David knew he was superior, and Bertie acknowledged it too. A few years later a contemporary was to say of them: 'It was like comparing an ugly duckling with a cock-pheasant.'

When Bertie began to stammer his father chaffed him, and this encouraged his brothers and sister to tease and imitate him. He became moody and silent, occasionally giving vent to violent temper and weeping. These were interpreted as signs of obstinacy and naughtiness and he was told that he 'really must pull himself together.'[9] He turned for solace to tests of individual effort, a favourite being running. The daughter of an official at Sandringham recalls seeing him, on a winter's afternoon in 1906, taking part in a paper chase through the park. There was determination in his every movement and written clear on his face. With every ounce of strength that he could muster he was fighting to be in front.[10] Nevertheless there were happier moments for him; the hour he liked best was when he and the others went to their mother's boudoir after tea. Resting in her dressing-gown on a sofa, she would chat with the children, read to them and teach them how to knit. Sometimes she would go to the piano and play popular tunes such as 'My Darling Clementine'. Bertie would stay with her as long as he could manage, watching her hair being prepared, telling her, in his lisping way, how pretty she looked;

probably not surprisingly at this age he showed a preference for female company.

Life was easier when the Prince was away, as he often was, shooting or fulfilling State duties in London and about the country. It was easier still when both parents were abroad, attending weddings and funerals, inspecting troops and visiting relations. The Prince did not relish these visits. As he was later to say, 'Abroad is awful. I know. I have been.' But duty bade him go, as the situation in Europe deteriorated and the King's health worsened. Then the way of life of the 'Big House' applied, and Grandpapa and Grandmama loosened the bearing rein. The children were bidden to big parties and receptions; they met famous people, among them Emperor William of Germany. They could race on their bicycles without being admonished for cutting up the paths with their tyres. There was the thrill of speeding downhill to Dersingham to buy sweets and of racing through the wood and down the slope to Wolferton station to watch the trains come in. The big disadvantage in the children's lives was that they seldom met children of their own age. They had few cousins – only the two shy daughters of their aunt Louise, Duchess of Fife, who lived in Scotland; and Olaf, son of Queen Maud and King Haakon of Norway, but he was far away and too young to count. When occasional young visitors came to the royal homes there was always a grown-up in attendance. There was one memorable exception to this isolation. Lady Leicester gave a children's party at Christmas time and Bertie was allowed to go. He met there a pretty little girl whose name was Lady Elizabeth Bowes-Lyon. She gave him the glacé cherry decorating her slice of iced cake.

3

Sunshine in the Garden

SATURDAY, 4 AUGUST 1900. London sweltered. The streets were empty, and but for the trade brought in by American tourists the West End shops would have closed their doors. Society had drifted away – to Cowes to sail, to Scotland to prepare for the grouse shooting, to their stately homes to check the harvest; the less fortunate had spent a few shillings on a cheap rail trip to the seaside. There was an added attraction to escaping from the dusty city streets: for the first time certain watering-places were allowing mixed bathing on specified beaches. The editors of the women's pages in newspapers were chary about the experiment, insisting that although 'knickers and very short basques to the tunics'[1] allowed of easier swimming, on mixed beaches the rules of decency must be observed – and skirts worn down to the knees. Holidaymakers who wished to observe feminity in less restricted circumstances travelled to Paris, the return fare being only thirty shillings.

Queen Victoria had held her last garden party and retired to Osborne. News from abroad was all depressing: in South Africa the Boer War lingered on; in China the Embassy staffs were beleaguered in Peking and an Allied Force had been sent out to relieve them. There was sadness on a personal front, too, over the death of her second son, Alfred, Duke of Saxe-Coburg and Gotha. Queen Victoria was alarmed at the idea of anarchists on the prowl in Europe. Apart from the attempt on the Wales's in May, on 29 July King Humbert of Italy was shot dead at Monza and on 2 August an attempt was made on the life of the Shah of Persia while visiting Paris. The frail old lady was convinced she was next on the list of victims. Those folk who were still in London, however, were concerned only with the heat and, as the evening came, they flocked to the Serpentine and thronged the open air cafés in Kensington Gardens.[2] One solitary aristocrat remained in the metropolis. Lord Glamis was constrained to remain in residence at 20 St James's Square. His wife was about to have a baby and on that Bank Holiday Saturday a girl was born. As soon as the health of Lady Glamis and her baby would allow, he retired to the peace of his Hertfordshire home, St Paul's Waldenbury, secluded in the quiet countryside to the west of the road between Welwyn and Hitchin.

Claude, Lord Glamis was the eldest son of the thirteenth Earl of Strathmore; he was forty-five. Nina Cecilia, his wife, was nearing her thirty-eighth birthday. She was the daughter of the Reverend Charles Cavendish-Bentinck, grandson of the third Duke of Portland. The couple had already had eight* children, all surviving except the first-born, Violet, who had died at the age of eleven. One more was to come to them, a son called David, born in 1902. To Lord and Lady Glamis their two youngest appeared more in the category of grandchildren. They were nicknamed 'the two Benjamins', in a class apart, babies when the brother next in age above them was in the schoolroom.

Lord Glamis, having been through the procedure so many times before, did not treat the registration of the birth of his ninth child with any degree of urgency. He overlooked the regulation that the matter must be attended to within six weeks and it was not until 21 September that he drove to Hitchin and called upon the registrar. His attention cannot have been upon the form, for he entered upon it that the baby had been born at St Paul's Waldenbury.[3] The family then moved *en masse* to Scotland, their destination Glamis Castle, Forfarshire, the Strathmore ancestral home. There the baby was christened Elizabeth Angela Marguerite. The second name was her father's choice for, with her big blue eyes and tiny hands, she reminded him of an angel; the third

* Violet Hyacinth – born 1882, died 1893; Mary Frances – born 1883, married Sidney, Baron Elphinstone; Patrick – born 1884, married Lady Dorothy Osborn; John Herbert – born 1886, married Hon. Fenella Hepburn-Stuart-Forbes-Trefusis; Alexander Francis – born 1887, died unmarried 1911; Fergus – born 1889, married Lady Christian Dawson-Damer, killed in action 1915; Rose Constance – born 1890, married Rear-Admiral Hon. William Leveson-Gower; Michael – born 1893, married Elizabeth Cator.

was her mother's, a devoted gardener, who had already chosen Violet, Hyacinth and Rose for her daughters.

Elizabeth spent much of her babyhood at St Paul's Waldenbury. Her opening views of life were of firelight throwing shadows on the nursery ceiling, of a high brass fender round the hearth, of pictures from story books hanging on the walls, of a screen decorated with scraps stuck there by elder brothers and sisters, of perambulations round the wide gardens where, in her memory, the sun was always shining. Her nurse was Clara Cooper Knight, known to the family as 'Alla', an odd similarity to Bertie's 'Lala'. She was only seventeen, young enough to take over the same role for the babies of the next generation, a quarter of a century ahead.

St Paul's was an ideal place for childhood. A woman who knew it well as the Edwardian days begun thus described it:

> About it there lingers a faint fragrance, like a whiff of potpourri of the eighteenth century. The redbrick Queen Anne house – with its fountains, its garden temples and its three converging avenues, cut through the wood in French fashion, either by Le Nôtre himself or by one of his pupils, each avenue leading the eye to some culminating point; here the tower of the village church; there two large statues . . .[4]

Those statues were of Diana and the Disc-Thrower, the latter known to the children as 'Bounding Butler'. There was peace even in the sounds that broke it – horses' hooves, the whistling of delivery boys, the tinkling music of a traction engine's wheels on a hard road, cock-crows and the cackling of hens at egg-time, the barking of playing dogs, birdsong, and the tiny sounds which only children hear. There was the magic intensity of smell which lasted from April until the fields lay bare, the potpourri of the scent of rose and magnolia, honeysuckle and violet, and the signal for full summer – the fragrance of new-mown hay.

The first big event in Elizabeth's life was the arrival of her brother David. The next, in 1904, was the death of her grandfather, who had been born in the reign of George IV. Her father became the fourteenth Earl of Strathmore and the owner of Glamis and Streatlam Castle in Durham. Streatlam had come into the family in 1767 through the ninth Countess of Strathmore, the daughter of George Bowes, who had made a fortune in coal, hence the family name of Bowes-Lyon. As young children Elizabeth and David regarded their residences thus: 'Glamis as a holiday place, Streatlam as a visit, and St Paul's as "Home".' When she was twelve Elizabeth confided in artist, E. Gertrude Thomson, that she and her brother could not 'bear' the name of Bowes. 'We never use it,' she said, 'we are just Lyon.'[5] Yet she had happy memories of Streatlam which lingered long after the castle was sold and demolished. Always musical, she loved attending the local band concerts there.

Elizabeth was a forward child, chattering away about nothing in particular from the age of thirteen months. Her mother undertook the early education of her 'Benjamins'. By the time she was seven Elizabeth knew most of the well-known stories of the Bible and British history. Lying on the floor, chin cupped in her hands, she would be lost in the dream-world of pages. David's only complaint later about this co-education was that his sister was too clever and that he was for ever struggling to keep up with her. Governesses arrived to teach French and German, and received a mixed reception. Their elder pupil thus decreed of them: 'Some governesses are nice and some *are not.*' A teutonic lady proved somewhat too Bismarckian for the relaxed atmosphere of the stately homes and was returned to the Fatherland. At the age of nine Elizabeth attended a day-school in London for two terms. Although she won a prize for literature, she was not moulded for the crocodile or the curriculum, and the experiment ended. Her mother was ever her best teacher, but she still set out from St James's Square for her drawing and music lessons. In September 1912 came a big break in her life. David went off to boarding school, leaving his sister very lonely, finding comfort in writing letters. Here is one that she wrote to Miss Gertrude Thomson, who had sent her an illustrated message:

> Never, never can I thank you enough for the *lovely* picture letter. I am having it framed, and shall hang it up in a conspicuous place. Everybody admires it awfully. Thank you millions of times for taking the trouble to do such a delicious letter just for me.
>
> David went to school for the first time on Friday last. I believe he is quite enjoying it. I miss him horribly.

Have you seen any teeny tiny frogs since you have been at St Paul's Waldenbury?

I do hope you can read my writing. I have got *such* a horrible pen. I hope you are very well. I have got to go to bed now.

Thanking you again many, many times for it.

Yours affec.,

Elizabeth[6]

Lord Glamis instilled into his children a love of, and interest in, outdoor life. He strode lightly round St Paul's garbed in leather, a pheasant's feather in his hat and a pruning-hook in his hand. He spent half his time lopping off surplus branches and making them into bundles. 'Good for the trees – and good for me,' he would say. He commented on his youngest daughter: 'Lady Elizabeth is most popular with all the tenants and the villagers of Whitwell . . . She was always more interested in her dolls' houses and her dolls than in how to tease the workmen on the estate and her tutors. Not that she was above mischief, as many of my tenants will tell you!'[7]

One employee who would not have agreed on the point of teasing was the chauffeur. He had but recently graduated from the stables to the garage and, while he was fully accustomed to the dangers to be encountered at the fore and aft ends of horses, he viewed with considerable trepidation similar positions on landaulettes. At the front end a handle was likely to kick like a mule and the back end was liable to omit explosions when surplus gases accumulated in the exhaust pipe. The motor car, its engine running, stood before the front door of St Paul's waiting for the embarkation of the Earl and Countess. While the chauffeur's attention was focussed on happenings within the house, Elizabeth and David placed a balloon under a front tyre and sneaked away to an observation point in the shrubbery. The stately departure was signalled by a bang and the conspirators, highly delighted, raced away to a secret hiding place. One such retreat was the loft of a centuries-old barn, reached only by a rickety ladder.

When, in 1923, the news broke of her engagement, a welter of stories about the young Elizabeth was extracted by the press from those who had known her as a child. Most of these concerned her insatiable appetite for sweet things, chocolate cake in particular, obtained either by speed or diplomacy. One cook took exception to unwanted exercise and complained that she was for ever chasing the 'little imp'[8] out of the kitchen. Certain stories pointed to her developing tastes and character. She adored acting and playing charades, and the dressing-up box was a treasured possession. When her pet bullfinch was devoured by the cat, she and David staged a dramatic funeral. A pencil box became the coffin. With slow tread this was borne into the wood and there David dug the grave. As he replaced the soil upon the box, his sister chanted a sad service born out of her imagination. Love for animals always showed, foremost perhaps in her love for her mischievous pony 'Bobs'. She had a pet black Berkshire pig. Unbeknown to her, her parents donated it for a raffle prize at a local fête. Horrified, brother and sister attempted to 'corner the market' in tickets, risking all their savings and borrowing recklessly from the staff, in their efforts to get the winning number. Sadly, Elizabeth lost her pig. There were signs of wilfulness and defiance. On being provided with new sheets for her bed, out of sheer naughtiness she cut them into strips with the nursery scissors; but such displays were rare – in the main she was best remembered for what her father termed her 'stately demeanour', earning for herself the nickname 'Princess'. She was the perfect hostess from the time that she could toddle, greeting visitors with charm and complete lack of shyness. She grew up in the days when newcomers to the area 'called' on their neighbours. Not all were welcome. Lady Strathmore, absorbed with her roses and at ease in her gardening dress, would sigh as some smart equipage, bearing mother and daughters 'done up to the nines', appeared on the drive. It was then that Elizabeth stepped into the breach, greeting the callers and keeping conversation going until her mother had changed into a more suitable garb and tidied her hair.

The Bowes-Lyons were not rich, to the degree that some of King Edward VII's friends were. They were victims of the slide in fortunes that had beset many of Britain's old families since the middle of the nineteenth century. Splendour, and 65,000 acres, had once been theirs, but death duties, depression and lack of business acumen were whittling away their fortunes. A revolution had taken place on the big estates. Those who had made fortunes out of coal, railways, engineering and cotton, and grown fatter still on the swollen profits of the Crimean War, were invading the stately homes. They had collected titles by well-placed gifts to charity, were in a great hurry to climb the ladder to aristocratic heights and, in their climbing, became more genteel than the gentry. While the employees on their estates often benefitted from the new flush of wealth, the mass of the poor country folk were far from happy. Common lands were fenced in, rights of way closed. It became a sin to snare a rabbit and sacrilege to kill a pheasant. *Punch*, ever watchful of the public's interest, lashed out: 'Even where the commons, open from time immemorial till lately, have been enclosed, you can go anywhere and do anything so long as you keep in the public highways, and don't go aside into the fields to gather mushrooms or pick flowers. Hurrah for the New Landed Interest!'[9]

After 1875 bad harvest succeeded bad harvest and the national loss of £80,000,000 led to a depression in commerce and trade as well as in agriculture. The price of corn, which had been 54 shillings during the Franco-German War, fell until it reached a low of 23 shillings. In the Middle West of America a vast new granary produced huge surpluses of grain for export. Beef was imported too. Tenant farmers were unable to pay their rents and landlords were unwilling, or unable, to reduce the amount. Farm after farm was thrown back on to the owners' hands and lay unproductive. At the ensuing auction sales prices were rock-bottom and new steam-powered equipment, which had cost hundreds, was knocked down for a few pounds. 1879 – 'black '79' – brought the crisis to a head for everyone. The gentry were forced to sell their London houses and forego the social Season as they struggled to save themselves from bankruptcy. Fathers warned their families of the dark future advising their sons to remember the advantage of a pension or to seek employment in the Empire, and stressing to their daughters the importance of marrying money. There came the difficulty, for large families were the fashion and the rule, and there were few accepted openings for sons beyond the army, the navy and the church: commerce was looked down upon and centuries of prejudice could not be wiped away in a day. Thus it was that once vast and well-preserved estates went under the hammer and were snapped up by international financiers to whom trade and the handling of money were a way of life. The Bowes-Lyons survived, finding relief in the brighter Edwardian days, but financially they had not escaped the wounding. A woman who met Lady Elizabeth at a children's tennis party noticed that her shoes were distinctly second-hand and her racket more suited to the catching of shrimps than to enduring a volley. Pocket money being difficult to extract from her father, Elizabeth had early become financially conscious. When she was seven she sent him the following telegram: 'SOS LSD RSVP ELIZABETH'.[10]

The Earls of Strathmore, the Lyons of Glamis, bore a tradition as good landlords quick to help those in trouble, and love and loyalty in return helped them through. As James Wentworth Day put it: 'At home in Angus they are an essential, friendly part of the background of life. They belong to the scene as much as the far-off, snow-whitened tops of the Grampian Mountains or the old Scots pines, red-trunked in the sunlight on the hills. They are "the family – the neighbours at the castle".'[11] Elizabeth cleaved to Glamis and its history in the Sidlaw hills and Strathmore valley. One of the oldest inhabited buildings in the United Kingdom, the castle has been in the Lyon family since the fourteenth century. She regaled herself with tales of feuding and raiding, imprisonment and torture. To Glamis in 1562 came Mary, Queen of Scots; 'the old Pretender' slept there in 1715, eighty beds being made up for his retinue. The Duke of Cumberland – 'The Bloody Butcher' – was an unwanted guest and, on his departure, Lord Glamis gave order that the bed in which he had slept be smashed to pieces. By contrast the four-poster used by Bonnie Prince Charlie was carefully preserved, as was the watch he left under his pillow when he fled in haste from the English. It was Stuart, Stuart all the way, and to hell with Hanover.

At Glamis the reception accorded to twentieth-century visitors could be in marked contrast with that at St Paul's. As they stood by the main door there might descend upon them a cascade of cold water. Brother and sister were playing a favourite game called 'repelling raiders'. In days gone by the falling fluid would have been boiling oil tipped from a cauldron. Ghosts glided in profusion through the upper passages. They came in a wide variety, some friendly and harmless, some sinister, the latter turning the dark hours into a nightmare for Sir Walter Scott when he slept in a lonely wing. There was Earl Beardie, a jovial medieval knight; the

Grey Lady, a smiling and beautiful apparition whose appearance was welcomed as a portent of good luck; the tragic spectre of Janet, widow of the sixth Lord Glamis, who was burned at the stake in Edinburgh; 'Old Nick' himself; and last, but not least, 'The Monster', the secret of whose story was confided only to the Glamis heir when he came of age. Elizabeth and David revelled in this spectral legacy and exploited it to the full, guests being treated to a lurid description of the night wanderers. Then, as they made their way to bed, the stories fresh in their minds, they might see in a dark corner, in the flickering shadow of an oil lamp, a body lying on the floor with a dagger deep in its chest and red stains on its clothing. They might even find a strange, still shape with its head resting on their pillows.

The summer holidays at Glamis were a gathering of the clan, brothers and sisters, cousins, uncles and aunts, enough to provide teams for cricket or make up a tennis tournament. There were picnics in the hills, long days with the guns and excursions to neighbouring houses. No lessons, all fun. There were other holidays to which Elizabeth looked forward with delight – the visits to her maternal grandmother, Mrs Caroline Scott, who lived in a beautiful house in a beautiful garden near Florence. The thrill of the boat and the train, the southern sunshine, the buildings and the culture, implanted in her a lasting love of Continental travel.

As the threat of war in Europe grew, Elizabeth passed her Junior Oxford examination. She was advanced and independent. Her passion was the theatre and, when David's holidays came round, it was on cheap seats that their spare cash was spent. For her fourteenth birthday present she asked to be taken to a hit show at one of London's largest theatres. The excitement there that 4 August 1914 was intense, unforgettable. When she woke up next morning Britain was at war with Germany.

4

'Bat Lugs' Goes to Sea

THE TIMES OF KING EDWARD VII were amongst the most difficult ever experienced by the Navy. With the new century the world was revolutionized. Only a handful of years after the introduction of the safety push bicycle, powered flight and radio were within reach, and infinite possibilities for submarine activity, telecommunications, scientific and chemical methods of destruction beyond imagination. Progress had brought other changes too – changes in the minds of men. The demand was being heard for social reform, better conditions in hospitals and schools, care of the old, trades unionism in factories, rights for women. These reforms would entail the outlay of vast sums of money – the building of a modern fleet capable of ruling the seas would also require such sums. The struggle was on.

For nearly half a century the British Navy had policed the world, gun-boats teaching tribal chiefs the power of the Great White Queen. Now progress had brought the probability of direct confrontation with a fleet as powerful as Britain's own. A fifth of the globe was coloured red. The safety and the future of the British Empire depended on the foresight of its naval leaders, resisting the inevitability of the old order changing and yielding place to new. All around them Britain did change, altering the ways of commerce and industry, educational establishments and the Army, leaving untouched only the city slums and the country villages. For the Army, the revolution was less shattering than for the Navy; in truth there was less to alter, and the Boer War had already given it a salutary lesson. Then regiments had given priority in baggage to mess silver over bandages. The truth had been learned the hard way.

King Edward was a modern-thinking man and saw the dangers ahead as clearly as any politician or military leader in the country. For 40 years, as adult Prince of Wales, he had travelled the Courts of Europe. That he was at loggerheads with his nephew, Emperor William II of Germany, was a tragedy and a handicap, but the confrontation would have come in any case, Bismarck having laid the foundation and William being the man he was. In the year of the Coronation, Admiral Sir John Fisher was recalled to the admiralty, becoming First Sea Lord in 1904. He was a dynamic man, convinced that Germany was intent on smashing Britain's Navy, and obsessed with the determination to keep Britain foremost on the seas. The King had complete confidence in him and gave him his full support. Changes of all kind came swiftly. The training period for cadets was increased from two to four years, divided between Osborne and Dartmouth. Plates were issued to the lower deck, relieving sailors of the primitive practice of eating with their fingers from tin basins, a change which was greeted with a roar from elderly admirals who forecast that the men would become 'sissies'.[1] Dreadnoughts, a new class of warship, highly armed and fast, and of eighteen thousand tons, were introduced. The concentration of naval strength was switched from the sunny, southern climes to the cold North Sea where, said Fisher, 'the fight will be'.[2] Savings had to be made to counter-balance the expenditure. This was done by cutting out dead wood, in the shape of outdated ships and outdated officers – 'fossils and ineffectives,'[3] Fisher labelled them. By thus wielding the pruning knife he cut the Navy clean down the middle. For the first time in history the service was divided against itself: there were those who agreed with Fisher, and those who did not.

One side of naval life did not change – the sadistic code of punishment and bullying. Cloaked as it was under the mantle of discipline and training, in truth it was the price which had to be paid by a nation which, for generations past, had sent its sons into the far corners of the earth, unaccompanied by their womenfolk. It was an unfortunate state of affairs which existed until Admiral David Beatty abolished it in 1917. Professor A. J. P. Taylor has written that it would be difficult to describe life at Osborne Naval College without exaggeration. 'Were such conditions to be discovered now in a Borstal institution, the Home Secretary would be driven from office overnight . . . The wretched boys were dragged from their beds at 6 a.m. in summer, 6.30 in winter. Thirty seconds for prayers and then, whatever the season, plunged into a tank of ice-cold water.'[4] At night one minute was allowed for undressing, the washing of teeth and jumping into bed. Any boy who failed to meet the deadline was summoned to the wash-house and there endured harsh application of the 'gong' rope. So they rushed and fought their way back down the passage and up the stairs, leaped into bed and there lay praying that their names would not be called out for punishment. The walls of the dormitories were so thin and in such poor repair that a hole could be kicked through them without hurting the foot. The food in the mess hall was unappetizing and insufficient and pocket money was restricted so that the diet could not be subsidized. Official punishment was terrifying. Sentence of a caning was passed on a Monday but the execution was delayed until Thursday, when a medical examination was carried out. The victim was then paraded in the gymnasium before the assembled officers and members of his term and strapped to a vaulting horse. Up to twelve strokes with a bamboo rod were flayed across him by a petty officer.

George, Prince of Wales, planned that all his sons should undergo naval training. In May 1907 David went to the Royal Naval College at Osborne. It was a shattering and wounding experience, contrasting violently with the sheltered existence at Sandringham and Marlborough House. In his own words, he felt 'like a lost dog'.[5] He was nicknamed 'Sardine', regarded as a freak because he had not been to preparatory school, as all the other boys had. He was the target for torments because he was the grandson of the King: his head was held firm on a window sill and the frame crashed down upon his neck – a cruel reminder of what could be the fate of sovereigns. He had to step off the pavement into the gutter when he saw senior cadets approaching. He had to run from the Common Room when those seniors entered. One day he did not move fast enough and a bottle of ink was poured down his neck. Another day it was decided that his hair would look better coloured red; he was anointed with red ink which streamed down on to his shirt. It was near to parade time: he could not attend in that condition and he could not sneak. So he was punished for absence: for the next three days he spent his spare time doubling round the stable yard, bearing a rod across his shoulders.

David did not say much when he returned to Sandringham at the end of term. He had always been the acknowledged leader of the schoolroom, and he was proud. He was shaken, but rebellious. Anyway he knew that if he complained he would be told that as his father had been through the naval mill, so would he. Yet there were vast differences in the two cases, the outstanding one being that when the then Prince George of Wales and his elder brother, Albert Victor, joined the training ship *Britannia* in 1877, they were accompanied by a very watchful tutor, the Rev. J. N. Dalton, and they had a cabin to themselves in the poop. David went to Osborne unaccompanied and slept in a dormitory with thirty other boys.

Bertie missed his brother very much and was lonely in the schoolroom at Sandringham. Out-classed and often teased as he had been by David, he was lost without the leadership. Mr Hansell's educational task grew even more difficult. An attempt to fill the gap was made by introducing young Harry into the class; Bertie was informed that he was now 'captain' and that he must show an example. But the experiment did not work, for Harry had none of David's sparkle in his character, nothing to spur Bertie on. Mathematics were the bane of his life; he simply could not master the fundamentals. When the strain of trying became too much he would lose his temper and then burst into tears. His father abruptly told him that he must stop behaving like a child of six. Hansell was instructed: 'You must be very strict and make him stick to it and do many papers.'[6] Still no effort was made to prepare him for the days ahead by allowing him to mix with other boys.

By 1905 the Wales's brood had increased to six. After the birth of Harry in 1900 their mother had written to her aunt Augusta: 'I think I have done my duty and may now *stop*, as having babies is highly distasteful to me.'[7] Yet twice more she underwent the ordeal, George being born in 1902 and John three years later. The Princess forestalled awkward questions by informing the earlier arrivals that the babies had flown in through the window and then had their wings cut off. The arrival of John meant that the Princess did stop producing for reasons both urgent and tragic. It was early noticed that there was something amiss with the child; epilepsy was diagnosed. A sweet and loving boy, he lived in a twilight zone and at the age of twelve was separated from his brothers and sister. Thus, for company, Bertie had Harry and George. Physically, Harry was more handicapped than Bertie. He, too, had knock-knees and was forced to endure the agony of splints. He also suffered from endless severe colds; he was slow at learning, coupled with the inherited family weakness of an ungovernable temper alternating, in his case, with fits of giggling. George, on the other hand, was a complete contrast to both of them. He was a lively child, considered by many to be the outstanding one of the family. He idolized David and copied him: he was not impressed by his parents and answered back. He was the most intelligent of the brothers and the brightest at lessons, and he was also musical. When he joined the classroom he quickly overtook his brother Harry, despite the age gap. Mr Hansell's hands were full.

In January 1909 Bertie, when just fourteen, joined David at Osborne. Mr Hansell forecast to the parents that, if he were treated as the other boys, the result would be disaster. Among the inhumanities which Bertie discovered was that, as a new boy, he was not allowed to talk with David. David got round this by meeting his younger brother at a secret rendezvous behind the playing fields, and there gave him advice and consolation.[8]

On arrival at Osborne Bertie was nicknamed 'Bat Lugs', on account of his outsize ears. He was pricked with pins to see if his blood ran blue. He was kicked by all those who wished to nurse the memory of having booted the grandson of the King. His ever-present problem was his stammer. If he were talking with his family or people he knew well there was little trace of it. But when speaking before an audience, he became obsessed with the fear that, having started a sentence, he would be unable to finish it. During his naval training there was always an audience, and an unsympathetic one at that. The initial letters which foxed him were G, N, K, and Q, which was why he referred to his father and mother as 'Their Majesties' instead of more usually 'The King and Queen'. One day 'Q' was his undoing. He was asked, in front of the class, what fraction was half of a half. The word 'quarter' simply would not come. His instructor assumed that he did not know and made sarcastic comment; the class sniggered.

Another handicap was his indifferent health, the spartan conditions exacerbating his tendency to severe colds and gastric trouble. Some degree of understanding must have entered the minds of his father and mother, for it was decided that his brother Harry should not follow him to Osborne. Instead, he was sent to Broadstairs and there cared for by Sister Edith Ward in a house lent by Sir Francis Laking, the royal doctor. At the end of summer 1909 Bertie was really ill. A chill developed into whooping-cough, and he was moved into isolation. This was sad for him as he missed a visit to Osborne by the Emperor and Empress of Russia and their young family, the task of showing them round the College being left to David. Thereafter Bertie was sent for convalescence to Alt-na-Guithasach on Deeside and regained his strength.

He looked forward eagerly to the holidays, but even then there was the fear of a bad report arriving and the subsequent summons to the study of York Cottage. His father had told the authorities at Osborne: 'Treat my sons like cadets and make them realize their responsibilities.'[9] His dearest wish was that they would be successful, and dark depression and anger came over him if the progress reports were not up to standard. In Bertie's case he was doomed to disappointment. Despite exhortation and the threat of extra studies, there were few encouraging signs. In the examination at the end of his final term, he emerged sixty-eighth out of sixty-eight contestants. Perhaps fortunately, there remains no record of his reception on returning to Sandringham for that Christmas of 1910.

To a more lenient mind there were grounds for excuse for his poor performance; it had been a disturbed year. On the morning of 7 May, as his Easter leave drew to its end, he had looked out of the schoolroom window at Marlborough House and seen the flag flying at half-mast over Buckingham Palace. King Edward VII was dead. The beloved Grandpapa, who had provided most of the fun he and the others had known, would never again laugh and joke with them in the 'Big House' at Sandringham. Two days later, in the uniform of a cadet, he stood at the salute on the garden wall of Marlborough House as the new King was proclaimed at St James's Palace. On 20 May he rode in the funeral procession, in a State coach with the Queen, David and Mary. It was a hot, sultry day and the strains of the Funeral March echoed in the streets as the procession made its slow way to Paddington, bound for St George's Chapel at Windsor. It was Bertie's first real experience of the overpowering grandeur of State ceremonial on an international scale, for he had been too young to recall clearly the funeral of Queen Victoria. Now he saw about him the Emperor of Germany; the Dowager Empress and the Grand Duke Michael of Russia; the Kings of Greece, Spain, Norway, Denmark, Portugal, Belgium and Bulgaria; the Crown Princes of Romania, Greece, Servia and Montenegro; the Duke of Aosta representing the King of Italy; Foreign Minister Pichon from France; and ex-President Theodore Roosevelt from the United States. This was to be the last gathering of the Sovereign powers of Europe, an echo of the nineteenth century, and they went their ways to await the armageddon of war.

Walking behind his grandfather's coffin into St George's Chapel was an experience Bertie was never to forget. He began to grow up. It was a necessary development, for Dartmouth was concerned more with the making of men than the training of boys. On his arrival at the senior College at the age of sixteen, he found that his enhanced status made little difference to the outlook towards him. The food was better there, the buildings sounder, but the punishments were even more vicious. Academically, he tramped along near the bottom of his class but showed little concern at his lack of progress. He was learning to adjust. He made more friends, his grit was noted and admired. He developed a liking for participating in mischief. Although not a leader in the larks planned by other cadets he was always in on the fun, and often the one to be caught and punished. On Guy Fawkes night he assisted in the letting off of a bonanza of fireworks, which was strictly against orders. At a College dance all the lights went out and there were driven on to the floor a flock of sheep and a terrified assortment of poultry. In a state of high excitement the second son of the King contributed largely to the ensuing chaos.

Bertie's stay at Dartmouth was enlivened by the great events which followed the coming of a new King. In June 1911 he was granted leave to attend the Coronation. He sat with his sister and younger brothers and watched David, now Prince of Wales, pay homage to his father, then shared the excitement of coming out on to the balcony at Buckingham Palace and, later, accompanying his parents on the State drives through London. In April 1912 he was confirmed in the church of St Mary Magdalene at Sandringham. In May he was with his father at the review of the Fleet off Plymouth. For him, the highlight was a trip in the submarine D4. 'We dived and went about three miles under water,' he wrote in his diary[10] which he kept religiously. It was during the review that he met for the first time a man who was to play a vital role in his later life. The First Lord of the Admiralty, Mr Winston Churchill, came on board the royal yacht to greet the King.

In December Bertie passed out of Dartmouth, this time managing to be sixty-first out of sixty-seven. His father softened somewhat. On 18 January 1913 Bertie joined the county cruiser *Cumberland* for the final phase of his training before becoming a midshipman. It was to prove the happiest period of his time as a cadet, but one weakness became immediately apparent and which stayed with him. As *Cumberland* rolled and twisted through the Bay of Biscay, he was very sick. Tenerife, Barbados, Martinique, Bermuda, Cuba, Havana. In Jamaica he faced a vital test: he was called upon to make a speech at the opening of a new wing of the Kingston Yacht Club. The ordeal was increased for him by the presence of a multitude of the young ladies of Jamaica, each intent upon touching him. He began to stammer, each clutch at his trousers increasing his predicament, but struggled on to the end. As a result of this experience he concocted a plan to lighten the burden of contact with the public. There happened to be on board a cadet who bore a striking resemblance to him and, by bribery and cajolery, he persuaded this boy to act as 'stand-in'. When *Cumberland* reached Canada, the Press were on the trail of the 'Prince'. The stand-in played his part to perfection, announcing that he was treated exactly the same as other cadets, except that he wore a bowler hat on Sundays! The highlight of the Canadian interlude was a trip to see Niagara Falls. It was on that day he first trod the soil of the United States of America. He loved Canada, the size of it, the lakes and in particular the fishing. Still it was apparent that he was a shy boy, a poor conversationalist and frightened of girls. At the ball given for the cadets he avoided the dance floor, retreated to a corner and from that point of vantage refused to move.

On 15 September Bertie became a midshipman – a 'snotty' – and he was known as 'Mr Johnson'.* He joined the battleship *Collingwood.* Here was fierce contrast with the comparative peace of the cadet cruise, the 'snotty' being regarded as the lowest form of marine life. There was no privacy; his total belongings were stored in a sea-chest outside the Gun-room, in a space occupied by twelve others. At night he slung his hammock above the chest and stowed it away in the morning. On one occasion it was cut down and he fell upon his sea-chest, severely damaging one eye. He coaled ship from the black hold of a collier. He was the errand-boy of his seniors. Discipline was severe and there were some unpleasant customs:

> When the senior members of the midshipmen's mess desire to be relieved for any or no reason of the society of their juniors, an ordinary table-fork is violently plunged into a wooden locker or partition and the operator shouts 'Fork in the beam'. By the time the fork has ceased its vibration every junior 'snotty' must be out of the room. As the Gun-room door is by no means a wide aperture and Admiralty forks do not quiver indefinitely, there was usually a jam of juvenile officers in the doorway, which was cleared with astonishing speed by the seniors applying vigorous chastisement to the rear anatomy of the burrowing laggards.[11]

So life continued until he was eighteen. On the plus side he had learned the meaning of discipline and the importance of good manners, and there had been implanted in him the basic strength of courage and perseverance. He had also learned how to make friends with men. Yet he had developed in a comparatively narrow world. It had been instilled into him that the Navy was everything, that the Navy could do anything and that the bridge was the stepping-stone to God. Osborne and Dartmouth existed only to train naval officers and beyond any doubt, obvious in the general result, they knew their drill. But Bertie was not destined to be a naval officer; in any circumstances he would progress into a role where he would be called upon to deal with the leaders of

* This *nom de guerre* was used for practical purposes, and used both by his supervisors and fellows.

countries who had no navy – in Vienna and Geneva nautical matters did not rate high on the priority list of indigenous values. He would require a global outlook and familiarity with the gamut of classes. David and Bertie were different as chalk is from cheese. The elder boy had resisted the naval inculcation, though the Navy had left its mark on him, some of those who knew him well believing that it was responsible for certain nervous habits and quirks in character. Nevertheless he was an individualist whereas Bertie was a follower, imbibing the atmosphere about him. At eighteen Bertie was in the position of never having visited the Courts of Europe, even though peopled with his relations. He lacked panache and withdrew from the limelight. He was ill at ease with women and lost in the social whirl. He knew nothing of politics or diplomacy, and nothing of the civilian rank and file. He had no small talk and his sense of humour was bawdy, though when he told stories he did so with such gusto that they were always well received, jokes about Gibraltar doing rude things to Malta, the ship's dog, and odd happenings on the China Station. He was convulsed with laughter when a senior officer lost his trouser buttons and was forced to appear at a function with his hands in his pockets.

It may then be asked why such a training should have been chosen for him. The answer is simple. It was an age when fathers wished their sons to repeat their own experiences. George V took it to extremes, desiring that just as he had been frightened of his father, so his sons should now be frightened of him. The highest accolade obtainable for the young was the approbation of their parents; while David rebelled, Bertie did his best to oblige. Again, the question must be asked, why did George V himself join the Navy? The answer is simple. He and his elder brother, Prince Albert Victor, were academically unfitted to enter a public school. Queen Victoria had wished them to go to Wellington College, in the founding of which the Prince Consort had taken such a lively interest. She wrote:

> The very rough sort of life to which boys are exposed on board ship is the very thing not calculated to make a refined and amiable Prince, who in after years (if God spares him) is to ascend the throne. It would give him a very one-sided view of life which is not desirable . . .[12]

As was often the case, she was right, but she was shown evidence that the training ship *Britannia* was the only solution for her grandsons. Thus, when Prince Albert Victor died in 1892 and George left the Navy, he was completely unfitted to take over the throne when the time came. So clear was this that a member of the household took it upon himself to write a letter to Windsor urging that steps be taken to prepare him. Despite twenty-odd years of opportunity he did little but shoot birds and stick stamps in an album. He was a Naval officer and there was no changing him. When King Edward VII was near to death in 1902, George had admitted he was not yet ready to take over but he still failed to see that the vital task of a royal father was to train his sons to reign and hold responsible positions.

There were other truths which George and Mary* did not see, outstanding among them being the menace of their cousin, Emperor William of Germany. In the summer of 1913 they travelled to Berlin for the wedding of William's only daughter, Victoria Louise. Among the twelve hundred guests were Würtembergs and Mecklenburgs, Holsteins and Hesses, Hanovers and Hohenzollerns. At the close of the festivities Queen Mary wrote:

> We left Berlin at 5.35 for London. William and Victoria [the Empress] accompanied us to the station. Took leave of them all with regret after charming visit. I cannot tell you how very much we enjoyed our visit to Berlin or how touched we were at the kindness shown us by William & Victoria and indeed by everybody. It was a most interesting time & so beautifully arranged in every way, nothing could have gone off better.[13]

* She took her proper name of Mary as her title.

5

The First War

THE GLAMIS FAMILY were quick to take up arms. Away they went in August 1914, three of Elizabeth's brothers in the Black Watch and one in the Royal Scots. Lady Rose Bowes-Lyon was training to be a nurse at a London hospital. Even Lord Strathmore, who was in his sixtieth year, went back into uniform. The London house was closed and Elizabeth and her parents squeezed into a packed train for Scotland. Lady Strathmore planned to convert Glamis Castle into a convalescent home for the wounded, but not only had she to organize a ward of sixteen beds and all the necessary facilities, she also had to prepare for the wedding of two of her sons, Fergus and John, who had decided to marry in September.

With autumn David went back to school, and Glamis waited. The breath-taking experience of the declaration of war, the departure from London, the weddings and the goodbyes were over. Many workers on the estate had left for the front; the convalescent hospital had as yet no patients. Elizabeth sat knitting, knitting, knitting, and making comforts for the 5th Black Watch, made up of local men. She said of those days: 'My other chief occupation was crumpling up tissue paper until it was so soft it no longer crackled, to put into the lining of sleeping-bags.'[1] On a day in December the first of the wounded arrived from Dundee and were helped to their beds in the panelled dining-room. For five full years those beds were all occupied, and the pace never slackened.

It was a disconcerting experience for the soldiers who came from all parts of Britain, from New Zealand, Australia and Canada, wounded in body or in mind. Most had never entered a castle before, nor met a Lord or a Lady. At Glamis they were received at the main door by Lady Strathmore and treated as if they were house-guests. Acclimatization was not easy. One soldier, helping to clear the table after dinner and bearing a high stack of plates, met Elizabeth in the passage. He stared at her and dropped the lot. She burst out laughing. It was the first Christmas which sealed the family and their wounded guests into a unity, a spirit of oneness which continued as the ambulances came and went. In the crypt stood a giant tree, sparkling with a hundred candles. Around its trunk was piled a mountain of presents, gifts from one Lyon to another, for every member of the staff and for every soldier. Some of those presents became treasured mementoes; some still are. When supper was over there was a sing-song, and words which had never been heard in the Castle before echoed round the grey walls.

Elizabeth played many and varying parts to those soldiers. She was stand-in for sisters and daughters, and girl-friends far away. She was a letter-writer, entertainer on the piano, nurse and parlour-maid, errand boy to the village shop. She was in great demand as a partner for card games, although it was noted she had a habit of winning, which caused many a wink. She could, at times, be a sergeant-major. Finding a man sucking at an empty pipe, she laced him down good and proper, demanding to know why he was short, for although the hospital had little money to spare no man was allowed to go without baccy. The impish element was still there. She would ride her bicycle among the men as they rested on the lawn and then, crossing her hands and shutting her eyes, end upside down in the rose bushes. She learned many lessons of life in those five years of apprenticeship. She learned that she must not show favour to one man more than another. She learned how to take sadness. She grew up.

The big moment of every day was when the 'postie' came up the drive. There was a scramble for letters from home, and messages from the front. In September 1915 Captain Fergus Bowes-Lyon was killed in the battle of Loos. Early in 1917 Michael was reported dead; after an agony of suspense word came that he was in a prison hospital in Germany. In 1916 Rose, who had been an indefatigable ward sister, married the Hon. William Leveson-Gower and Elizabeth became her mother's other right hand. Then the Countess fell ill and her youngest daughter had to bear the full burden of running Glamis. It might have been her 'passing out' examination: she passed with flying colours.

1919. The last of the wounded prepared to leave, signed the visitors' book and handed over their goodbye gifts. Elizabeth, spaniel at her heels, watched them go. Words came back to her: 'There's a long, long trail a-winding . . .' 'Goodbye, Dolly, I must leave you . . .'

On the morning of 29 August 1914 the hospital ship *Rohilla* anchored off Aberdeen and the Aberdeen Boys' Brigade Ambulance Company carried Prince Bertie ashore on a stretcher. He was taken to the Northern Nursing Home, suffering from appendicitis. Six days before, after keeping the afternoon watch on HMS *Collingwood*, steaming off the north coast of Scotland, he had collapsed with violent stomach pains and in the sick bay was injected with morphia. Transferred to the hospital ship at Wick, he was examined by Sir James Reid, the royal doctor whom the King had despatched hurriedly north. He confirmed appendicitis and on 9 September Bertie was operated upon. Convalescing in the loneliness of York Cottage, Sandringham, he was overcome by depression and frustration. He felt wasted, completely 'out of it'. David was in France and, although forbidden the front line, was habitually making his way there; his younger brothers were away at school; his father and mother were fully occupied with a daily stint of war duties. He longed to be back on *Collingwood* but the gastric trouble continued. In December a Naval Medical Board determined that he was still unfit to go to sea. The King's surgeon, Sir Frederick Treves, who had served Queen Victoria and Edward VII, was of the opinion that he ought never to go to sea again.

His father, perhaps becoming more sympathetic towards his son, refused to accept the pessimistic report and, noting Bertie's frustration, arranged for him to work at the Admiralty. He was received by Mr Winston Churchill and initiated into the work of the War Room, but although he was glad indeed to be back in uniform the monotony of office routine wearied him. Young men of his age, many of whom he had known, were falling fast in France and all he could do was to attend their memorial services. He bearded the Second Sea Lord, persuaded him and, in the middle of February 1915, he was back on *Collingwood*. Life had its frustrations at Scapa Flow too, described by one officer as 'gallons and gallons of water surrounded by miles and miles of damn all'.[2] After short forays into the North Sea, ships remained in harbour for ten days. There was almost 'damn all' for Bertie to do: forbidden to take part in the physical exercises practised by the remainder of the crew he had to content himself with an occasional game of golf. Fortunately, being now a senior Midshipman, his duties were less arduous and uncomfortable.

His next lapse in health came in May coinciding with the loss of the *Lusitania* off Ireland with twelve hundred lives, an event which upset him deeply. Sudden and unheralded gastric attacks sent him to the sick bay and in July he was transferred to the hospital ship *Drina*. On one point he insisted – that if the Fleet were ordered to sea, he would be allowed to rejoin his ship. The doctors did not agree, but his father backed him, knowing what effect any other course would have on his son's nerves. The gastric condition continued and in the autumn Bertie spent some time convalescing on Deeside. Previously, at Alt-na-Guithasach, he had learned to fish in Lock Muick, taught by his tutor, who was an expert, and by the gillies. Thanks to them be became a polished fisherman and not a 'water flogger'. He was completely absorbed in the sport, and completely relaxed: it was noted that with a fishing rod in his hands, his stammer disappeared. He moved to Sandringham after a month and while there received the disturbing news that his father had been thrown from his horse while inspecting troops in France; it later emerged that the King had suffered a double fracture of the pelvis. The accident brought him recurring pain, resulting in increased irascibility and lack of patience.

A bright spot for Bertie, and one which did him a power of good, was a visit to his brother David, who was with the Guards' Division at La Gorgue. He inspected the battle grounds of the previous September. He watched a British bombardment of the German trenches and later was at the receiving end when the enemy retaliated, learning at first hand the grim realities of war. He watched houses crumbling, saw the inmates come from back doors and race for safety. Return to 'light duty' at the Admiralty saw him with a renewal of the confidence which recent months had drained. He helped his convalescing father by relieving him of minor public duties, then came the welcome news that he had passed his examinations to become a Sub-Lieutenant. He bounced up, convinced the doctors that he was fit for service and early in May 1916 he rejoined his ship.

He was just in time. On the evening of the 30th *Collingwood*, in the First Battle Squadron, slipped out to take her place among fifty-one British ships of war. The course was east, towards Jutland. It was a milk night, the sky bright with stars and the sea sparkling their reflection. Next day there was mist, restricting visibility. At two in the afternoon came the call for 'Action'. 'Mr Johnson', suffering some discomfort from an ill-advised over-indulgence in soused mackerel, leaped from his bunk. This was 'it' and any lingering gastric handicap faded clear away.

At 4.50 the signal came that the enemy fleet was heading north. 'Full speed ahead'. Bertie was second officer in No. 2 Turret, 'A', twelve-inch guns, the fore turret of *Collingwood*. From this viewpoint he watched the British Fleet cut the still, grey-green water into wide, white Vs. The mist was thickening, visibility down to four miles. At 5.37 *Collingwood* opened fire on some light German cruisers. 'The second salvo hit one of them which set her on fire; she sank after two more salvoes were fired into her. We then shifted on to another light cruiser and helped to sink her as well.'[3] Thereafter Bertie saw what battle at sea could mean. He saw the wreck of *Invincible*, broken in two, bows and stern rising from the water, her crew trapped in the eddies below. *Ambuscade* was out of action, steam pouring from her funnel. *Queen Mary* was early hit, 'within 30 seconds breaking up and sinking in a wild confusion of red glare and smoke so thick that it looked solid.'[4] One of her Midshipmen was blown off his gun-turret into the sea. He caught hold of a floating hatch and clung there for half an hour while enemy shells exploded all around him. He was rescued.

At 6.28 the outline of the German cruiser *Derfflinger* showed through the mist, her position fixed by her gun-flashes. Bertie was sitting on top of 'A' Turret when a salvo from her straddled *Collingwood*. He ducked. 'What the hell's the matter with you?' roared a senior officer. 'Coming down now, sir,' answered 'Mr Johnson'.[5] But that was easier said than done. A portly petty officer, who had also been having a 'decko' at what was going on, reached the narrow entrance to the turret first and became jammed there. A second salvo whistled overhead before pressure from above and below released him. *Collingwood* put three salvoes into

Derfflinger with deadly effect. Great holes were torn in her side and flames poured from her quarter-deck; she slipped away to be swallowed by the mist. For an hour desultory fire continued at shadowy German shapes, in all eighty-four rounds being expended. Two torpedoes came at *Collingwood,* one passing astern and a second only thirty yards ahead, skilful use of the helm successfully evading them.[6]

It was nine o'clock when nightfall put an end to action. *Collingwood* was forty miles south of the Skaggerak and the same distance from the Danish coast, and for the few dark hours she steamed south. At four there was action again when a zeppelin was spotted at 12,000 yards. When fired at, it turned away. At noon on 2 June *Collingwood* was back at Scapa Flow and immediately coaled and ammunitioned.

Bertie was mentioned in despatches, his name appearing among those of 'Officers commended for their Services'.[7] He had 'made it'. All the sweat and stammering and punishments had earned him his reward, but he was somewhat disappointed that his ship showed no outward traces of the engagement. He confided in the Prince of Wales: 'When I was on top of the turret I never felt any fear of shells or anything else. It seems curious but all sense of danger and everything else goes except the one longing of dealing death in every possible way to the enemy.'[8] And he wrote to a former tutor: 'The Jutland battle was a great thing to have been in, and it certainly was very different from what I had expected. We of course in the *Collingwood* saw a good deal more than some of the other ships, and we fired more than they did. We were not hit at all, which was very lucky, though we were straddled several times. One shell dropped over the forecastle, missing us by inches!'[9]

Bertie was now convinced that his 'inside trouble' was over, and through the summer of 1916 he looked forward to further action. But at the end of August the pain struck again. He was ordered to rest at Windsor, where three royal doctors agreed he had a duodenal ulcer. The only small consolation for him was that Queen Mary's insistence on a balanced diet certainly suited his stomach better than the rough naval menu. In November he reported for staff work at Portsmouth, but again found shore duties frustrating. Still, he had some moments of excitement and pride. He took his father's equerry, Sir Charles Cust, out for a trip in a submarine. When it dived it stuck firmly in the mud on the bed of the Solent. 'A great experience,'[10] commented Bertie, once the bows were cleared and the surface reached. When he was twenty-one in December he was invested by his father with the Order of the Garter.

In May 1917 Bertie was back on sea duty, reporting to the battleship *Malaya* where, to his delight, he met an old friend and supporter of Osborne days, naval doctor Louis Greig. But it was clear that his insistence to serve was out of proportion to his physical capacity to do so; in July he was back in hospital. This time, on his own decision, there was no return to his ship. He was operated upon for his ulcer and the cause of his trouble was removed. Some asked, and with reason, why the operation had not been allowed before but, with the sea denied him, Bertie determined on a new course, and transferred to the Royal Naval Air Service.

Before joining Bertie had changed his name. In July King George V had proclaimed that henceforth 'Our House and Family shall be styled and known as the House of Windsor.' Queen Mary's family had switched from Teck to Cambridge. Her elder brother, Adolphus, Duke of Teck, who had married Lady Margaret Grosvenor, became Marquess of Cambridge; their children – Bertie's cousins – being the Earl of Eltham, the Ladies Mary and Helena Cambridge, and Lord Frederick Cambridge. Mary's younger brother, Alexander, whose wife Alice* was daughter of Leopold, Duke of Albany, Queen Victoria's youngest son, was created Earl of Athlone; their children became Lady May Cambridge and Viscount Trematon.

The swap had come about because of rumours and beliefs that that the royal family must be German-biased because of their close ties with that country. After all the Prince Consort had declared that he was a German through and through and would always remain one. Both George V and Bertie were most touchy on the point of 'the German connection'. Similar feelings had, in 1914, brought about the retirement of Admiral Prince Louis of Battenberg from the Navy. In 1917 matters were exacerbated by the pro-German attitude of Princess Alice's brother, the Duke of

* Died 1981.

Coburg, hence George V's decree. The Kaiser took satirical revenge by dubbing the play *The Merry Wives of Windsor,* 'The Merry Wives of Saxe-Coburg and Gotha'. It was therefore with considerable relief that the royal family felt themselves clearly labelled British.

6

Engaged

THE ROYAL NAVAL AIR SERVICE and the Royal Flying Corps were in progress of conversion into the Royal Air Force when Bertie began his service early in 1918. He was posted to Cranwell, near Grantham, the station still being known as HMS *Daedalus* and under naval discipline. Naval doctor Louis Greig, friend and mentor, and his wife went with him, and they took a small house in the village of Rauceby. Bertie's coming aroused little comment among the Lincolnshire folk, though there was some surprise at learning that the King's son pumped up his own bath water, dug the garden and that he'd brought some wire netting at the local shop so that he could keep chickens. His job was to supervise the many young men in training at Cranwell. He liked the work and was intensely interested in it, but the combining of the two services presented many problems of clashing customs and characters. In the spring Bertie wrote to a friend; 'The whole of my show is upside down . . . I am pretty fed up . . .' Luckily for him he was transferred to a cadet unit at St Leonards-on-Sea in July.

It was his great ambition to serve in France before the war ended. That ambition was achieved on 23 October when he flew across the Channel and reported to RAF Headquarters. A few days followed of intense excitement and round-the-clock activity. Then the war ended – and with it the job of the King's second son. Somewhat despondently, he wondered what next lay in store for him. He was to be pleasantly surprised. He was chosen to ride beside the King of the Belgians on his triumphant entry into Brussels on 22 November. It was the first time Bertie had represented his father on a State occasion, and he did it very well. His next ambition was to learn to fly. He was not particularly enamoured of the idea of flying; simply he did not like appearing in RAF uniform unless the white wings were upon it and objected to being classified a 'quirk'. He obtained permission and two Avros were sent over to France to allow him to 'get the feel'. Returning to England early in the New Year, he began serious instruction at Waddon Lane Aerodrome, Croydon, in March. He proved an adept pupil and earned his wings on 31 July, his test flight taking him over Windsor Castle. Next day he was gazetted a Squadron Leader, which was to prove his last promotion as a full-time serving officer. He was very popular with the mechanics, to whom he was known simply as 'Bertie'. One of them, fiddling about with an Avro, was asked by a friend if he would go into town. 'I'm busy for a bit,' he replied, 'Bertie's mooching round the house tops.'[1] A red letter day came when he took his brother David up for a flip but the staff on the ground were mightily relieved when the two young men next in line to the throne got safely back: the King was unaware of their escapade.

In October Bertie, accompanied by his younger brother, Harry, went to Trinity College, Cambridge. His subjects for study were political economy, civics and history. Since to date the principal learning drummed into him had been connected with knots (of various kinds), naval custom, the weather and explosives, the time had indeed come for a widening of outlook and interest. The two Princes stayed with Louis Greig, his wife and children in 'Southacre,' an ugly house with a nice garden off the Trumpington Road. Domestic life was much as it had been at Rauceby and, once again, the gardener saw much of Bertie. Constantly referring to him as 'Your Royal Highness', the old man was told: 'Only once a day, please. I am sick of it.'[2] He had a bicycle for the mile journey to College. He also had a motor cycle, of which he was exceeding proud. He made no dramatic impact on the town or the Backs or the Common Room; the episode he remembered best during this pleasant interlude was being fined 6/8d for smoking in the street while wearing academic dress.

Bertie was still far from being a hundred per cent fit. There were frequent moods of depression, and he became easily discouraged when beaten at sports or defeated by academic subjects. He was forbidden to fly solo. Partly because of his stammer he still dreaded making speeches and, when called upon to speak at the

Royal Academy Dinner, wrote to his mother: 'I am longing to get the Academy Dinner over, and that dreadful speech . . .'[3] His days bore little resemblance to those lived with panache by his grandsons, Princes Charles, Andrew and Edward. While his elder brother was abroad, captivating millions of people with his charm and prejudicing his future peace of mind through the cruel burden of duties with which the Government loaded him, Bertie grew to maturity in peace, under modest conditions, away from the spotlight. He relied to a considerable extent on Louis Greig. Greig was, in part, playing the role which Baron Stockmar had carried out for Prince Albert of Coburg prior to his marriage: in 1838 the German doctor had accompanied Albert to Rome, the object being to toughen him up and to put polish on him. After his time with Bertie was over, Greig was to say: 'My principal contribution was to put steel into him.'[4]

Bertie went down from Cambridge at the end of the Easter term of 1920. In June his father created him Duke of York, with the additional titles of Baron Killarney and Earl of Inverness. He took his seat in the House of Lords on the 23rd. The stress of the occasion proved almost too much for him and he swayed as he advanced towards the Woolsack. The Lord Chancellor, Lord Birkenhead, saved the situation and brought a return of composure by whispering in his ear: 'Been playing much tennis lately, Sir?'* The King, by honouring his son, had shown his appreciation of his work and progress but he never fully came to understand Bertie's inner problems, which were partly of parental making. More irascible than ever after his riding accident in France, off song with David, irritated by a demanding mother who was for ever plaguing him with problems about Russia and Greece, George V was not an easy man to live with. Queen Mary and Bertie took the brunt of his ill temper and carping at the changed way of life which followed the war's ending. Daughter Mary was the apple of his eye and could do no wrong, while soldier Harry and sailor George took their own lines, as younger children are apt to do. Although Bertie was often away, on the Continent and about Britain, helping his father out with public duties, the intervals at Buckingham Palace and Windsor

* The Duke, partnered by Louis Greig, won the RAF Doubles Competition in July.

definitely played on his nerves. In addition there was the problem of female company. King George V dreaded the thought of modern misses skipping around the Palace, with their liking for cocktails, gramophones and weekend parties. Bertie was late in developing a taste for the ladies, but the time came and his choice fixed upon Grace Vanderbilt, daughter of Mrs Cornelius Vanderbilt, an American hostess of considerable ambition.[5]

On the evening of the first RAF summer ball, Bertie and some cronies dined at the Berkeley, then strolled across Piccadilly towards the sound of music from the Ritz. Elizabeth was dancing with James Stuart, MC, twenty-three-year-old son of the Earl of Moray, and recently appointed equerry to Bertie. When the music stopped Bertie summoned him and asked the name of his partner. When the music began she was in his arms.

At twenty Elizabeth was in marked contrast to most of the gay young things who danced and flirted through the wild post-war days. The Countess of Airlie knew her well: 'She was very unlike the cocktail drinking, chain-smoking girls who came to be regarded as typical of the 1920s. Her radiant vitality and a blending of gaiety, kindness and sincerity made her irresistible to men. One knew instinctively that she was a girl who would find real happiness only in marriage and motherhood.'[6]

Bertie set himself to win Elizabeth and took every chance that came his way to meet her. It was no easy task: Elizabeth was in demand and elusive. The one thing she demanded of young men was absolute emotional fidelity, and several hopefuls were cast aside because they were suspected of flirting. There was no danger of this with Bertie: he rather took after his father who, having once at a dance snatched a kiss from his cousin, Marie of Edinburgh, considered that this would, of natural course, lead to marriage. He also had great tenacity and did not mind if she treated him somewhat cavalierly at times. When he called at her house to take her out to dinner or a dance, the message might come down from her dressing-room that she was not yet ready. So Bertie would chat with her mother. Elizabeth was very dependent on the judgment and ruling of her mother in particular. Lady Strathmore liked Bertie very much but saw his weaknesses and the absolute necessity of finding him the right wife. Lord Strathmore thought him a thoroughly nice young chap. There was no question of any of them being impressed by the aura of majesty.

In the autumn Bertie made progress – he was invited to stay at Glamis and motored over from Balmoral. He said nothing then but recruited an emissary to spy out how the land lay. The blunt message came back that if Bertie had anything to say he must say it himself. He had a try in the spring of 1921 but the words came hard and he was rejected. Still, he didn't give up hope.

Lady Airlie was Lady of the Bedchamber to Queen Mary and discovered from the Queen that the Prime Minister had indicated that foreign marriage by the Princes would not be tolerated by the British public. Queen Mary added: 'I don't think Bertie will be sorry to hear that. I have discovered that he is very much attracted to Lady Elizabeth Bowes-Lyon. He's always talking about her.'[7] She added that she did not know much about her. Lady Airlie was able to fill in the details. Thereafter she took it upon herself to further the romance. Both Bertie and Elizabeth would frequently call in at her flat for a chat, which gave her the chance she required. She found that Elizabeth was frankly afraid of the public life which lay ahead of her if she married into the royal family. Bertie could talk of nothing but Elizabeth, but he was no Lothario. The Countess commented: 'His humility was touching. He was deeply in love but so humble.' As the months passed Queen Mary became convinced that Elizabeth was the one girl who would make Bertie happy. 'But,' she said, 'I shall say nothing to either of them. Mothers should never meddle in their children's love affairs.'[8]

That summer a common interest developed for Bertie and Elizabeth. It centred round the care of the young, less fortunately placed than themselves. She was deeply involved with the Forfarshire Girl Guides: at twenty-one she was appointed District Commissioner of Glamis and Eassie Parish; London headquarters reported that she was an excellent officer and took the keenest interest in her work. Bertie's mind was working on the same, but more advanced lines, stemming from his experience of training during his active service with the RAF. He wanted to knock down the barriers between the classes, pronounced as they were, and to show that members of the royal family were as much interested in service for the under-privileged as they were in the activities of the privileged. Working with the Industrial Welfare Society he organized a scheme for annual summer camps at which two hundred boys from the public schools came together with a like number from industrial firms. These camps became an institution and a key interest in Bertie's life. For their first ten years they were held at New Romney in Kent, thereafter at Southwold in Suffolk. Bertie planned to spend at least one day under canvas at each camp and integrate himself into the programme of sports and community singing.*

It happened that Princess Mary was also deeply interested in the Guide Movement and the shared enthusiasm led to a friendship with Elizabeth, who was accordingly asked round to Buckingham Palace on occasion. Naturally she came to the notice of the King and Queen, two parents with marital affairs very much in their minds but with little practical experience of how to set about such things beyond consulting the pages of the Almanac de Gotha. Interest increased when Elizabeth was chosen to be a bridesmaid at the wedding of Princess Mary and Viscount Lascelles at Westminster Abbey in February 1922.

Queen Mary liked what she saw of the Scottish girl and, mindful no doubt of Lady Airlie's words decided not to 'meddle' exactly but to probe more deeply. During her visits to Deeside in the autumn, she motored over to Glamis. Lady Strathmore was ill and Elizabeth did the honours. Her behaviour, her presence and her detailed knowledge of the Castle's history created a most favourable impression.

Society began to talk and to conjecture. The more irreverent section – descendants of those who had referred to Victoria and Albert as 'Joseph and Eliza' – had labelled the Queen's family 'the Teck snobs', and not without reason. What Society recalled, with clarity, was the almighty row which the Duke of Teck had raised when his son Adolphus became engaged to Lady Mary Grosvenor, daughter of the first Duke of Westminster, simply because she had not got the magic letters before her name. Now Society pondered on whether Queen Mary would part with a son to the daughter of a Scottish Earl. In fact, after the Glamis visit, she was

* In June 1981 Queen Elizabeth the Queen Mother gave a party at Clarence House to mark the Diamond Jubilee of the Duke of York's camps, at which she welcomed members who had attended the very first camp.

thinking in terms of Lady Elizabeth Bowes-Lyon becoming Queen of Britain. She was considering her as a wife not for Bertie but for the Prince of Wales.

Right as she was to put all thought of renewed German connections aside, wrong indeed was she in the choice of David. That young man's affaires were already leaving his grandfather's aberrations far behind, though he matched his penchant for married women. When he attended balls on his overseas tours, he would let his fingers play up and down the bare backs of 'colonial gals' – and 'colonial gals' were unaccustomed to such freshness, somewhat shocked at the regal style. David missed few opportunities, from Canada's icy mountains to India's coral strands. When at home, he succumbed to the magic of the tinkling piano in the smoky nightclub, and the bubbling glasses.

To Elizabeth such behaviour was anathema and any man who went too far too soon found himself travelling in the opposite direction. On second thoughts Queen Mary, assessing Elizabeth anew, came to the conclusion that, once rejected though he had been, Bertie was the man for Elizabeth. And Bertie was steadfast and determined in his pursuit. Wherever Elizabeth was, he was not far behind. They found they had other things in common. They shared the love of the countryside, of Scotland and of history. They could talk together, moving into a world of their own. Their families became fully united in the wish that they would marry. In January 1923 Bertie was invited for a weekend visit to St Paul's Waldenbury. On Sunday, the 14th, Elizabeth and he were excused church, an unusual occurrence in the Bowes-Lyon menage. They went for a walk and came back engaged. That afternoon a telegram for the King and Queen arrived at Sandringham. It read: 'All right. Bertie.'

7

The Abbey and After

AT TWELVE MINUTES PAST ELEVEN on the morning of 26 April 1923 Lady Elizabeth Bowes-Lyon left her father's home, 17 Bruton Street, in a State Landau to be married at Westminster Abbey. She forgot her gloves. That was her only mistake in a day of faultless performance. Bertie left Buckingham Palace at 11.13. It was to be an incident-free day for him also, except for a few awful seconds when, mistakenly, he thought his chief supporter, brother David, had mislaid the ring.

Despite the April showers, London was packed as it had rarely been since Alexandra of Denmark arrived to marry her Bertie, the Prince of Wales, in 1863. It was estimated that there were a million people lining the streets. Had the ceremony been broadcast, some of them might have stayed at home listening to their crystal sets or loud speakers, but the suggestion by the BBC that it should be was rejected by the Chapter of the Abbey on the grounds that it was too revolutionary.

There was a jubilant cheer when the bridegroom came in sight. Beside him sat the Prince of Wales, nervously fingering the chin-strap of his busby. He knew the question which everybody was asking: when will the Heir make the same ride to the Abbey?

> A pause, and then the biggest thrill of all. The bride's carriage is approaching. Such a sweet, composed little bride, leaning forward in her seat and smiling seriously. Her lace veil so prettily draped about her head, leaving the face uncovered, the bare arms with their tiny Victoria sleeves, the dainty satin-slippered feet. She looked almost ethereal, just a trail of white and silver as she passed into the dim vastness of the Abbey, attended by

> her maids, who surrounded her like a sea-mist, all white and green, with white flowers in their hair.[1]

Her dress was on simple Botticelli lines, covered with Nottingham lace. She carried a wreath of white roses and heather and, as she walked with her father from the west door, she paused and placed it on the tomb of the Unknown Warrior. She was watched by a throng of the famous. Queen Alexandra was there, playing one of her last star roles; and, beside her, the Dowager Empress of Russia. Statesmen were in force: Mr Bonar Law, the Prime Minister; Lloyd George; Stanley Baldwin; Winston Churchill; Lord Curzon; Austen Chamberlain; Neville Chamberlain; and Mr Asquith, with his brilliant wife, Margot. Lady Diana Cooper took the prize for beauty.

The bride promised to obey. The Archbishop of York paid tribute to the groom: 'You, sir, have already given many proofs of your care for the welfare of our working people. You have made yourself at home in the mines and shipyards and factories. You have brought the boys of the workshop and the public school together in free and frank companionship. You have done much to increase the public sense of the honour and dignity of labour.'[2]

It was as she came, radiant, from the Abbey that the reporters dubbed her 'the Smiling Duchess', a title which stayed with her until she became Queen. The crowds had thickened even more, a hundred deep in places: it was fortunate that the drive back to the Palace had been extended to include St James's Street, Piccadilly and Constitution Hill. Pipes were playing Scottish tunes and the voices of thousands sang the words. Every window on the route was packed, and the waving of flags and bunting and handkerchiefs was as if a breeze blew through a multi-coloured flowerbed. At the end of the journey came Elizabeth's first experience of appearing on the balcony to hear the roar of greeting rising from far down the Mall.

For the next scene, the wedding breakfast, King George came into his own, staging a reception which would have done credit to his father or his grandmother. The menu cards were red and gold. The King's cypher was encircled by the rose, the thistle and the shamrock, linked by gold ribbon. Below were the crests of Bertie and Elizabeth in crimson and gold. It was a souvenir to keep and to treasure for ever. The meal lasted for an hour and a half, of dishes that had been planned many weeks before and had taken days to prepare: Consommé à la Windsor; Suprêmes de saumon Reine Mary; Côtelettes d'agneau Prince Albert; Chapons à la Strathmore; Jambon et langues découpés à l'aspic; salade royale; asparagus et crême mousseuse sauce; Duchess Elizabeth strawberries; patisseries in sugar baskets; and fruit. The wedding cake was nine feet high. In it were concealed gold charms, and there were some very non-regal tricks and scrimmaging among the guests to gain possession of them. The high jinks continued until the bride and groom left the Palace in a landau for Waterloo Station. Old shoes flew through the air, confetti fell and the Princes battered one another with bags filled with paper. The King's salutation to his daughter-in-law then brought home a realization of her place in the royal family. Already by her marriage an HRH, she was also the fourth lady in the land, after the Queen, the Princess Royal and Princess Mary. Elizabeth brought a style of her own to her new family. A contemporary impression of her at the time of marriage describes her thus:

> In appearance she is petite, with a neat and graceful figure, and her prettiness is absolutely flower-like in quality. Her surprisingly dark hair is worn parted in the middle and with a fringe on the forehead. Her intensely blue eyes are thickly fringed with black lashes. Her complexion is beautiful. Her manners are exquisite; she carries herself with dignity but without the least suspicion of being stiff. One of her greatest assets is a low-toned charming speaking voice. She has little that is modern in her appearance, yet is always attractively dressed, with a touch of the picturesque and of her own individuality in her clothes. She is one of the few who could remain unshingled without looking old-fashioned.
>
> But what stands out more vividly than beauty of feature and delicacy of colouring is her particularly happy expression that is ever ready to break out into a radiant smile. It speaks of what all her friends know her to be possessed of – an unselfish nature, simple and affectionate; a mind and character incapable of unkindness of thought and action; a complete lack of affectation and pose; a candid sincerity and an

> ingrained gentleness. She has an unfailing wish to make things pleasant for others; she has an active and responsive sense of humour and a pretty and infectious laugh. She is full of the joy of life that is as spontaneous as the sunshine.
>
> These qualities form the basis of her personality. Her tastes are chiefly for an outdoor life. She rides and goes well to hounds, although she has not hunted nearly so much as she would have liked. She is a keen tennis player, sharing this taste with her husband. She is an exceptionally beautiful dancer even in these days when good dancers abound, and she has much fondness for reading and music. Her particular gift is playing the piano, and if she has a vanity – and probably every woman has at least one – it rather centres round her hands, which are very artistic, with long tapering fingers and a pretty wrist.[3]

The first part of the honeymoon was spent at Polesden Lacey, the lovely home of the Hon. Mrs Ronald Greville, a famous hostess of Edwardian days and friend of the royal family. For the second part the couple travelled to Glamis, where a boisterous reception awaited them; unfortunately, while there, Elizabeth developed whooping cough. The third part they passed at Frogmore in Windsor Park, and doubtless reminding Bertie of his boyhood summer days there, as he swotted at the lessons which were so hard to master. In June they moved into their new home, White Lodge, Richmond Park. This was the choice of the King and Queen, based not on what might suit the newly-weds but on their own links with the past. The nostalgic call of days gone by was influencing them, the happy moments remembered, the sad ones forgotten. At White Lodge Queen Mary had spent her childhood; from there she had gone to tea at East Sheen Lodge and received a proposal of marriage from George; there she had had her first child. But also from there she had gone into exile to Florence when her family were under financial pressures and there her father had spent his last two years, a virtual prisoner and mentally unstable.

The house was antiquated: there was no electricity and no central heating. The long corridors were drafty. The kitchens were pure Gothic and the stables intended solely for horses, totally unsuitable for cars. Communication with London was difficult and the journey back and forth from town added the best part of two hours to the duration of any appointment. Fogs were an added hazard in days when car lamps lacked penetrating power. There were other snags – staff problems, high running costs and, most telling of all, lack of privacy. Despite these domestic difficulties, marriage came to Bertie as the miracle of liberation. The hands of the clock ceased to rule. Now, if they had no engagement, he and Elizabeth would have supper on a tray before the fire. In the Palaces, meals had begun as the clock chimed, there was little chatter and less laughter. It was therefore with some trepidation that Elizabeth faced the ordeal which falls to the lot of new brides – entertaining her in-laws to supper. Queen Mary liked plain food. To the despair of her chef at Buckingham Palace, she would cross out his suggestion for some ambitious gateaux and substitute stewed plums and semolina. Elizabeth was thus faced with the problem of contriving a menu which was interesting yet basically simple. She succeeded, and received the congratulations of the Queen.

One great blessing which Elizabeth brought to her husband was a better relationship with, and understanding of, his parents. George V was pleasant enough if those around him agreed with his views, but highly critical and even sarcastic if they did not; Bertie had followed the easier route, as in fact George V had with Edward VII. George was not basically a strong man but he had the acumen to recognize strength when he saw it. He sensed the great power and determination of Elizabeth, and avoided confrontations. Accordingly, the two got on very well together. She laughed at his jokes, which was a sure way to his heart, as he fancied himself a comedian. She could even be late for Palace meals without fear of a reprimand. One evening she was two minutes behind time. She apologized profusely. The King said that it didn't matter a bit, adding, with a wink, 'I think we must have sat down two minutes early.'

The couple were blissfully happy together. Duff Cooper (later Lord Norwich) went to the theatre with them. He wrote to his wife: 'The Duke and Duchess of York were there. They are such a sweet little couple and so fond of one another. They reminded me of us, sitting together in the box having private jokes, and in the interval when we were all sitting in the room behind the box they slipped out, and I found them standing together in a dark corner of the passage talking happily as we might. She affects no shadow of airs and graces.'[4]

It was a contrast for both of them. Elizabeth came from a family of strong and polished men, soldiers, successful members of the British social scene, who had not undergone the subjugating experiences which had been the lot of Bertie. For his part, he had really never known care and attention, and he was transported to have someone of his very own ministering to his needs. He was her 'gentil knight', tender and thoughtful in his ways, qualities unusual in the strain of Queen Victoria; the likelihood is that they reached him through his beloved grandmother, Alexandra.

Their honeymoon privacy ended abruptly when they moved into White Lodge. Every post brought a shoal of requests – that Elizabeth should visit this hospital, be patroness of that society, lay a foundation stone, open a ward, help a children's home, further a needlework scheme, open a garden fête or a bazaar. The line on the graph of public engagements at Buckingham Palace shot up. Every request was carefully examined; Elizabeth was most conscientious and, because it was all new to her, the sorting-out procedure took a great deal of her time. One of her baptismal engagements was the annual outing of the Fresh Air Fund in Epping Forest, when a thousand poor children were given a day of fun in the open. Elizabeth turned her attention to the coconut shy. She knocked one down and photographs of her in action were seen round the world. The result was that her daily mail increased even further.

One of her first official engagements with her husband was to visit the Royal Air Force Pageant at Hendon, a day which had special appeal for Bertie. Initiation into historic ritual came when the couple accompanied the King and Queen to Edinburgh, staying at Holyrood where a State Reception was held. Wherever they went, they carried the mantle of completeness in just being together out into the public world. They were not spurred on by ambition: their only aim was to do an important job well, and according to the rules, and thereby help the whole royal family. The demand for them was such that a move from the White Lodge became imperative. In 1924 Princess Mary offered her brother and his wife the use of her London home, Chesterfield House, and with relief Bertie and Elizabeth moved in.

For him, despite the pressure, public appearances became less of an ordeal. When he was called upon to speak, the words came more easily now that Elizabeth was beside him, as though she were imparting some of her own power. She was not playing a nurse role, as she had done in the convalescent home at Glamis during the war years – she was a partner and, in her quiet way, very much in love. Yet there is no doubt that her experience at Glamis stood her in good stead: she had learned to understand. James Wentworth Day wrote: 'He was shy. He stammered. Her gaiety conquered his shyness. Her moral support was tremendous. She taught him music, she helped him to forget his stammer, she gave him confidence in his own speech. "When he rose to speak she flashed a quick smile. It was their mutal 'telegram'. It gave him just that spur which he needed." That is how a friend at Buckingham Palace summed it up for me.' He later met the Duke and Duchess at a private dinner. He sat next to Elizabeth and she captivated him with her chatter. When, at a signal from the host, the ladies rose, she whispered to him: 'Now we are only three women and you are only three men, so don't stay too long over the brandy and leave us to gossip among ourselves. We've lots to talk about.'[5]

Soon after their marriage she and Bertie were invited to a luncheon party and one glance at the list of guests told them that, conversationally, the occasion would prove hard going, for those attending were inclined to be stiff and pompous. Elizabeth whispered to a woman whom she knew: 'Can you laugh? I mean laugh as though you mean it? Laugh to order, in fact?' Yes, she thought she could. 'Well,' said Elizabeth, 'will you laugh with me at luncheon whenever I raise my left eyebrow?' For a short time the two practised and ended in fits of laughter. When they sat down at table, the procedure was followed and peals of mirth echoed out throughout the meal.[6]

The summer of 1924 was one mad rush of royalties. In May the King and Queen of Romania arrived in London. The King and Queen of Italy followed and then Ras Tafari, Prince Regent of Ethiopia, later Emperor Haile Selassie, whom Bertie welcomed at Victoria. The Wembley Exhibition opened. Bertie and Elizabeth went there with David, Prince of Wales, and headed for the amusement park. David and Elizabeth sat together in the front seat of car No. 2 of the Giant Switchback; the picture taken of them, wind-blown, thrilled, gripping the handle-bar, was one of the happiest ever taken of the pair together.

Bertie and Elizabeth made two overseas trips together in their early married life. The first, to Belgrade, in October 1923, was for two reasons. One was that King Alexander and Queen Marie of Yugoslavia had had a baby son, to be named Peter; Bertie and Elizabeth were chosen as godparents. The other was that King Alexander's cousin, Prince Paul, was to be married to Princess Olga of Greece, a close relative of Queen Alexandra. (Olga had a younger sister named Marina, who was destined to marry Bertie's brother George and become Duchess of Kent.) So off they went from Victoria Station, on the long, romantic journey across Europe, Elizabeth seeing lands that were new to her. In a way it was a trip into the past, to meet a host of new relations all entwined in the tree of Victoria and Albert. It was great fun, the Palace in Belgrade was packed with guests, the ceremony was that of a century before, and there was no hot water. Bertie had sole charge of the baby during the service. He wrote to his father: 'You can imagine what I felt like carrying the baby on a cushion. It screamed most of the time which drowned the singing and the service altogether.'[7] There was good reason for the screaming of his godchild. The elderly Patriarch whose duty it was to immerse him in the font let go his hold on the scrap of humanity, condemning him to an unscheduled bath from which he was rescued by the prompt action of Bertie. Their second trip was to East Africa. Although there were a number of royal occasions and duties for them to attend en route, it was in the main a holiday. They had both determined to see as much of the world as they could before starting a family. Elizabeth was keen to see beyond the confines of Europe, and fascinated by the thought of penetrating into the heart of Africa, while Bertie was set on trying his hand at big game hunting.

These overseas trips had great significance for both of them, in particular Bertie. In Britain, whether in their own home or guests of other members of the family, they were enveloped by the etiquette of royalty, always confined to the programme of engagements, always surrounded by the Household and ever on call. But together in a railway compartment, in the cabin of a steamer or cramped in a tent on safari, there was a new feeling of real togetherness. On home engagements for royalty there are seldom upsets and unexpected happenings, but away on tour anything could happen, and did, and they would have to sort things out for themselves. There was relief, also, at being away from the supervision of the Palace, of being able to make decisions of one's own on the spot, without the fear of correction. The sense of intimacy spread to those who accompanied them, no longer men and women doing their spell of in-waiting, but friends on a royal trip. Travels meant that Bertie and Elizabeth came nearer to one another, more self-reliant and assured. In the 1920s communications and coverage of events by the media were very different from today, and royals on tour moved out into a world of their own. There was an air of honeymoon for Bertie and Elizabeth as they made their final arrangements for the African visit.

On 1 December 1924 they left London for Marseilles, there embarking on the P. and O. liner *Mulbera* and heading east. A member of the liner's crew recorded:

> She bubbled over with happiness all the time. Perhaps her greatest thrill was to cross the equator for the first time. The Duke and several dozen others had never crossed the line before, so we prepared them for the usual ceremony after leaving Aden. The Duke took his punishment with the rest of them, and you should have heard the little Duchess laughing as one after the other was barbered and tumbled into the ship's pool. We were sorry to say goodbye to the Duke and Duchess when they left us at Mombasa.[8]

Mombasa proved a fitting introduction to Africa. For their benefit a festival called *ngoma* had been staged, consisting of five thousand natives taking part in a wild dance. They beat tom-toms and blew horns. Some sported gilt crowns, enriched by lighted candles, but below neck level, there was often little but the scantiest of grass skirts. As the dance had already been going on for three days, the movements of the participators, owing to tiredness and an in-take of liquid refreshment, were weird and extravagant.

The railway line had been built at the turn of the century with £5,000,000 of British money; it rose to 7600 feet. To allow of a better view, the Duke and Duchess were provided with a seat erected on the front of the engine and from there, securely strapped in, they caught their first sight of ostrich and zebra, baboon and wildebeeste. After a short round of visits and engagements in Nairobi, Bertie and Elizabeth came to the high point of their holiday – a five-week safari.

> They drove north to Embu, into the empty spaces and the private days to which they had so looked forward. They ran into a cloud-burst. Five inches of rain fell on them in half an hour; it was touch and go whether they got through the fords. War dancers were waiting for them at their harbour. They spent the night in a little circle of huts. Next morning it was still raining. They set off for Meru. The water in the rivers rose and rose. It penetrated too deeply into the engine of one of the cars: it was pronounced beyond cure, and had to be abandoned. So seven people went on in one Buick. After a rest and a dry, the real safari to Siola began. They travelled light and lived in tents. Each morning they were up soon after five, trudging on until the high sun told them it was time to rest. There was so much for the Duchess to photograph: the vistas out towards distant Mount Kenya, the glorious butterflies, the richly coloured birds. But it was the nights that were the magic, the blue-black velvet of them just beyond the tent flap. The cool air smoothed away the tiredness, discomforts, the bruises of the day; the few lights burned and one by one went out. The silence was an experience on its own. Then a lion would roar, a hyena cry and the zebras gallop by.[9]

The game bag included two rhinoceroses, two buffaloes, a lion and a lioness and smaller fry such as gerenuk, oryx, impala, lesser kudu and dik-dik. Stories of the safari filtered back to London and caused an uproar in the press, on a number of counts. It was a time of quickly changing values, the old order yielding place to new. Already the shooting of big game was facing increasing criticism, the knowledgeable realizing that the demands of sport, coupled with poaching for the value of ivory, skins, feathers etc., would soon mean there would be no game to shoot. And here was the second son of the King, ably assisted by his wife with her .275 Rigby, thinning the wild ranks even further. There were other criticisms: the religious-minded took strong exception to shooting on the Sabbath; monarchists considered that the second in line to the throne should not risk being trampled to death by a rhino; mothers voiced the opinion that a young wife should be thinking of having a baby rather than adventuring on the trail. The King was perturbed. Elizabeth took the hint and waived the rhino she was licensed to shoot.

Bertie and Elizabeth fell in love with Kenya. To their delight the Colony wished to present them with a farm, thus giving them the excuse for return visits, but the King did not agree with the idea. He wrote: 'What would you do if the farm didn't pay? The only way would be to buy a farm yourself (and you have no ready money) like David did in Canada and I thought that was a mistake.'[10]

In the middle of February the pair moved on to Uganda, crossing wide Lake Victoria from Kisumu to Entebbe. At Kampala, the native capital set on seven hills, Bertie invested King Daudia, the Kabaka of Buganda, with the KCMG. Here was a touch of real old imperial splendour, a fabulous pavilion having been erected for the occasion, before which the warriors danced. Then on through the valleys where King Solomon's men once collected peacocks for the Queen of Sheba, to the shores of Lake Albert where they began one of the most interesting stages of their long journey. The paddle-steamer *Samuel Baker* was waiting to take them along the White Nile. She was more of a local bus than a royal yacht, drawing only four feet of water and rolling 'like the very devil' in any swell. Besides a variety of passengers, she carried timber and potware, bales and casks, hides and tusks. She called in at all the villages along the bank, loading and unloading passengers and cargo, tooting and clanking, being greeted at each step by the local population – for the passing of the *Samuel Baker* was a great event, doubly so with a royal Duke and Duchess on the passenger list. It was baking hot, and Bertie and Elizabeth slept on deck despite the menace of mosquitoes. One whole night was spent in mid-stream, as the rudder-post had been bent in the shallows. Then on they chugged to Nimule in southern Sudan; a change into cars was necessary here since the river was unnavigable on its race from the high plateau to the plains in the north. Ninety very uncomfortable miles followed, over narrow, stony tracks, but their reward came at Rejaf, where lay waiting for them the comfortable river steamer *Nasir* to take them on the fascinating thousand-mile haul to Khartoum. This really was a pleasure cruise after the hard miles they had come – little to do but to lie in the shade, sheltered from the scorching heat, watching the frieze of the banks slip by, spotting the many animals which came down to the water's edge to drink. Khartoum came as a noisy contrast: triumphal arches in the streets, brilliant receptions in the evenings, the nights full of lights. At Port Sudan they boarded the liner *Maloja* and on 19 April were back in London.

Bertie had been at the top of his form throughout the trip, trekking fifteen miles a day and more, often wet through, a very different man from his sailor days. The truth was he benefitted from a life without mental stress – as applied, to varying extent, to all the children and grandchildren of Edward VII, whose mother had said that her heir was not a man born to endure worry and strife. It was fortunate that he had grown in stature that summer, for David was abroad on tour and the health of both the King and of Queen Alexandra was causing anxiety, thus leaving the Yorks to cope with a multitude of public duties. In February the King had suffered from influenza, followed by bronchitis with high temperatures. His doctors had insisted upon a Mediterranean cruise, which put him to rights; but it was the first knock on the door for George V. Queen Alexandra was in her eighty-first year and very tired, no longer able to make her Rose Day drives through London's crowded streets. She passed the green summer days of 1925 in her beloved Norfolk but, as the leaves came from the trees, she weakened. She was preparing for her birthday when a heart attack struck her. Bertie raced down to Sandringham to say goodbye to his beloved grandmother; fog held up his train and he arrived too late. Yet, before she went, Alexandra was told a secret which gave her great happiness. It was that Bertie and Elizabeth were going to have a child. The baby, a girl, was born on 21 April 1926 at 17 Bruton Street. She was named Elizabeth Alexandra Mary.

8

Conflicts

Bertie said, one day in 1926, that his only claim to fame was that he was the father of Princess Elizabeth. Made in a light-hearted way, the remark was then sadly true although he basked in a brilliant light, for no royal child has ever aroused greater interest than his daughter. From the day of her christening the picture postcards of her poured from the presses, and the newspapers carried every snippet of news about her: as she came to talk, her mother kept an album of the things she was supposed to have said but had not. The fact remained that the time had come for the second son of the King, now thirty years old, to do something to make an impact on his own account. In this direction he was faced with many difficulties. Firstly there was the handicap of the stammer, 'the curse which God has put upon me,' as he described it, and which so inhibited him. Secondly, there was the attitude, towards him and towards life, of his parents. Thirdly there was the competition of his brilliant elder brother, David, to be faced and, in general, the widening gap of understanding and interests which showed between them.

Bertie had tried every known remedy to cure his speech defect, consulting no fewer than nine specialists. Always, in the end, the same answer came up – the basic cause was nerves, a rather discouraging answer, since there was nothing tangible with which to grapple. He was about to give up and accept the inevitable when urgent need arose for him to be able to deliver an important speech. In 1926 the Australian Premier, Mr Stanley Bruce,* asked the King if one of his sons would open the New Parliament House at Canberra, and the name of the Duke of York was put

* Later first Viscount Bruce of Melbourne.

forward. The King, not unnaturally, was uncertain whether Bertie could tackle an event of such importance, and even Mr Bruce feared the same. For his part Bertie was very keen to visit Australia and New Zealand yet, if he were to go, there was no course open to him but to seek still another cure, though he dreaded the thought of it. Then his Private Secretary met a Mr Lionel Logue, an Australian who practised in Harley Street. He had previously run an elocution school in Perth, done wonders with wounded soldiers returned from the war, and used a system of diaphragm breathing which had proved of great help to children suffering speech defects. It was Elizabeth who persuaded her husband to have one last try at a cure. When Bertie entered the consulting room, Mr Logue saw 'a slim, quiet man, with tired eyes and all the outward symptoms of the man upon whom habitual speech defect had begun to set the sign. When he left at five o'clock, you could see there was hope once more in his heart.'[1] Briefly, what Mr Logue did was to instil into his patient one idea – faith. He convinced him that the trouble was not an incurable permanency but a passing handicap which could be put to rights. He made it completely clear that the final answer must lie in Bertie's hands: he could be shown how to effect the cure, but the working of the cure lay with himself.

Bertie attended the consulting room every day in addition to spending an hour or more on breathing exercises, and the results were truly remarkable. He spoke with his father who, noting the improvement, agreed that he should go to Australia. Bertie now found, to his amazement, that in these interviews he ceased to stammer. Previously he had always stammered when talking with the King which had put him in a weak position. The King had always held that, just as he had been frightened of his father, so should his sons be frightened of him. They were, from childhood, through adolescence and into maturity. David, in rebellion, took refuge in isolation. Bertie did what he was told and thus, with the advantage of having Elizabeth, was more favoured. The two youngest, George and Harry, still looked upon their father as a tyrannical headmaster, but regularly risked his ire. One evening Harry sneaked out of the Palace, dance pumps in his pocket, to meet a young lady in a night club. An equerry spotted him on his return. To make matters worse, Harry was five minutes late for breakfast; he took one glance at the anger on the King's face and fainted. George and Mary were really beginning to feel their power. Ever since their own marriage they had played a secondary role, Edward VII and Queen Alexandra stealing all the starlight and giving the orders. George was only a second son, Mary a poor relation. They were both very much aware of this and Mary, in particular, had much ground to make up if she were to move into the shadows of Victoria and Alexandra. On King Edward's death Queen Alexandra had kept up the *status quo ante*, elevating her grandson David to be the star elect. Now Alexandra was dead and George and Mary had reached the goal of parading on the gravel outside Sandringham itself, 'the Big House', instead of being tucked away in York Cottage. They were masters of all they surveyed, including, still, their family.

David took a line of his own, kept himself to himself and never went to Sandringham. His speeches showed his originality in thinking. He wrote them all himself, sitting at a little red typewriter at his quarters at York House, St James. He puzzled over problems of equality – why should Britain be able to afford luxury liners to ferry the international set across the Atlantic while the men who built them lived in squalor by the dockside? Why were the people of Wales – his people – eating out their hearts in unemployment? Why was more not being done to help the men who had fought the war to end all wars? While the King strove to retain the aura of the nineteenth century, his eldest son fought as fiercely for the twentieth. David, Prince of Wales, was the most popular man in the world: he was Britain's best ambassador and Britain's best salesman. But mentally he was tiring, as Prince Albert the Consort had tired at the same age. Every year from 1919 to 1931 he was despatched to wave the flag around the world but thereafter his journeys were restricted to more familiar places nearer home, like Salzburg and Formentor. This was strange, for Britain, in her financial crisis, needed a top salesman and the diplomacy of a senior ambassador to counteract the ambitions of the rising dictators.

The gap between King George and his heir was wide. Apart from differing ideas in their concept of kingship and the foreign policy to be followed by Britain, there was a clash over the people with whom David mixed and, in particular, the women. One evening early in 1918 the maroons went off, warning of an air raid, and those in the streets took shelter. A young lady, homeward bound with her escort, slipped into the hall of a house in Belgrave Square. The guests poured down from above and the couple were invited to share the safety of the basement. Among the guests was HRH the Prince of Wales, on leave from the Front. He spotted the girl, looking somewhat lost amid so many strangers. He began to talk to her. He fell in love and in that state so remained for the best part of sixteen years.

She was Winifred May Dudley Ward, and called Freda. Freda's father was a rich industrialist, Charles Birkin, of Lamscote, Radcliffe on Trent, Nottinghamshire. Her mother was Claire Lloyd, daughter of Alexander Howe of New York, a flamboyant lady, with large hats; she married off her three daughters well. The Birkins were a familiar sight, riding, on the back seat of a large tourer, on the road from Radcliffe to the city then known as 'the Paris of the Midlands'. In 1913 Freda had married William Dudley Ward,* MP for Southampton, and nephew of the Earl of Dudley. They had two daughters.

King George and Queen Mary knew all about Freda. As Queen Victoria had done, in similar circumstances, they enquired closely and secretly into the romances of their sons, the King going as far as opening files, though Queen Mary disclaimed 'meddling'. The King followed the Sandringham practice of poking fun and derision at unpopular alliances. And Freda was unpopular, and never received. As Queen Alexandra had dubbed Miss Chamberlayne, her husband's American girl friend, 'Miss Chamberpots,'[2] now her son labelled Freda 'Miss Loom' or 'the lacemaker's daughter'.[3] The trouble with delightful Freda was that she was 'commercial' and married. George would not allow the breath of trade to blow in the family circle. This was one point on which his views were contrary to those of his own father, but he did feel the same way as his father about divorce, conveniently forgetting that the marriage of Prince Albert's parents had ended that way and that three of Queen Victoria's grandchildren had suffered the same fate.

As the years passed the close liaison of David and Freda began to affect, imperceptibly but surely, the status of the Yorks. Firstly,

* Divorced 1931.

as David and Freda obviously could not marry and showed no signs of breaking up their friendship, there could be no heir to the throne from the Prince of Wales, which left the claim of baby Elizabeth unchallenged. Secondly, the older generation of professional and service folk, and the staid middle classes, watching David's aberration, turned their favours towards Bertie and Elizabeth, with their spotless way of life and happy family circle. Here they saw the perfect marriage, and it was well time that there was one in the royal line: looking back through the years there was not one in sight. Owing to revulsion at his illness, Queen Charlotte refused even to see her husband, George III, during the last six years of her life. George IV's union with Caroline of Ansbach was one long, undignified quarrel. William IV's marriage with Adelaide was an arranged affair, designed solely to produce an heir to the throne. Despite the propaganda poured out by the widow, the marriage of Victoria and Albert was a sequence of tantrums and disappointments. With the possible exception of Leopold, who died young, all their sons strayed, and often, from the marital bed; their daughters managed little better. Looking now at Bertie and Elizabeth people saw the one example of pure romance and obvious happiness, refreshing when compared with the peccadilloes of Bertie's brothers.

Confirmation of the happiness of their marriage and the characters of the pair came from members of the family and from those who had long served in the household. Princess Marie Louise, whose own marriage had ended in divorce, described Elizabeth as the perfect wife and mother. In talking to the Countess of Strathmore, she said: 'How lovely Elizabeth is.' Lady Strathmore replied: 'Yes, lovely in every way. I have never heard an ugly word pass that child's lips.'[4] Lady Cynthia Colville, Woman of the Bedchamber to Queen Mary for thirty years, paid her tribute to Bertie: 'I invariably felt that the Duke of York's wisdom, kindliness and sterling commonsense were the constituents of a delightful and competent personality.'[5] Lady Airlie quoted an unusual remark of George V: 'Bertie has more guts than the rest of his brothers put together.'[6] The King wrote to his son: 'The better I know and the more I see of your dear little wife, the more charming I think she is and everyone falls in love with her.' Robert Lacey summed up the marital relationship: 'He [Bertie] had been brought up in an environment where human emotion was suppressed, where raw love, anger, pain or exultation were not regarded as topics of polite conversation, and he was content to live out his own adult life within the same inhibitions. This affected his relationship with his wife and family, and in particular with the daughter who was his heir. It was certainly a much more cheerful arrangement than the one his parents had reached. Fun was the hallmark of King George VI's family life, fun conscientiously aimed at and persistently maintained.'[7]

In sharp contrast to the Yorks and their circle, one particular danger for David was the society with whom Freda allied. Their friendship led to frequent visits to Nottinghamshire, and there the danger lay, in particular in the hunting field. The Prince of Wales thus described the fields:

> Intermixed with the local landed gentry . . . was a lively sampling of dashing figures; noblemen and their ladies; wealthy people who had discovered that the stable door was a quick if expensive short-cut into society; a strong injection of Americans from the famous eastern hunts; ladies whose pursuit of the fox was only a phase of an even more intense pursuit of romance . . . good riders on bad horses; bad riders on good horses . . .[8]

This motley collection was tough – tough in social rivalry, tough in love, tough with money, tough out hunting and tough in their pleasure seeking. Before the feeling of mercy for the fox crept in with the years, the hunting folk were stars, gathering in their Bentleys and Sunbeams to drink a stirrup cup of cherry brandy before the Manor House. And the outstanding star for the spectators, at meets and point-to-points, was David, not a great horseman, but a brave one. Yet David was not, in truth, tough enough for the circle in which he moved. His training and his 'miserable childhood', as he termed it, had not fitted him for the cut and thrust of social rivalry; he was too apt to wish to please. The time came, though, when he strayed occasionally from Freda. Fidelity often exists in ratio with the degree of temptation, and in his case temptation was very high. An insight into his prowess in this direction came on an occasion when he was sailing to New York. Forewarned of danger, his equerries kept guard on his cabin, but a siren slipped through the net and slammed the door; she was nabbed as she emerged in the early hours. Admonished, she was unrepentant. 'He wasn't much good,' she said, 'but it's not every night that one sleeps with the future King of England.'[9]

As the King's health declined, his irascibility increased. One day he roared at David: 'You dress like a cad. You act like a cad. You are a cad. Get out!'[10] So acrimonious did the relationship become that the heir threatened to renounce his rights.[11] David found the strain too much to bear, and he was not the only one. Queen Mary wearied of the continual carping. On the way back from Sandringham in their Daimler, she announced at Royston that she would get out and continue her journey by train unless the unpleasantness ceased.

Even shy and retiring Bertie and his charming wife were not to be allowed extravagant slices of the royal cake. Never was this more clearly demonstrated than when they returned from their world tour of 1927. They had been away for six months, travelling in the battle-cruiser *Renown* via Panama and Fiji to New Zealand. They had visited Tasmania and Australia, from Sydney to Perth, and made the journey home by Mauritius and Suez. On their arrival the royal family greeted them at Victoria Station. The King turned to the man who, six weeks before, had opened Australia's Parliament at Canberra and instructed: 'When you kiss Mama, take your hat off.'[12] It was a quite unnecessary deflation of an ego which needed the reverse.

That world tour and the experiences in New Zealand and Australia really laid the foundation for the Yorks' public successes: it was something new in its style. George V and Queen Mary had paraded about the Empire some years earlier, but their travels came into a very different category – they were programmed affairs, spiced with little humanity. They adhered to their terms of reference, saluted the flag, met only the right people, cut ribbons and were always on time. The royal personality most usually seen on tours was David, but his wanderings were more in the nature of 'road shows', the reception being much the same as if he had been Rudolph Valentino. Students mobbed him, teenagers screamed at the sight of him and the young ladies fought fiercely to win the honour of being able to say that they had danced with the Prince of Wales. Bertie and Elizabeth managed to extract the best from the examples of both George and Mary, and of David. They were neither too pompous nor too free and easy; they appeared more like ordinary people, despite the fact that they were wrapped in tinsel. The knowledge that they had left a baby at home appealed enormously. True, Mary had left a young brood behind her when she visited Australia, but no one thought of giving her teddy bears to take home to her infants, whereas Elizabeth was inundated with toys for Lilibet. Time and again the pair won affection by attention to the little things, by deferring their departure from an engagement until they had met all those who had come to see them, by defying the weather so that they would not cause disappointment, by speaking to those who had at one time served the royal family, by never forgetting a name or a face. They worked together as a team and, in so doing, drew closer to one another.

Their success began at Auckland, New Zealand, and continued through the North and South Islands. On that first day the crowd broke through police cordons and surrounded the royal car; the Duchess's clothes were so fingered that there were doubts whether her wardrobe would survive the lengthy tour. On the second day of the visit Mr Joseph Coates, Prime Minister of New Zealand, was talking to a well-known Communist agitator who told him: 'I've done with this bloody communism.' On being asked why, he replied: 'Why, they're human! Yesterday I was in the crowd with the wife, and one of the children waved his hand, and I'm blessed if the Duchess didn't wave back and smile right into my face, not two yards away. I'll never say a word against them.'[13] The Australian welcome was unforgettable. A cacophony of sounds rang over Sydney harbour – guns, bells, steam whistles, ships' sirens, bands and cheering all striving to be heard. There were little gestures which appealed to the Australians too. At Newcastle it was teeming with rain: Bertie and Elizabeth were noted whispering together; then the car hood came down, to the detriment of the lovely lady's hat.

The train journey which took Bertie and Elizabeth from South Australia to Canberra lasted from Friday afternoon to Sunday morning. When they reached the new capital the sun was shining brightly, there was a nip of frost in the air and fifty thousand people had arrived from all over the Dominion by car and special train. The doors of the great Parliament House were closed. The Duke and Duchess drove up in a carriage and four, escorted by outriders and postilions – a scene from Westminster played out exactly that ninth of May on the wide plain with the blue mountains as a backdrop. He was in naval uniform and she in a flowing cloak of silver-grey chiffon trimmed with fur. The greatness of the occasion had had its effect on him, and he had slept badly; it was good that Elizabeth was with him. Dame Nellie Melba, Australia's immortal operatic soprano, sang the first verse of the National Anthem. Then the crowds joined in and a flurry of pigeons rose into the sky. Bertie opened the door with a golden key. Once inside, he unveiled a statue of his father who, on that same day twenty-six years before, had opened the first Federal Parliament of Australia. They took their places in the throne-chairs on the dais. Bertie rose and spoke, and he spoke very well, without hesitation. It was indeed a great day for both of them.

On 23 May the engines of *Renown* began turning for the long journey home via Mauritius. Three days later at sea, at two o'clock on a stiflingly hot afternoon, the engines stopped. There had been an overflow of oil and a serious fire had broken out in a boiler-room. Four badly burned seamen were carried away and a fire-fighting squad went into action. The danger lay in the fire reaching the main oil supply, in which case there would be no alternative but to abandon ship, an unpleasant prospect with land three days away in one direction and four in the other. Plans for flooding the ammunition chamber and for abandoning ship continued. Nearer and nearer the flames approached the main oil tanks. They were within a few feet when the perspiring fire-squad at last got them under control. It was ten o'clock before Elizabeth was certain that they would not all spend the night in a life-boat on the vast and very empty ocean.

In June they reached London, after covering thirty-four thousand miles. They were met by the King and Queen. It was then that Bertie was instructed to take his hat off before he kissed his mother. For Bertie and Elizabeth the incident was softened by the joy of reunion with their baby and the thrill of entering a new house. After three years of marriage they at last had a home of their own – 145 Piccadilly. But it was noticeable that thereafter there were no more global excursions for the Yorks. This was strange as Elizabeth had shown, in that year of 1927, that she was a star of the first magnitude, and Bertie's behaviour was impeccable. There was never a breath of scandal about him, no gossip, no exploits with girls as in the case of his younger brothers, George and Harry. When his photograph appeared in the press it either showed him inspecting a factory, playing games with the boys at his camps or, more often, playing second fiddle to his wife and daughter. There was an air of steadfastness about him which appealed to the middle classes, who were tiring of the pictures of Society disporting themselves at the fashionable night clubs. Britain was in an economic plight, the hunger marchers were on the move and the quiet and serious attitude of the Duke of York was welcomed.

The King was watching his own popularity rating closely. He kept well in with the Church, held close check on royal spending and always had a smile for children. He benefitted by contrast with the leaders of Europe. The public saw a benign and bearded monarch, the grandson of Queen Victoria, ruling over a fifth of the globe, set on a path of peace, and compared him with the upstarts across the Channel. In November 1928 the King's popularity and reputation soared to the heights: he became severely ill with septicaemia, the result of a chill, and nearly died.

> As the public was made aware of the seriousness of the King's illness, profound anxiety was shown in the Press and gradually communicated itself to every house and cottage in the land and throughout the Empire. Crowds assembled regularly outside the Palace in the bitter cold, to wait for and to read and re-read the bulletins, and thousands would remain silently observing for long hours the comings and goings of doctors and messengers and watching the lights in windows which they believed to belong to the King's suite of rooms.[14]

In December he was operated upon, but it was not until February that he was taken to Craigweil, near Bognor, to convalesce. While there he entertained a guest whose presence did him a power of good. It was Princess Elizabeth and she was better than any medicine.

The Yorks had again proved of the greatest help during this

troubled time, Bertie being a Counsellor of State and Elizabeth a constant and cheering visitor. It was her idea to send Lilibet to Craigweil. There had grown between the small girl and the ailing and irascible King a strong bond of friendship and understanding. She was not in the least afraid of him. She played groom to his horse, leading him round the carpet on all fours by the beard. She found that she could see his room at Buckingham Palace from the nursery at 145 Piccadilly and every day at a set time she would wave him good morning. She was his favourite person. At breakfast when at Sandringham he would talk away at her, airing adult views of which she took no notice, which suited him exactly. They had one difference of opinion; he stamped from the room. He was called back. Anticipating forgiveness, he returned. Instead he was told sharply that he had forgotten to close the door. At Craigweil they went for walks together, she prattling away beside the wheel chair. One afternoon, when he was getting better, they made sand castles. The Archbishop of Canterbury saw these and was of the opinion that they should be preserved for posterity.

No sooner was the King fully recovered than the Yorks were in the limelight again: it was announced that the Duchess was to have another baby, due early in August of 1930. Every year the Yorks spent that month with the Earl and Countess of Strathmore at Glamis Castle. On the 5th the Home Secretary, Mr J. R. Clynes, arrived, his duty to ensure that the newcomer was a true child of the royal mother. He was a guest of the Countess of Airlie at nearby Cortachy. The days, the weeks, dragged by and still no call came for him. The question of entertaining Mr Clynes became quite a problem. On the evening of 21 August a black thunderstorm blew up. Rain swept the valley, lightning lit the twilight and thunder echoed from the battlements. A telephone message brought the Labour statesman from Cortachy. After a Caesarean operation, the baby was born at twenty-two minutes past nine, a girl, soon to be named Margaret Rose and known in the family as 'Bud'. Bells rang out and, in defiance of the rain, a bonfire was lit on the top of Hunter's Hill.

Only sixteen years lay between the day when Kaiser Wilhelm of Germany precipitated the First World War and the birth of Princess Margaret, a short bridge indeed between the old world and the new. And now, in 1930, the seeds of war were once again sprouting in Europe, showing clearly in Germany, Italy, Spain and the Balkans, though it was perhaps too soon for many people, to whom Armistice Day was a recent memory, to realize that the catastrophies were about to begin again.

In Britain home troubles were to the fore. There was a financial crisis, unemployment was rising, industry was stagnating and national defence lagging behind the safety limit. The Government was doing very little about these things. There was another problem receiving very little attention. It was – what would happen when King George died? The standard reply was – there is always the Prince of Wales, but few realized that David, in his late thirties, was a very different man from the idol of ten years before, had lost much of his drive and the magnetism of his personality.

George V was very much the King, holding the reins in his hands, determined to be a father figure to his people and to be liked, set resolutely against change. Yet it was clear to some, and certainly to the doctors, that he had not long to live. There was need, therefore for a successor to be trained on the accepted lines, and this was not being done. Not one successor but, for safety's sake, two, since the Prince of Wales lived a reckless life. David unburdened himself to Lady Diana Cooper one night at the dinner table. Having complained of his miserable life and childhood, Lady Diana recalled: 'He described the gloom of Buckingham Palace; how he himself and all of them "froze up" whenever they got inside it; how bad-tempered his father was; how the Duchess of York was the one bright spot there. They all love her and the King is in a good temper whenever she is there.'[15] In fact, relations between the King and his heir had reached a state when communication between them no longer existed.

The King's main difference with the Prince lay in the latter's liaisons with married women. He just could not understand why David did not marry a suitable girl. He himself had been given no say in the choice of a bride, marrying May of Teck because Queen Victoria had decided that he should do so, although there was clearly no romantic attachment between the two. But the union had provided a bond of companionship and love, there had been an ample supply of children and there had been no infidelity on either side. His only daughter, Mary, had acquiesced in marrying his friend, Lord Lascelles, and produced two sons – the King did not consider it any of his business what the relationship was behind the bedroom door; children and outward appearances were paramount. Bertie had in fact been encouraged to marry Elizabeth Bowes-Lyon. All this, the King believed, showed that he knew what he was doing for his children. Why, then, could not David follow in the footsteps of his brother and sister? The same logic applied, but to a lesser extent, to the younger sons, Harry and George.

The pressure for him to marry had been on David since 1914. A suitable Princess had been produced, approval given on all sides, but not even the urgings of his beloved grandmother, Alexandra, had influenced him. He had been asked what objection he had. He replied: 'Only that I will never in any circumstances marry any woman unless I love her.'[16] It was a resolute attitude for a young man whose only experience of life had been restricted to the naval college and the university.

By the 1930s the full tragedy of his long association with Freda Dudley Ward became apparent. He was in contact with her daily and she filled his life. No woman would have considered marrying an heir to the throne whose affections were so firmly cemented; the 'lacemaker's daughter' blocked the way. Despite the restriction on brides brought about by the anti-German feeling of the First World War, there were still suitable candidates for marriage to be found, for example Princess Marina of Greece. There certainly could be no objections to her, either on the grounds of parentage or looks. But David was 'otherwise engaged' and the chance slipped by. The royal family did not know it at the time, but the final hope of David finding an acceptable wife faded in June 1931 when, at an evening's end, an American woman turned her hypnotic eyes upon the Prince of Wales. Those eyes contained a message which there was no mistaking. The owner of the eyes was Mrs Ernest Simpson, whose christian name was Wallis. She was flat fore and aft; her neck was long, her forehead high, her shoulders square. She had blue eyes, a flawless skin and carried herself well. She was intelligent, ambitious for power and money, and somewhat ruthless with men but she knew how to exploit love and there was magic in her eyes, hypnotism in her touch. She bewitched David.

King George soon found out about her, and was frightened. He opened files dealing with various periods of her life which, especially while in the Far East, had on occasion been lurid. He was not enamoured of Americans and Wallis clashed with his ideas of suitable female companionship for his heir – in any case she was married, had been divorced and was thirty-eight. But he could not summon up the courage to do anything about it and have the matter out with his son; instead he fretted and worried. He said to old friends who urged him to act: 'There's nothing I can do with the fellow.' He burst out to his wife: 'I pray to God that my eldest son will never marry and have children, and that nothing will come between Bertie and Lilibet and the throne.'[17]

It therefore appears clear that George V had considered the possibility that his eldest son would not succeed him; David had already threatened to renounce his rights on several occasions. Yet the King did nothing to prepare his second son: Bertie remained in the background, his main interest in his family. He was content to do any job well that was assigned to him. An important opportunity arose for him to learn more of the family business. In 1931 his name had been suggested as Governor-General of Canada by Mr R. B. Bennett, the Canadian Prime Minister. This would have been a splendid chance for him to widen his experience of leadership, to learn more of politics and diplomacy and generally to appreciate the outlook and customs of both Canada and the United States. The Labour Government, on principle, was opposed to the appointment, Mr J. H. Thomas, Secretary of State for the Dominions, giving a somewhat lame excuse that it would conflict with democratic ideas across the Atlantic. Lord Stamfordham, Private Secretary, dismissed this as rubbish. But the King gave in to politics, Bertie would not press his claim, and the chance was lost.

Despite the disturbing conditions all around them, Bertie and Elizabeth spent the first half of the 1930 decade cocooned in the serenity of family life. They had a settled home at 145 Piccadilly and the upbringing of their children was their major concern. Whenever their appointments would permit, they made a point of being home in the evenings. Nurse Knight would bring Lilibet and Margaret down to the drawing-room, there were games on the hearth and a recitation of the day's events. Then came the ceremony of the bath. A frequent visitor to these evening sessions was David, showing a new side to his character. He would call in on his way home to York House, join in the games and became the favourite uncle. One game which they played was Winnie-the-Pooh. Elizabeth would read a passage from a book and then it was the job of the audience to mime the characters of which she had read. David relaxed and was clearly finding something he sorely missed. One evening he told his sister-in-law: 'You make family life so much fun.'[18]

There was one gap in the lives of Bertie and Elizabeth – they had no country retreat where they could spend the weekends, and no quiet garden in which the children could play. David had Fort Belvedere, a strange castellated building six miles from Windsor Castle. He adored it and spent much of his time restoring the building and laying out the garden. Bertie accordingly approached his father, stressing the importance of the adored Lilibet having somewhere to play in private and to learn about the country. He was granted the Royal Lodge at Windsor, which had once been a tea house of Queen Adelaide, wife of William IV. The place was a complete mess, both internally and externally, as had been Fort Belvedere, and it appeared that the King, by granting grace and favour residence to his sons, was not only insuring that they were kept busy with decorating and gardening, but also getting State properties restored on the cheap.

Bertie and Elizabeth forced their way in to inspect the building through a tangle of weeds and undergrowth and gained access through a greenhouse. They found the fine Georgian hall, designed by Wyatville, criss-crossed by ugly partitions. Here indeed was a challenge. Nevertheless there was an air of grandeur about it which appealed to them and they gladly accepted the King's offer. It was their first real attempt at home-making from scratch and they set about the task with the enthusiasm which Victoria and Albert had applied to the building of the new Balmoral. The hall became a vast drawing room; two wings were to be added, to accommodate children and staff. The grounds consisted of fifteen acres – an overgrown fruit and vegetable garden, a forest of unpruned shrubs and a wilderness at the end of a wide lawn.

Elizabeth's love of gardening, inherited from her mother and fostered in her as a child, had a chance now to show itself; she had sadly missed her hobby since marriage. Economies deemed necessary by the financial crisis had prompted Bertie to give up hunting and sell his horses. Elizabeth saw the chance of giving him a new interest. Soon gardening filled all his spare-time hours, and would for the rest of his life. His experience was small. As a boy, his participation had been limited to planting cabbages in neat lines, dressed from the right and ready for inspection by his father. It was both a lesson and a drill, not destined to inculcate a love of the soil, though he had enjoyed gardens at Rauceby and Cambridge. Now, if at a comparatively late start, he had advantages and capabilities which enabled him to reach near-professional standard in a short time. Firstly, since the Royal Lodge grounds had been so neglected, he had a garden with infinite possibilities. Secondly he had top experts at hand to advise and assist, such as landscape gardener Sir Geoffrey Jellicoe and Eric (later Sir Eric) Savill, creator of the Savill Gardens at Windsor, one of the most remarkable pieces of landscape gardening in the country. Thirdly, he had inherited from Prince Albert the Consort the gift of planning and detail and the power to master any subject to which he turned his mind. Fourthly, and not least, he had ever beside him a woman who knew and understood flowers and, in particular, roses. Even so, he learned the hard way. He and Elizabeth spent their weekends in attack with sickle and scythe, axe and saw. In *Royal Gardens* George Plumptre described how they planned: 'From his work at the Royal Lodge Geoffrey Jellicoe gives a very telling insight into the achievements of the Duke and Duchess of York in their garden there. It was working with the Duke of York in the 1930s which was largely responsible for Jellicoe's developing interest in what he was later to call the psychology of landscape. At the Royal Lodge it was strikingly clear that the Duke and Duchess had definite and enthusiastic ideas about what they were striving to achieve in their garden, guided by three influences: the historical background to their home, its physical character and setting, and their personal desires and ambitions. It was the inspired fusion of these three motives which accounted for much of the royal couple's love of the place and which held the key to their success.'

Bertie quite soon became a pundit on rhododendrons; an expert employed by the Commissioner of Crown Lands commented, 'Nobody could stump him.' He had the collector's passion for exchanging information with other enthusiasts and the depth of his knowledge was shown in a letter which he sent to the Countess of Stair, after a visit to Lochinch Castle in the spring of 1935, in which he used 'the language of rhododendrons':

> Dear Lady Stair,
>
> I must write & thank you both so much for asking me to come to Lochinch. I did so enjoy my visit & you gave me such an *Agapetum* (delightful) time.
>
> It was a great disappointment to me that my wife was unable to come too, & she is miserable at having missed the two *Formosum* (beautiful) days we had there. I am glad to tell you that she is much better, though I found her looking *Microleucrum* (small and white).
>
> It was nice of you to say that I deputised well for her on Saturday but I feel that she could have done everything much better, as she has the *Agastum* (charming) way of *Charidotes* (giving joy). As we had arranged our visit for her, she *Pothinum* (much desired) to be there, & it was very sad for her to have missed it. However it is *Sperabile* (to be hoped for) *Timeteum* (to be honoured) with a future invitation.
>
> As to my visit, I am overjoyed *Eclecteum* (to be chosen out) and *Aberrans* (wandering) *Cyclium* (round) so many *Erastum* (lovely) and *Arizelum* (notable) gardens in so short a time, has left me *Charitostreptum* (gracefully bent) with a *Recurvum* (bent back), & somewhat *Lasiopodum* (woolly footed). I must say I am filled *Coeloneurum* (with impressed nerves) at all the *Agetum* (wondrous) & *Aperantum* (limitless) beauties of the gardens *cyclium* (round) Lochinch.
>
> But despite being *Asperulum* (slightly roughened) & having had time to examine my feet, *Denudatum* (naked) and *Detersile* (clean) I am glad to find that they are neither *Hypoglaucum* (blue beneath) *Hypolepidotum* (scaly) nor *Hypophaeum* (grey) but merely *Russatum* (reddened). This *Rufuscens* (becoming reddish) will have *Comisteum* (to be taken care of) otherwise they will not be *Eudoxom* (of good report) for *Clivicola* (living on hillsides) in August. As a diversion I much enjoyed our

chase after those *Tephropeplum* (ashy grey colour) *Dumicola* (dwellers in thickets) which we were lucky enough to find *Telopeum* (conspicuous) *Lochmium* (from a coppice). Knowing you to be an *Ombrochares* (lover of rain) I hope you will soon get some to revive the Species of Rhododendron; which as we are told by one Wallace: 'Of course it is over', and to make the snipe bogs *Paludosum* (marshy). It is too kind of you to have given me so many *Axium* (worthy) & *Eucallum* (beautiful) plants which will be *Eritimum* (highly prized) by me & are most *Apodectum* (acceptable).

After this I feel I cannot write English any more. It was really too kind of you to have had me to stay & I did so enjoy every moment of it. Thanking you both again so very much.

Yours very sincerely

Albert.[19]

After they moved into the Royal Lodge, Elizabeth began collecting modern paintings, sharing the interest with Winston Churchill whose book, *Painting as a Pastime*, she sent as presents to her friends. She bought a study of George Bernard Shaw by Augustus John and examples of Wilson Steer and Walter Sickert; those of the latter show a young man and a girl in fancy dress, and a conversation piece of George V and his racing manager, Major Fetherstonhaugh. Much later, when the war was over, she purchased a seascape by Monet which had once belonged to 'Tiger' Clemenceau, Premier of France. In time she added paintings by Matthew Smith and Paul Nash. Today, a great favourite is the study of her husband by Simon Elwes; another is one of the then Princess Elizabeth by E. Moynihan.

An external adornment to the Royal Lodge arrived in 1932 when the people of Wales presented Lilibet, on her sixth birthday, with a model of a traditional Welsh cottage. Fifteen feet high and with six rooms, complete down to the bathroom with hot and cold water, it was set up in a formal garden. Then dogs and ponies were acquired and, as the gardens took shape and the builders finished their task, the Yorks had a perfect country retreat. No wonder that later Queen Elizabeth II was to say the sun always seemed to be shining when she was a child.

In 1934 George became engaged to Princess Marina of Greece and was created Duke of Kent. Marina was the daughter of Prince Nicholas, son of King George I of the Hellenes, brother of Queen Alexandra. She was beautiful but considered somewhat advanced in her outlook: she earned a rebuke from Queen Mary for smoking a cigarette on the Channel steamer on her way to London. George and Marina were married in November at Westminster Abbey and Lilibet was a bridesmaid. Harry, who had been created Duke of Gloucester in 1928, looked as if he were set on the same course and the following year married Lady Alice Montagu-Douglas-Scott, daughter of the Duke of Buccleuch.

There was other royal news which did not appear in the newspapers, was hidden from the public and only reached the Royal Lodge on the grape vine. In the spring of 1934 the Prince of Wales jettisoned both his current girl friend, Thelma, Lady Furness, and his long-time companion, Freda Dudley Ward, never even bothering to say goodbye to either. He flushed them out of his life, leaving Wallis Simpson sitting alone on her pinnacle.

The occasion which attracted the most public and family attention, and which called for detailed planning, was the Silver Jubilee of the reign of King George and Queen Mary in May 1935. It turned out to be a success beyond all dreaming; Britain and the Empire let the King know beyond any doubt how they revered him. Despite ill health and endless worries, George V had understood exactly the required image of kingship in his time. The reception gave him great happiness. He wrote in his diary:

> A never-to-be-forgotten day, when we celebrated our Silver Jubilee. It was a glorious summer's day, 75° in the shade. The greatest number of people in the streets that I have ever seen in my life, the enthusiasm was indeed most touching. May & I drove alone with six greys . . . The Thanksgiving Service in St Paul's Cathedral was very fine. 4406 people present . . . On our return we went out on the centre balcony & were cheered by an enormous crowd . . . By only one post in the morning I received 610 letters.[20]

Yet on that memorable drive in the May sunshine there was a carriage which attracted almost as much attention as that of the King and Queen. In it were the Duke and Duchess of York and their daughters. Elizabeth was in powder blue, Lilibet and Margaret in rose pink with matching bonnets. People were already asking, would the elder girl one day be Queen?

George V tired quickly after the excitement of the Silver Jubilee. His decline in strength was hastened by the deaths of old friends and relations, and by ceaseless worry over Mrs Simpson. He saw it was no ordinary love which his son had for her, but begged his wife to promise that, after his death, she would not receive the American. Queen Mary could not in any case bring herself to interfere. On Christmas Day the King sent out his last message to the people over the radio. Lilibet and Margaret were at Sandringham to cheer him up, but their mother was in bed with pneumonia at the Royal Lodge. Snow fell and the King was confined to his room. He weakened fast. At dinner with the Household on the evening of 20 January 1936 Lord Dawson of Penn, the King's Physician, picked up a menu-card and wrote on the back: 'The King's life is moving peacefully towards its close.'[21] The words were telephoned to the BBC in London. At five minutes to midnight King George V died.

9

The Great Uncertainty

'THE SUNSET OF HIS DEATH tinged the whole world's sky . . .'[1] Queen Mary wrote in her diary.

As, with her children around her, she stood by the bed and realized her husband was dead, she stooped and kissed the hand of the new King, Edward VIII. None of her family had appreciated that George V would die so soon and they were all overwrought, dumbfounded. Yet before morning some slight portent of the changes ahead showed itself: a fragment of tradition was thrown out into the Norfolk night. Since Sandringham was first built the clocks had been kept half an hour fast in order that the then Prince of Wales might gain precious time for shooting, and in order also to offset his wife's unpunctuality. This difference between Sandringham time and Greenwich time had caused a misunderstanding and a delay among those hurriedly summoned to the house as the King weakened. Now Edward VIII ordered that the time should immediately become Greenwich, and in haste the man responsible for the maintenance of the many clocks worked at the re-adjustment, moving from room to room.

Next morning the new King flew to London for the Accession Council – the first monarch to fly. Bertie, now the Heir Presumptive, went with him. Once arrived they saw the newspaper placards. The spotlight was on Lilibet; one headline ran: 'Now second in line of succession to the throne, one day she may be Queen of England.'[2]

Queen Mary, in order to avoid the long-drawn-out drama which had preceded the funeral of Edward VII, had requested that her husband's body should not remain unburied for more than a week. Among Bertie's worries was whether his wife, convalescing after pneumonia, should travel to Norfolk and return with the funeral procession. He went to the Royal Lodge to discuss it with her. Elizabeth's reply was typical. Yes, she would go, and risk the dangers of the wintry weather at Sandringham. She decided that Queen Mary, indomitable as she was, might need her support for, although the Duchesses of Kent and Gloucester were there, they were but newly married while Elizabeth had been a member of the family for thirteen years. The strain the old Queen had borne during the past few days had been such that some around feared she might crack. So it was that with Queen Mary in the carriage which followed the King's coffin to Wolferton Station were her daughter, the Princess Royal, and the Duchess of York, now the first lady in the land.

It was a clear, frosty morning as the funeral train pulled out for London. The engine's smoke rose high and white into the sky; Sandringham watched it and said a last goodbye. At King's Cross the royal ladies stood stock still in their black shrouds for eight minutes as the coffin was loaded on to a gun-carriage.

There followed the incredible scenes which immortalized the lying-in-state in historic Westminster Hall. A million people queued to pay their homage, a seemingly endless line as they moved, pace by pace, along the south bank of the Thames, over the bridge and so to Westminster. One evening the four sons of the dead King stood guard at the corners of the catafalque. For the funeral service at Windsor Lilibet was with her parents, a sad little figure peering down into the darkness which had swallowed her beloved grandfather.

His new position as Heir Presumptive brought various elevations for Bertie. He was promoted to Vice-Admiral, Air Marshal and Lieutenant-General. His income was increased to £50,000 a year. He was always on call if his brother needed assistance with his multifarious duties, one of his first tasks being to make a survey of the Sandringham estate and suggest how the expenses there might be cut. Edward VIII regarded the royal home in Norfolk as a 'voracious white elephant', swallowing too big a slice of the available funds. Bertie, who loved the place, did not wish to see the old order changed, least of all a cut in staff, but he made many sensible suggestions, most of which were later adopted. The result of King George's death showed more clearly in Elizabeth than in her husband. The smile came less often; there were traces of a new air of authority about her, becoming in the mother of the girl who was next in line after her father. But she was thinner, the price of pneumonia and the strain of the funeral. To put right the after-effects of her illness, she and her family went in March for a convalescent holiday to Compton Place, Eastbourne, a house belonging to the Duke of Devonshire.

All the time there was the worry of the chatter about the King and Wallis Simpson and their weekends at Fort Belvedere. Edward had started his reign in a blaze of energy, assiduously attending to his work. Then began a delay in the return of papers. It was said that vital despatches were being left about the Fort in places where visitors might read them. The attitude of Wallis Simpson grated on those few who had the opportunity to observe her. She was too confident. Her quick repartees jarred on the wives of the famous and the ladies of the Establishment. She was tart with servants, some of whom had served their apprenticeship under Queen Victoria and were set in their ways as to how things should be done. She clearly had considerable control over the King: she would kick him hard under the table when he was to stop talking, and gently when he was to go on. She knew little of English ways, less of Scottish, and seemed to regard the King's job as synonymous with that of a department store director, where sharp direction brought results and all issues could be settled by the correct publicity.

On 9 July Wallis took a step forward: her name appeared in the Court Circular, recording her presence at one of the King's dinners. Among the guests were Sir Samuel Hoare, the Marquess of Willingdon, the Winston Churchills – and the Duke and Duchess of York. There were clear opinions in the minds of the people who mattered, yet not a word was spoken, not a finger raised. The King's sisters-in-law barred Wallis from their doors but in fact the necessity of receiving her was thrust upon Elizabeth. Edward had bought an American station wagon which appealed to him enormously and he decided to drive over from the Fort to the Royal Lodge to show it to Bertie. There was a demonstration drive, a walk in the garden, tea in the drawing room. 'It was a pleasant hour,' wrote Wallis, 'but I left with a distinct impression that, while the Duke of York was sold on the

American station wagon, the Duchess was not sold on David's other American interest.'[3] The impression was correct – Elizabeth was not to play hostess again. 'Who is she?' asked Lilibet as the station wagon drove away.

Wallis Simpson began divorce proceedings. The action was undefended and her husband moved out of their London house. Then in August came the cruise of the *Nahlin*, down the Dalmatian coast and into Grecian and Turkish waters. Custom decreed that the King should be at Balmoral for the shooting, but Edward wanted sunshine and fun. The unsettled state of Europe dictated that he holiday at sea, so two British destroyers accompanied the yacht. He attempted to travel incognito as the Duke of Lancaster, but the peoples of the lands which he visited would not have that, and nor would the foreign press. Reporters dashed along the coasts and the headlines ran round the world. Only the British press kept silent. 'Long live love,' yelled the locals as the *Nahlin* moved into ports where the passengers might picnic and bathe. What more startling contrast with the stately Mediterranean cruises of King Edward VII and Queen Alexandra, when protocol was followed to the letter, fleets dressed overall, receptions were held in palace gardens and all were sartorially perfect. Edward VIII was seldom dressed in anything but shorts, was photographed with the ladies about him wearing the latest in swim suits. He met foreign rulers for meals in cafés. Those of his staff with him, trained in the old ways, were horrified. The help of Wallis was sought to persuade the King to wear a shirt when appearing before the crowds. She shrugged it off, saying it was not her responsibility. At times she appeared bored with the pleasure cruise.

The King arrived back in London on 14 September. That was the moment when the nettle should have been grasped and the position clarified. Those who should have done it were the members of the royal family. The responsibility lay squarely on the shoulders of Queen Mary. If she demurred, then the task fell upon the Duke of York, backed by his wife, for it was their child who would inherit. Edward went to dinner with his mother, half-expecting a rumpus as a result of the sensational reports in the American press. Not a critical word was spoken. She talked to him just as she had done when he came home from school as a boy:

'Didn't you find it terribly hot in the Adriatic?'[4] and enquired after the health of King George of Greece. She wrote in her diary: 'David got back from abroad looking very well and came to dine with me and we had a nice talk.'[5]

The Yorks were at Birkhall, enjoying a quiet autumn holiday with their children. The King arrived at Balmoral; in his party was Wallis Simpson. She slept in the bedroom formerly occupied by Queen Mary; she interfered with the kitchen arrangements and kept servants up late. There was dancing and high jinks but little communication between the Castle and Birkhall. Then Bertie learned that changes had been made both in staff and management at Balmoral. He wasn't told until they were an accomplished fact. Why, he wondered, had he not been consulted, as he had been about Sandringham? He was deeply hurt; a special relationship had existed between the royal family and Balmoral since the days of John Brown: the staff were more like friends than servants. But all Bertie did was to write to his mother: 'David only told me what he had done after it was all over, which I might say made me rather sad. He arranged it all with the official people up there. I never saw him alone for an instant . . .'[6] And still there was no confrontation.

In October Wallis moved into a rented house at Felixstowe in Suffolk. Her petition for divorce was due to be heard at Ipswich on the 27th: if all went well, she would be a free woman by the time the Coronation took place the following May. Somebody had to move. Queen Mary was being inundated with letters from old friends of herself and her husband, and from every corner of the Commonwealth, and these letters urged her to take action and take it at once. But she did not wish to become involved; she wasn't a person to initiate an urgent campaign. She chatted and complained to a number of 'extraneous persons,'[7] with no results. At last, in desperation, she passed the ball to the Prime Minister, Mr Stanley Baldwin.

After a stay at Glamis, the Duke and Duchess of York returned to London. Major Alexander Hardinge, the King's Private Secretary, called upon them bearing vital news. He reported that 'on 20 October the Prime Minister had, after deep consideration and much searching of heart, sought an audience of the King, and, having shown him samples of the letters which had been received from many sources deprecating His Majesty's association with Mrs Simpson, had begged him to persuade her to have the divorce proceedings withdrawn.'[8] The King had replied that it was not his right to interfere with people's private affairs: the case must go on.

Wallis received a decree *nisi* but now all manner of folk in a position to know the facts – Ministers, Press Lords, legal experts, Bishops, members of the Household – joined in the clamour, each with his own plan for salvation; Bertie and Elizabeth still held their peace. The King carried on with his engagements and Wallis, chaperoned by her aunt, was a weekend guest at Fort Belvedere. It was these visits which caused the American press to heat up the headlines even further, while a French newspaper commented, '*L'Amour du Roi va bien.*' British publications still refrained from comment, but the moment of explosion was near at hand. It is possible that Edward, caught between the power of Wallis's presence and his own reluctance to precipitate a crisis, persuaded himself that a divorce would solve everything, that people would come round once the irregularity of Wallis's married status was eliminated. Perhaps, and more likely, he was just unable to cope with a problem of such emotional complexity.

On 13 November the King received the following letter from his Private Secretary, Major Hardinge:

> Sir,
>
> With my humble duty.
>
> As your Majesty's Private Secretary I feel it my duty to bring to your notice the following facts which have come to my knowledge, and which I *know* to be accurate.
>
> (1) The silence of the British press on the subject of Your Majesty's friendship with Mrs Simpson is *not* going to be maintained. It is probably only a matter of days before the outburst begins. Judging by the letters from British subjects living in foreign countries where the press has been outspoken, the effect will be calamitous.
>
> (2) The Prime Minister and senior members of the Government are meeting today to discuss what action should be taken to deal with the serious situation which

> is developing. As Your Majesty no doubt knows, the resignation of the Government – an eventuality which can by no means be excluded – would result in Your Majesty having to find someone else capable of forming a Government which would receive the support of the present House of Commons. I have reason to know that, in view of the feeling prevalent among members of the House of Commons of all parties, this is hardly within the bounds of possibility. The only alternative remaining is a dissolution and a general election in which Your Majesty's personal affairs would be the chief issue, and I cannot help feeling that even those who would sympathize with Your Majesty as an individual would deeply resent the damage which would inevitably be done to the Crown – the cornerstone on which the whole Empire rests.
>
> If Your Majesty will permit me to say so, there is only one step which holds out any prospect of avoiding this dangerous situation, and that is for Mrs Simpson to go abroad *without further delay* – and I would *beg* Your Majesty to give this proposal your earnest consideration before the position has become irretrievable. Owing to the changing attitude of the press the matter has become one of great urgency.
>
> I have the honour . . .[9]

Edward was shocked and angered. To him, the suggestion seemed to be that Wallis should be escorted to a port by a detective, handed a wad of five pound notes and despatched into oblivion. He did not reply but had no further dealing with Major Hardinge: in the days ahead Mr Walter Monckton acted as his liaison with Downing Street. Action was not long delayed. On the 16th the King saw Mr Baldwin and told him of his decision either to marry Wallis or to abdicate. That evening he dined with his mother and sister and, charged with emotion, told them the same. Next day he told his brothers.

> Bertie was so taken aback by my news that in his shy way he could not bring himself to express his innermost feelings at the time. This, after all, was not surprising, for next to myself Bertie had most at stake: it was he who would have to wear the crown if I left, and his

> genuine concern for me was mixed with the dread of having to assume the responsibilities of kingship. He waited a few days before confiding his thoughts to a letter. He wrote that he longed for me to be happy, adding that he of all people should be able to understand my feelings; he was sure that whatever I decided would be in the best interests of the country and the Empire.[10]

Bertie was now a really worried man; he had talks with the Prime Minister and with Queen Mary. He did not want to succeed to the throne. He said that, if the job were forced upon him, he would do his best but he feared that the whole fabric might crumble. Queen Mary later revealed: 'He sobbed on my shoulder for a whole hour – on a sofa.'[11]

On the 29th Bertie and Elizabeth left London for long-standing engagements in Scotland. It was a dismal Sunday evening and they didn't wish to leave the centre of action. 'I feel like the proverbial sheep being led to the slaughter,'[12] was Bertie's comment. In Edinburgh he was installed Grand Master Mason of Scotland. Elizabeth attended a reception for the wives of Masonic officers, re-opened the Deaconess hospital and received the Freedom of Edinburgh. Together they went to a variety concert at the Empire Theatre. She warmed to the cheers and bowed out as the smiling Duchess of York. They boarded a sleeper, London-bound, on the evening of 2 December. They reached Euston Station as the morning crowds were milling their way to work and, to their shock and amazement, they saw the newspaper placards blazing out the words – MARRIAGE OF THE KING.

Bertie hurried round to Marlborough House, his mother's new home. Surrounded by newspapers, she was deeply shaken and almost bereft of words, but she kept her comments short. 'Really,' she said, 'this might be Romania.' She hurried off a note to the King: 'This news in the papers is very upsetting, especially as I have not seen you for ten days – I would much like to see you; won't you look in some time today?'[13] Meantime the shock wave had hit Fort Belvedere, where Wallis was staying. She saw the papers early and told Edward that she must leave England that day. He agreed. Quickly arrangements were made. A telephone call to Mr Herman Rogers, a friend who lived at Cannes, settled that she could find shelter at his villa there, Lou Viei. Lord Brownlow agreed to accompany her as escort. Her own car was sent to Newhaven for stowage on the Dieppe boat; she was to follow in Brownlow's Rolls. She had hardly time to pack. Sadly, she agreed to leave her beloved dog, Slipper, behind – thereafter he never left the King's heels.

It was dark when Wallis left, on the start of what was to prove the most sensational escape-run through France since the Empress Eugenie fled the Tuileries in 1870. Tired out, depressed beyond measure, the King drove to London. He saw Mr Baldwin at Buckingham Palace and repeated his decision – marriage or abdication. Then he went to Marlborough House to dine with his mother. The Princess Royal and the Duke and Duchess of York were there. He told Queen Mary, Bertie and Mary (Elizabeth was out of the room) that he could not live alone and must marry Wallis. He asked Bertie to come and see him in the morning. After a further conference at the Palace, he left for the Fort after midnight. There was still a crowd round the Palace gates and a cheer of encouragement went up from his supporters. The Daimler went on through the western suburbs. That was the last time His Majesty King Edward VIII saw London as King.

Next morning, Friday 4 December, as he had been instructed to, Bertie contacted his brother to find out when he could see him. There followed a series of evasions, as yet not fully explained, which had vital bearing on the issue at stake. These evasions were thus described by Bertie in his diary:

> I rang him up but he could not see me & put off till Saturday. I told him that I would be at Royal Lodge on Saturday by 12.30 p.m. I rang him up on Saturday. 'Come and see me on Sunday,' was his answer. 'I will see you & tell you my decision when I have made up my mind.' Sunday evening I rang up. 'The King has a conference & will speak to you later,' was the answer. But he did not ring up. Monday morning came. I rang up at 1.0 p.m. & my brother told me he might be able to see me that evening. I told him, 'I must go to London but would come to the Fort when he wanted me.' I did not go to London but waited. I sent a telephone message to the Fort to say that if I were wanted I would be at the Royal Lodge. My brother rang me up at ten

> minutes to 7.0 p.m. to say, 'Come & see me after dinner.' I said, 'No, I will come & see you at once.' I was with him at 7.0 p.m. The awful & ghastly suspense of waiting was over. I found him pacing up & down, & he told me his decision that he would go. I went back to Royal Lodge for dinner & returned to the Fort later. I felt having once got there I was not going to leave. As he is my eldest brother I had to be there to try & help him in his hour of need. I went back to London that night with my wife.[14]

The apparent reason for the delays and prevarications was that there was a strong lobby, composed of politicians and members of the press, of the opinion that Bertie was not up to the task of kingship. The premise for this was, on the surface, strong. He had been weak as a child and backward at the naval colleges. He had been invalided out of the Navy. The signs of upset, both physical and mental, had continued, and his stammer had been a permanent drawback. He had conducted only one major royal engagement, that of the world tour in 1927. He had shown little forcefulness, or insistence on preparation for the ruling role, being content to live at the Royal Lodge, gardening and studying historical records. He had kept in the background throughout the Wallis Simpson affair and taken no drastic steps to safeguard matters if his brother abdicated. In addition, he had himself said that he could not do the job. It was said that he would be a 'rubber-stamp' King, entirely unfitted to cope with the war crisis blowing up in Europe and of re-livening the loyalty of the shaken Empire. Mistakenly, he was dismissed by some critics as a 'plain bore', filling a gap at a time when dynamism and magnetism were needed.

Of course it was not a legal necessity that Bertie succeed to the throne. It was customary, not essential, for the Heir Presumptive to follow on but it was up to Parliament to decide on the successor in the Abdication Bill. It had already been necessary to put considerable pressure on Bertie to convince him that he should become King: his fears were not confined to himself, but increased by knowledge of the burden he would lay on Lilibet's shoulders when he died. But it would be a very different matter if the decision were taken out of his hands and settled without his knowledge: that would have broken him. It was just such a question that was being discussed at Fort Belvedere during the days of prevarication.

The man who was being put forward as the next King was Bertie's youngest brother, George, Duke of Kent. Harry, Duke of Gloucester, was passed over: he did not fit the bill – somewhat slow, he was a professional soldier, devoted to his career and not enamoured with 'princing', as he called the royal round. George was thirty-four. He was strong, well built, suave in the manner of the thirties, quick on the answer and suffered none of the health drawbacks which plagued Bertie. He was married to a beautiful and delightful wife, Marina; he already had a son, Edward, ready to take the role of Prince of Wales, and the Duchess was about to have another baby. It was well known that George had an irresistible urge to pursue a pretty face and stern action had been taken on a number of occasions to free him from the attentions of certain young ladies. But what was not known was that he had succumbed to the temptations and dangers of drugs, that he had been saved by his eldest brother who had taken him to the Fort and helped him break with their use.[15]

Behind the closed doors of the Fort another struggle now took place and moved gradually in favour of the Duke of York. Obvious backers were Baldwin and Dr Lang, the Archbishop of Canterbury, both mature men of staid outlook and out of sympathy with the way of life of Edward VIII. Cosmo Lang had been keeping a watchful eye on developments since the Wallis Simpson affair began and had exerted his influence in a number of directions. He had been a close friend of George V, listened to what he had to say, and knew that George V had prayed the throne be kept for Bertie and Lilibet. The attitude of responsible men was expressed by a contemporary who knew Bertie well:

> He was in no way a bore. He was born out of his age. He was very serious-minded and only liked doing things for under-privileged people, which was at the time right against the swim of the tide, especially among those in royal circles who were mostly renowned playboys. No – not a bore, but *not* in sympathy with the thirties.

Yet the detractions of Bertie were very real and it was meet they should be considered. His health record was a real worry. People were saying that if he could not stand up to Navy life as a young man, could he stand up to the strain of kingship in middle age? But Bertie had one card which tipped the balance in his favour. It was no personal asset of his own: it was his wife. For thirteen years Elizabeth's charm and thoughtfulness had been seen throughout the country in a ceaseless round of routine royal engagements. She had brought happiness into hospital wards and missions, homes for children and welfare organizations, schools and universities. She had backed charities and been a welcome guest at women's societies. She was a religious woman and her views were well known to the heads of the Church. She was adored by the armed forces and was the darling of the Scottish regiments. Her magic stretched across the social spectrum, from the under-privileged to the leaders of the world and, of particular importance, to the heads of the Commonwealth who had voted unanimously against Wallis Simpson. Statesmen had noted her powers: shortly after she became Queen she was chatting with Mr Ramsay MacDonald. Looking at the King, he said, 'He's coming on magnificently.' Smiling with delight, she queried: 'Am I doing all right?' 'Oh you . . .' he replied simply, saying more clearly than words could express that she had been taken for granted from the start.

The weight of opinion in power was that Bertie should become King. When he was at length called to Fort Belvedere on the evening of 7 December his brother told him his decision was that he 'would go'. That decision had been made perfectly clear on the night of the 3rd, it had been repeated to Mr Baldwin on the 5th, and there was no going back. Yet no word had been sent to Bertie – even the Government connived in keeping him in ignorance: the probability was that they were waiting for the final selection of successor. And, most strange of all, Bertie was not allowed to see Walter Monckton, acting as the King's adviser. So he was left with the impression that his brother had in fact been wavering on the point of abdication. He had throughout believed, and prayed, that Edward would change his mind. He was spared knowing the truth: Edward had been kind.

Bertie had enough worries on his mind as he drove back from Windsor to London with Elizabeth late on the night of the 7th. She was developing influenza. Next morning she retired to bed and there stayed throughout the days of drama which followed. Bertie was summoned to dine at Fort Belvedere. In his own words, it was a dinner 'I am never likely to forget'. Ostensibly the object of the meeting was to discuss disposition of family property, but another point arose. Wallis, who had been visited by her solicitor, Mr Goddard, was doing her best to stop the abdication: she was prepared to renounce her love and move out of France into oblivion. This move brought other guests to the Fort. Round the table were Mr Baldwin; Sir Edward Peacock, Receiver-General of the Duchy of Cornwall; Mr Walter Monckton; Mr George Allen, solicitor to the King; and Major Thomas Dugdale, the Prime Minister's Private Secretary. Then the Duke of Kent arrived uninvited. 'What the dickens are you doing here?' asked Edward. 'Whether you want to see me or not, I have come,' the Duke replied.[16]

The meal threatened to be a melodramatic affair but the King, now under a still greater strain because of Wallis's move and exceedingly angry and perturbed about it, summoned up a reserve of strength, and he sparkled. He was, said Bertie, the life and soul of the party. He wore a white kilt, watched over the needs of each of his guests and kept conversation rippling, 'telling the PM things I am sure he had never heard about unemployment centres, etc.'* Bertie whispered to Monckton: 'And this is the man we're going to lose!' Baldwin was on his other side; Bertie, looking at his brother, said to the Prime Minister: 'Look at him! We simply cannot let him go!' After dinner he commented: 'I would never have been able to do that! I can't do this job . . .'[17] Even at this late stage in the crisis he was still hoping for a miracle.

He was at the Fort again next day. 'I had a long talk with D[avid], but I could see that nothing I said would alter his decision. I motored up to London with Walter Monckton (much to our mutual surprise) as D. had been very suspicious previous to my talk with him, & we were then able to discuss what we liked in confidence. I went to see Queen Mary &, when I told her what had happened, I broke down & sobbed like a child.'[18]

On the 10th Bertie and his younger brothers witnessed the signing of the instrument of abdication. 'Perfectly calmly, D. signed five or six copies of the instrument and then five copies of

* As a result of his recent controversial visit to Wales.

Queen Victoria in the last year of her life with
Prince Henry in her arms, Prince Albert in the foreground,
Princess Mary and Prince Edward

(*left to right*) Prince of Wales,
Princess Mary,
the Princess of Wales
holding Prince John,
Prince George,
Prince Henry (seated),
David and Bertie

Prince Albert of Wales

far left:
Bertie, on special leave from Dartmouth, attends King George V and Queen Mary at Portsmouth for the Review of the Fleet, 1912

Whilst at Cambridge Bertie became a keen motorcyclist

Elizabeth at the end of the First World War, which she spent nursing wounded soldiers in the hospital at Glamis

The Duchess of York returning to Buckingham Palace as the fourth lady in the land after her wedding

above right: A relaxed Duke and Duchess of York fishing in New Zealand during their visit in 1927

The royal family, with Queen Mary, on the balcony at Buckingham Palace celebrating the coronation of King George VI

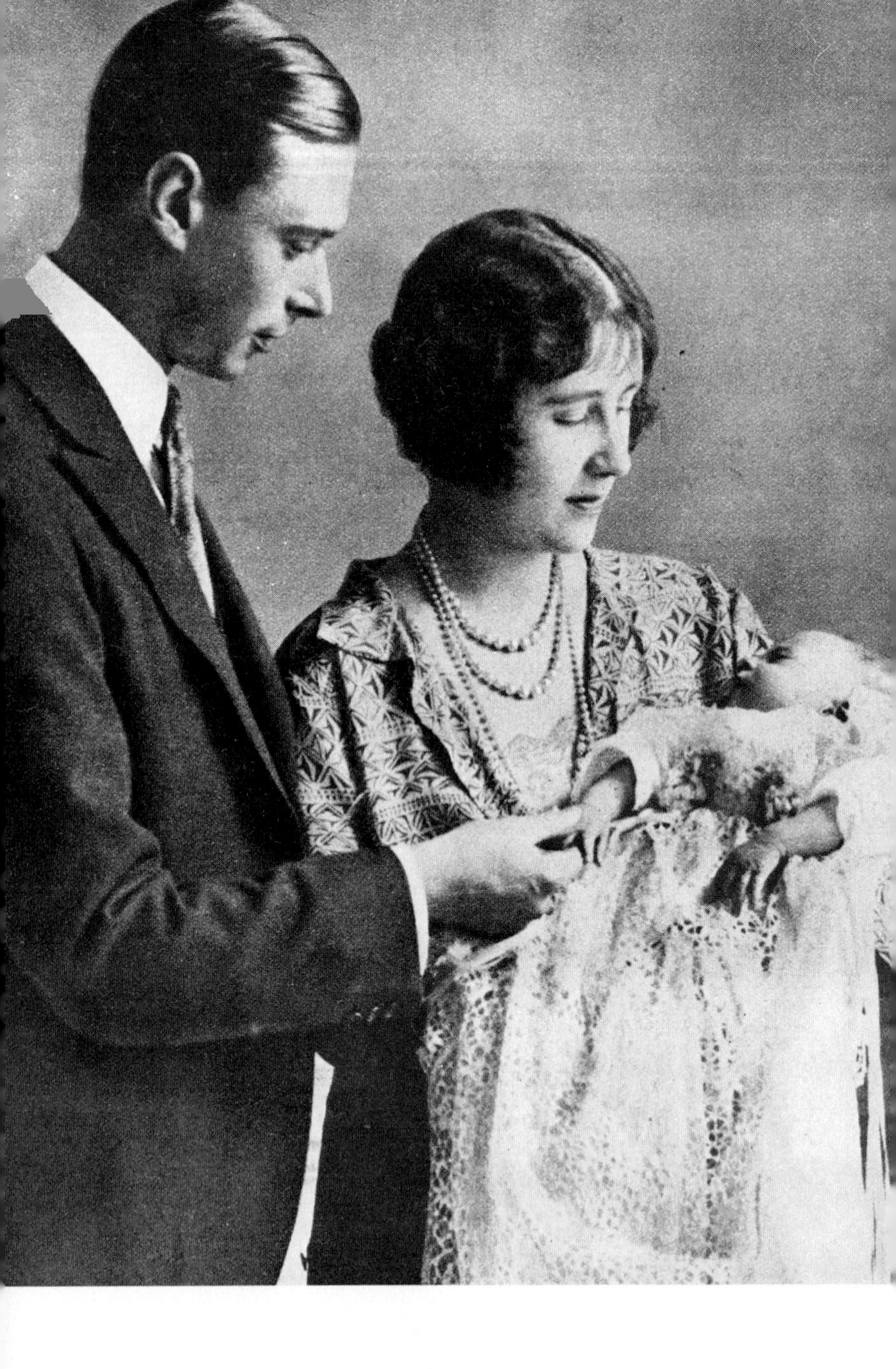

David, as Prince of Wales

Speculation that the little Princess Elizabeth might someday reign began long before 1936. The then Duke and Duchess of York with their baby at the time of her christening

Mrs Wallis Simpson, shortly after becoming Duchess of Windsor

Queen Elizabeth set a fashion for parasols in France and America. Seen here at Buckingham Palace

King George VI in North Africa

The King and Queen inspect bomb damage to Buckingham Palace

Relaxing (*Lord Salisbury*)

The Royal Lodge gardens

11th February 1952. The coffin of King George VI

his message to Parliament, one for each Dominion Parliament. It was a dreadful moment & one never to be forgotten by those present. One or two curious incidents happened later re the servants.'[19] When Bertie arrived back at 145 Piccadilly that evening there was a large crowd outside the house and they were cheering madly. Tired out, Bertie was overcome with emotion.

Friday, 11 December Bertie labelled 'that dreadful day'. He became King George VI, taking his fourth name in memory of his father.* The day was spent preparing details of the Accession Council and Proclamation. Queen Mary called upon Queen Elizabeth, who was still in bed. She brought the invalid an anti-germ-impregnated handkerchief.

That evening there was to be a farewell dinner for the ex-King at the Royal Lodge, the guests being Queen Mary, the Princess Royal, the Dukes of Gloucester and Kent and the Earl and Countess of Athlone. On his way there Bertie called in at the Fort. There the servants addressed him as 'Your Majesty' and he found it hard to believe they had the title right. Lord Mountbatten was there. Bertie confided in him of his reluctance to succeed, and his unpreparedness: 'I have never seen a State paper.' Edward assured his brother that he would not find it a difficult job at all. For the dinner party Queen Mary wore a brightly coloured dress, the first time that she had been out of mourning since her husband's death: it was her effort to cheer up a cheerless evening. Conversation hung heavy and before the meal was over the car arrived to take Edward to Windsor Castle for his farewell broadcast. On the back seat was Slipper, Wallis's dog, greeting him with delight. So he went through the fog, to the hill and the grey walls, to face the great ordeal, with a precious possession of the woman whom he loved beside him to give him strength and distraction.

Soon those at the Royal Lodge heard the clear voice come over the radio:

> A few hours ago I discharged my last duty as King and Emperor, and now that I have been succeeded by my brother, the Duke of York, my first words must be to declare my allegiance to him. This I do with all my heart . . . But you must believe me when I tell you that

* The ex-King was created Duke of Windsor the following day.

> I have found it impossible to carry the heavy burden of responsibility and to discharge my duties as King as I would wish to do without the help and support of the woman I love . . . And I want you to know that the decision I have made has been mine and mine alone. This was a thing I had to judge entirely for myself. The other person most nearly concerned has tried up to the last to persuade me to take a different course. I have made this, the most serious decision of my life, upon a single thought of what would in the end be best for all. This decision has been made less difficult to me by the sure knowledge that my brother, with his long training in the public affairs of this country and with his fine qualities, will be able to take my place forthwith, without interruption or injury to the life and progress of the Empire. And he has one matchless blessing, enjoyed by so many of you and not bestowed on me – a happy home with his wife and children . . .

Edward came back from the Castle and, with a great sense of relief filling him, he felt that the tension had eased between him and his family. Queen Mary was a changed woman now, hardened, in complete control of herself, firm in decision. Had she achieved that frame of mind two years earlier there might not have been an abdication. Now she was worried about the fog which hung over the Thames – she said her goodbye and left with her daughter. Her written comment was: 'The whole thing was too pathetic for words.'[20] Bertie, Harry and George stayed on with their brother until it was time for him to leave for Portsmouth, to travel to Boulogne on HMS *Fury*. Midnight came. They walked with Edward to the door, as they had so many times when he was about to depart on a journey. Edward bowed to King George VI. Bertie kissed his brother and the two parted as Freemasons.* Then Edward climbed into the car with Walter Monckton and Slipper and the fog swallowed them.

Edward had had little thought of what would happen to him in the days ahead. He had taken it for granted that somehow his staff would care for immediate requirements but, as he said, they

* In 1924 the Duke of York accepted the charge, as Grand Master, of the Masonic Province of Middlesex. In 1936 he was installed Grand Master Mason of the Grand Lodge of Scotland.

seemed to evaporate; even his valet refused to accompany him – he had not known where he was going to rest his head that night until just before the final broadcast. It was left to Wallis to arrange that he be the guest of the Rothschilds at their home at Enzesfeld, near Vienna. As the half-light came over Boulogne and the long train prepared to pull out for Austria, Edward wired Bertie: 'Hope Elizabeth better. Best love and best of luck to you both. David.' He would have left England all alone, with only Slipper for company, had not Sir Piers Legh, his equerry since 1919, decided that something must be done, and volunteered to escort his master to Austria. This was the position for a man who had had every detail of his daily requirements catered for since he left Dartmouth. In the final count there was to be no reward for the long years of service.

10

The Trial of Strength

MID-DECEMBER HAD OFTEN BEEN a time of crisis for the royal family since Prince Albert the Consort died at Windsor on 14 December 1861. It happened again in 1936. Since the beginning of the month the newspapers had been packed with the news of the Abdication; but there was one fortunate point about its timing – Christmas was coming. Almost with a sigh of relief, the public switched to a new priority: preparing for the festive season. The picture which most of all spread a sense of continuity and peace was of the new King and Queen and their two daughters leaving by car for Liverpool Street to spend Christmas at Sandringham. Queen Mary went with them. She wrote: 'Left London with Bertie, E, and their children for dear Sandringham to spend Christmas there, my staff running it this year . . . Happy to be back in the old Home.'[1] She was a welcome guest, never interfering but always ready with advice that only she could give.

Norfolk was just the tonic the King needed. He felt really wanted there. The staff assembled to receive their presents and the crowd of the 'faithful' gathered around the church of St Mary Magdalene for the Christmas service. But for poor Queen Mary reaction came. The death of her husband, the unremitting worry over the actions of her eldest son and his association with Mrs Simpson, the change in her homes – all these proved too much for her and she retired to her room, not to bed but to sit and ponder on the critical days, and to regain her strength. She still could not understand David. 'All *this* thrown away for *that*,' she would exclaim. But there came a welcome present, for her and for all of them. On Christmas Day the Duchess of Kent gave birth to a daughter, to be named Alexandra Helen Elizabeth Olga Christabel: Alexandra in memory of 'the beloved lady' who had been the goddess of Sandringham for over sixty years; Elizabeth in honour of the new Queen; and Christabel because of the day of her birth.

The peaceful interlude lasted until the New Year, when a reaction from Edward's supporters began to make itself felt. There was disappointment that there had been no royal broadcast on Christmas afternoon: the King's message had become a major radio attraction since George V began the practice in 1932 – 'Through one of the marvels of modern science, I am enabled this Christmas Day to speak to all my people throughout the Empire . . .' – but the new King had had little time to prepare such a talk, he felt that as yet he was too unknown to the public to undertake such a task and he was tired out, which still had a deleterious effect on his speech. In addition, the BBC had not had time yet to perfect a technique for patching over his pauses. Still, a message from him was sorely missed. Then the critical remarks about Edward VIII made by Dr Cosmo Lang, Archbishop of Canterbury, though intended to ease the situation, back-fired and the ex-King's supporters counter-attacked further. Pens were dipped in vitriol and the Archbishop was labelled 'the auld Lang swine'. Four lines were widely circulated:

> My Lord Archbishop, what a scold you are!
> And when your man is down how bold you are!
> Of Charity how oddly scant you are!
> How Lang, O Lord, how full of Cantuar!

A rumour began that the King would not attend a Delhi Durbar, India's ceremonious State reception to welcome a new monarch, a rumour which was to prove true. King Edward had indicated that he would attend such an historic occasion and George VI also wanted to do so, but the weight of advice was against him. Contrary to the avowal in his brother's broadcast, George had to learn the business of being King from scratch and it was considered inadvisable for him to be away from Britain for long so soon after his accession, particularly in view of the unsettled conditions in Europe, the probability of a change of Government and the opposition to his visit of the Indian Congress Party, who had announced that it would take no part in the Durbar, although it was an event looked forward to with enthusiasm by millions of Indians. For many thousands of British, whose life-work was bound with India and who plied regularly from Tilbury to Calcutta, the probability of a cancellation came as a grave disappointment.

The rumours built up through the opening months of 1937 until they came near to being out of hand. John Wheeler-Bennett commented: 'Coming from none knew where, passed from mouth to mouth, in some cases unheedingly, in others with malignant intent, there swept through London a wave of idle and malicious gossip which embraced not only the general health of the King and the royal family but also his ability to discharge his functions as a Sovereign.'[2] It was said that the King's health was so frail he would not be able to stand up to the ordeal of the Coronation and that the service would be curtailed until it bore little resemblance to the traditional ceremony: some went so far as to whisper that there would be no Coronation. It was widely believed that George VI would never be able to speak in public. We have a 'rubber stamp' King, said his critics, a cypher, a mere tool of the politicians. Based on the contrast between George and the panache of Edward VIII, much of this talk is readily understandable but it was grossly inaccurate. At last a man stood up and said so. The Rev. Robert Hyde, who had known George well for nearly twenty years and who had been closely associated with the Duke of York's Boys' Camps, thundered: 'Those of you who hear this gossip, do not heed it. It is unkind, unworthy and untrue.'[3] And it was untrue. After three months of reigning, George was showing signs that he was master of the situation. His health had never been better. True, he was still receiving treatment for his speech defect from Mr Lionel Logue, but that was only natural in view of the ordeal which lay ahead. True also was it that the discovery of the multifarious duties of kingship had come as an almost unbearable shock and he had been driven once again to say to his advisers that he could not do the job – the Teck temper flared, as it had done when he was over-taxed with studies as a boy. But he was a born trier and he gave his everything to winning. From nine in the morning until seven in the evening he worked at his papers. He was apt to open mail himself and had to be persuaded not to waste his time answering the letters of cranks. His penchant for detail and accuracy showed clearly, for he would sign no paper unless he fully comprehended it. And if he didn't understand a paper or a question, he would put it on one side and discuss it with his wife in the evening or at the weekends, relaxing in the garden at the Royal Lodge. Now the deep truth of Edward VIII's parting words could be seen: 'And he has one matchless blessing, enjoyed by so many of you and not bestowed on me – a happy home with his wife and children.'

The toughness of Elizabeth never showed more clearly than it did in the opening days of 1937. She wrote to Dr Cosmo Lang: 'I can hardly now believe that we have been called to this tremendous task and (I am writing to you quite intimately) the curious thing is that we are not afraid.'[4] It was their courage which saved the day. Twenty-five years later a close observer, Mr John Gordon of the *Sunday Express*, summed up the part which she had played: 'She gave guidance, support and tactful leadership to her husband at a most critical time, which may well have saved the Monarchy . . .'

As well as deriving strength from each other and their family, there is no doubt that both George and Elizabeth lived guided by faith. Belief was part of their make-up, so that they would not confront difficult tasks without first praying for strength and blessing. Both Elizabeth's parents were deeply religious, and nightly prayer was something all their children were taught. At Glamis there were prayers every day in the private chapel, the women attending wearing white lace caps, such caps being provided in the bedrooms of lady guests. On Sundays Lady Strathmore would preside at the harmonium. George never missed services at Balmoral and Sandringham and would look around the churches to see if there were absentees among his staff and tenants. If he spotted one – and he never missed – he would later make enquiries about their health. Edward VII had done the same, but he would come in halfway through the service assuming a look intended to suggest he had been held up by urgent State business. He took his Kingship with him into the pew, but George and Elizabeth gave instructions that they were to be treated as ordinary members of the congregation, the only difference being that they left first. George valued religion as background music to his life; he was a regular listener to the *Lift up your hearts* programme on the radio and read books such as Bishop Carey's *Prayer*. He once devastated a new lady-in-waiting at dinner by turning to her and demanding what she thought of the ten commandments. He liked to follow procedure exactly. Once, when he was ill, he had no alternative but to take the Sacrament seated; profuse apologies to all concerned followed. Though belief was strong it had no narrow boundary: the Nonconformist and Roman Catholic churches were held in great respect. When George's friend, Arthur Cardinal Hinsley, died in 1943, the King was most vexed that his advisers laid down he should not attend Requiem Mass, on grounds of precedent. He wrote to Queen Mary: 'I know how much he had done to bring his church into line with our churches here & I was going to see him & thank him personally . . . I feel that it was a great chance missed when relations are definitely better.'[5] Elizabeth, too, felt that public avowal was important, and regularly lent her support to religious institutions and charities.

Elizabeth's practical abilities were put to the test in those first months of her husband's reign. She gave priority to the welfare of the King, watching his health and ensuring that he had relaxation. She gained a closer insight into the business of the country than had any Queen Consort before her: when things went wrong in State affairs, it was she who smoothed matters when her husband got home at night. The slow smile would come on, the eyes would meet his. 'Now Bertie . . .' she would say. In addition, she had to familiarize herself with the running of Windsor Castle, Balmoral, Sandringham and Buckingham Palace, to which they moved in February. She had to adjust the upbringing of her children to suit their altered status. And she had to keep up with her public programme, realizing that to be seen was a vital part of their initiation. It was comforting indeed to hear the cheers when she and her husband made their State drive through the East End of London on 13 February, and to see the reception accorded them when they attended the Grand National at Aintree.

Overshadowing every day was the preparation for the Coronation. The customary time granted to a new Monarch was between a year and eighteen months. Although Victoria had been allowed only twelve, being crowned in June 1838, Edward VII and Alexandra had had nineteen months, the Coronation being postponed due to the King's illness. He died in May 1910; George V and Queen Mary were crowned in June of the next year. However, it being considered essential that the Coronation date fixed by Edward VIII should be adhered to, George VI and Elizabeth were allowed only five months.

In many ways it came harder for her than for him. There were hundreds of points to settle and each day those responsible for the staging of the ceremony queued either to seek the answers to questions or to receive approval for steps taken. For one thing, and not a minor consideration, the King's wardrobe was preordained: the Queen had to decide the style of the robe and the dress which she would wear, and also those for her children and her Ladies. For her Coronation robe Elizabeth followed the design used by Queen Alexandra, with train and cape combined. Handley Seymour made the Coronation dress and at the Royal School of Needlework in Kensington ten women sat at a long table working on the embroidery, emblems from all corners of the Empire. Robes of purple velvet edged with ermine were designed for the young Princess; Norman Hartnell created the stiff white satin dresses for the Maids of Honour; and the four Duchesses, who were to hold the canopy over the Queen at her crowning, were dressed by Molyneux.

The stands went up. '*Too* ugly,' commented Queen Mary, 'and the poor daffodils are squashed and hidden underneath.'[6] Taking place only a few days before her seventieth birthday, Coronation Day was to be one of the most historic of her life. She broke with a tradition which had existed since Plantagenet times. No Queen Dowager had ever attended the crowning of her husband's successor, but Mary had asked her son if she might do so and take her place in the procession. His was a wise decision, for her presence lent an air of continuity to the ceremony and was a big added attraction.

There were other firsts about this Coronation. It was to be the first one broadcast and arrangements were being made to send out the first outside television broadcast in the world. Although George had a deep-seated antipathy to the microphone, both he and Elizabeth were deeply interested in new technology and in new ways of reaching the people. Kings and Chiefs, Presidents and Premiers, arrived each day and were met with ceremony at

London's stations. Service contingents began to arrive from overseas – Australia, New Zealand, Canada, India and Burma. Vast electric chandeliers were hoisted into place in Westminster Abbey and wide carpets arrived for the nave. Along the route the flag poles went up and the gilding was done. The banners hung proud in the wide streets and the Union Jacks and the bunting made patchwork quilts of the alleys. Festive lights went on and the Fleet came up the river. After a quiet weekend at the Royal Lodge, George and Elizabeth drove to Buckingham Palace on the evening of Sunday, 9 May. There, in their private apartments, they met the Archbishop of Canterbury and knelt with him in prayer. 'From that moment,' Dr Lang recorded, 'I knew what would be in their minds and hearts when they came to the anointing and crowning.'

There was something strange, almost unbelievable, about the Coronation of King George VI and Elizabeth his Consort. It left behind it, commented *The Sphere*, 'a memory of jewelled magnificence, a gigantic diamond for the chaplet of British history.'[7] Over three million people struggled to get a glimpse of some part of it. This happened spontaneously, despite the wave of criticism and despondency which had plagued the early months of the year. The forecast had been that the ceremony would be a flop. What caused the hundreds of thousands to camp out in the streets, in inclement weather, for twenty-four hours and more?

The drawing power did not come from the King alone. Maybe it was a deep-seated reaction to the Abdication. He was not the kind of man to be a magnet for crowds. The gilt and trappings were of obvious appeal to many, but not to the tune of three million. The presence of Queen Mary was a decided boost, for she was a link with the past, and the beauty of the two Duchesses, Marina of Kent and Alice of Gloucester, drew an army of fans. Princesses Lilibet and Meg could add lustre to any occasion. Perhaps it was the image of family they unconsciously projected that appealed so widely.

It was early on the morning of Tuesday, the 11th, that the firstcomers began to pick their pitches along the ceremonial route. Many office workers did not head home that evening but made their bivouacs on the pavement. By eight there was not space to sit down round Nelson's Column in Trafalgar Square. The last trains coming in from the suburbs were packed. The smell from the frying pans was strong in St James's Park; the revellers came from the restaurants and children slept unheeding under their tarpaulins.

King George kept a detailed diary of the happenings of Wednesday, the 12th.[8] It began for him before the dawn:

> We were woken up very early, about 3 a.m., by the testing of the 'loud speakers' which had been placed in Constitution Hill; one of them might have been in our room. Bands and marching troops for lining the streets arrived at 5 a.m., so sleep was impossible. I could eat no breakfast & had a sinking feeling inside . . .

By first light there were fifty thousand people in the Mall alone. At five the barriers to a packed Whitehall were closed. An hour later the peers began to arrive at the Abbey. George and Elizabeth got up at seven. They looked out from the Palace upon the biggest crowd ever assembled in London. At 8.30 a.m. the doors of Westminster were closed upon the guests, and between then and 10.30 a.m. all the other processions arrived at the Abbey, bringing the royal family, Mr Baldwin and the Dominion Prime Ministers, the representatives of Foreign Powers, the Speaker and the Lord Mayor of London.

As the setting was completed at Westminster, George and Elizabeth left Buckingham Palace in the State Coach, built for George III in 1762, and drawn by eight Windsor greys. Yeomen of the Guard flanked it; before and behind were divisions of a Sovereign's Escort of Life Guards. The cheers scattered the birds in St James's Park, echoed round Admiralty Arch and reached their climax in the funnel of Whitehall. At eleven precisely the Westminster Choir began the anthem, 'I was glad when they said unto me . . .' as the King and Queen came through the west door. George chronicled:

> Elizabeth's procession started first but a halt was soon called, as it was discovered that one of the Presbyterian chaplains had fainted & there was no place to which he could be taken. He was removed, however, after some delay & the procession proceeded & arrived in position. I was kept waiting, it seemed for hours, due to this accident . . .

There came the Recognition, the ceremony of presenting the King to his people. The Archbishop of Canterbury, accompanied by the Lord Chancellor, Lord Great Chamberlain, Lord High Constable and Earl Marshal, moved towards the four points of the compass, the King turning himself in each direction so as to be seen. The Archbishop cried: 'Sirs, I here present unto you, King George, your undoubted King . . .' And the answer came from the congregation, 'God save King George.' After the Anointing, the King's heels were touched with the Spurs, and then the lord who carried the great Sword of State handed it over to the Lord Chamberlain and received another sword in a scabbard of purple velvet. This was laid upon the Altar, before being delivered into the King's right hand and then girt about him by the Lord Great Chamberlain. Then the King arose and the Armill and the Robe Royal were delivered by the Officer of the Great Wardrobe to the Dean of Westminster and put upon him. The King then sat down and the Orb with the Cross was brought from the Altar and delivered into his hand by the Archbishop. Thus the ceremony progressed to reach the most dramatic moment of the day – the placing of the Crown on the head of the King by the Archbishop of Canterbury. The congregation shouted, 'God save the King', the peers put on their coronets, the trumpets sounded, and the guns at the Tower of London roared out their salute.

For George, all proceeded according to plan until he reached the Coronation Chair, and then things started going very wrong:

> Here various vestments were placed upon me, the white Colobium Sindonis, a surplice which the Dean of Westminster insisted I should put on inside out . . .
>
> Before this I knelt at the Altar to take the Coronation Oath. I had two Bishops, Durham, & Bath & Wells, one on either side to support me & to hold the form of Service for me to follow. When this great moment came neither Bishop could find the words, so the Archbishop held his book down for me to read, but horror of horrors, his thumb covered the words of the Oath.
>
> My Lord Great Chamberlain was supposed to dress me but I found his hands fumbled & shook so I had to fix the belt of the sword myself. As it was he nearly put the hilt of the sword under my chin trying to attach it to the belt.

> The supreme moment came when the Archbishop placed the St Edward's Crown on my head. I had taken every precaution as I thought to see that the Crown was put on the right way round, but the Dean and Archbishop had been juggling with it so much that I never did know whether it was right or not.
>
> As I turned after leaving the Coronation Chair I was brought up all standing, owing to one of the Bishops treading on my robe, I had to tell him to get off it pretty sharply . . .[9]

After the Homage, the beating of the drums, sounding of the trumpets and the shouts of 'May the King live for ever', the Archbishop went to the Altar and the Queen, supported by the Bishops of St Albans and of Blackburn, made her way to the steps for a prayer. She was then anointed and received the Queen's ring, before the Archbishop set the Crown upon her head with the historic words, 'Receive the Crown of Glory, Honour and Joy'. Watching her with intense interest were her daughters, sitting in the gallery with Queen Mary, the Princess Royal, the Duchesses of Kent and Gloucester and Queen Maud of Norway, the King's aunt.

At a quarter past two the procession began its long way back to the Palace. And it was a long way – along Victoria Embankment and up Northumberland Avenue, into Pall Mall, right into St James's Street, right again into Piccadilly and left into Regent Street, and then via Oxford Street and Park Lane to Hyde Park Corner and Constitution Hill. And as the huge crowds cheered and the flags waved from the packed windows, the rain came down. Out there, at the focal point, so great was the enthusiasm that people simply ignored it and the spectacle remained unspoiled. But back at the Abbey there was a very different story.

The rain pelted down. The vast crowds, who had achieved their object of seeing the procession pass, rushed for shelter, blocking narrow streets, seeking escape in doorways and even in the Abbey itself. All the elaborate arrangements for getting the guests away went aft agley. There were seven and a half thousand of them; many had not had a meal since the previous evening and were nearing exhaustion. Jammed in the canvas tunnels at the Abbey exits, they were stifled – officers drew their swords and cut holes in the canvas to let in air. Chauffeurs were in a dilemma and, when they did get through, often found themselves at the wrong door. Cars were commandeered and aristocratic tempers flared. Five hours after the ceremony was over a solid mass of guests a hundred yards long still waited at one exit. Lord Derby was most displeased.[10]

At the Palace all was frenzied excitement as the King and Queen and the royal family came out on to the balcony. Daring young men climbed the Victoria Memorial to get a better view. And there the crowds stayed until midnight, through the King's broadcast – when, speaking well, he said, 'The Queen and I will always keep in our hearts the inspiration of this day . . .' – and through five encored appearances on the balcony.

The following days were a marathon of endurance for George and Elizabeth. On the day after the Coronation there was a drive through London's streets, gaining them a tumultuous reception, and a State Banquet. On the 14th they distributed medals to the Empire troops. On the 15th there was a reception for foreign envoys. On the 19th they drove to Guildhall for the City's magnificent luncheon. Next day came the journey to Portsmouth and the review of six miles of warships – that was the evening when the happy words came over the radio from the commentator: 'The Fleet's lit up.' Before the month was out George and Elizabeth had attended the Empire Day service at St Paul's Cathedral, had been entertained to dinner at 10 Downing Street and had been the guests of London County Council at County Hall.

3 June was the anniversary of George V's birthday. On that day HRH Prince Edward, Duke of Windsor, married Wallis Warfield* at the Château de Candé in France. She looked beautiful indeed and seemingly untouched by the ordeal through which she had passed. But, in the marriage announcement, the letters 'HRH' were not before her name. They never were to be. The rift never healed and was still open when the Duke died, thirty-five years later to the day.

The Coronation was the first major step up the regal staircase for King George VI and Queen Elizabeth. For him, there came a wave of confidence. He admitted that he was a happier man now that he could say what should be done, instead of for ever trying

* The name to which she reverted on her decree becoming absolute.

to interpret what was required of him, as had been the case in the days of his great-grandmother, his grandfather, his father and his elder brother, all supreme egotists convinced that their way of seeing things was the right and only way. Fate had thrown down a challenge and he had met it. There was deep satisfaction in that. There was satisfaction for Elizabeth also. It was he who had borne the brunt of the criticism, which she considered unfair. Already her judgment had proved correct. She rejoiced in seeing him make up his mind, and invariably being proved right. A lady about the Court commented, after he had gone, that few people realized how much Elizabeth depended upon him, seeming, as she did, to be ever in the lead.[11] There was, however, one fundamental difference between the two. George was content to do the job of being King, carrying it out as best he could from day to day. Elizabeth looked into the future. On the day of the Abdication Mr Maxton, ILP member for Glasgow, Bridgeton, had said in the House of Commons that the 'Humpty Dumpty' of royalty had had a great fall and that there was no way of putting Humpty Dumpty back on his wall. It was Elizabeth's intention to do all she could to bury that remark in oblivion.

There was little time for her to make drastic changes in 1937, for she was on the go throughout the summer and well into the autumn on Coronation work. But later she gained a wealth of experience about the ups and downs of the royal roundabout, from the splendours of the opening of Parliament to bomb scares in Northern Ireland. It was a period of trial and learning, for there was a vast difference to be bridged between being Duchess of York and being Queen. What her personal views were when she was Duchess had not, in reality, mattered much: there had been no attempt to record them, and her utterings at the routine engagements which were part of her daily rounds were of an innocuous nature. That had all changed. Now that she was Queen her inexperience of the role had to be considered. A Court official was ever by her side to ensure that she did not make some casual remark which might be upsetting to politicians or foreign envoys but still the news media went so far as to employ lip-readers to discover the nature of her asides. That she made no slips, behaving like a Queen born to the task, was a triumph for her and a great relief to the Palace, but it was not a role easily learned and brought home the truth of the fear which she had expressed before her engagement, that she would 'never, never again be free to think or act or speak as I really feel that I ought to think or act or speak'.

She saw the task of restoration and re-gilding from a woman's standpoint; it called for an admixture of stateliness and the common touch, swinging from radiance and tradition at affairs about the throne to 'walkabouts' amid the home-made jam at Women's Institute fêtes. She reduced the problem to a nutshell and came to see the importance of two groups of men – the photographers and the dressmakers. George, who had much of his father in him, was averse to change; he wanted Elizabeth to remain as she was when he married her. So George V had done: when Mary experimented with large summer hats, there were clicks of disapproval; when she shortened her skirt to display more of her well-shaped legs, there was more active opposition. She gave in, adopted a uniform with round hat and stick for tapping, and remained with it for the rest of her life. George VI was more amenable, and his wife was a better persuader than her mother-in-law. As she had interested him in the joys of gardening, so did she rouse his interest in clothes, and he became something of a connoisseur, as he did in all things upon which he turned his attention.

As Duke of York, George had been controlled by the strict conservatism of his father, but as King, in the words of John Wheeler-Bennett, he 'achieved a standard of *soigné* impeccability which it would be difficult to surpass'. He had the right build to show off a suit or a uniform and all his movements were elegant. He was a stickler for correctness and never missed an error. Attending the Gillies' Ball at Balmoral he spotted immediately that the pleats of the kilt of one of the pipers were pressed the wrong way round. He was an expert on decorations and medals and how they should be worn. On one occasion, spotting that his godson, King Peter of Yugoslavia, was wearing a thin gold watch-chain, he enquired whether it was part of the uniform. When informed it was not, he told King Peter to take it off. 'It looks damned silly and damned sloppy.'[12]

Elizabeth's first chance to spread her wings in matters of dress came with the State Visit of King Leopold of the Belgians in November 1937. Mr Norman Hartnell was invited to make the dress for the banquet to be held in King Leopold's honour, his first experience of making an important dress for a member of the royal family. The King met him at the Palace and showed him round the galleries, making a special point of stressing the beauty of the clothes in the Winterhalter portraits. The designer took the point and the final result, an outstanding success, was 'a *robe de style* of gleaming silver tissue over hooped *carcase* of stiffened silver gauze, with a deep *berthe* collar of silver lace encrusted with glittering diamonds'.[13] The King was delighted.

For everyone in 1937 came the blessing of a traditional Christmas at Sandringham, this time without the tragedy of a dying King or the upset of the Abdication. George broadcast: 'The Queen and I feel that we want to send to you all a further word of gratitude for the love and loyalty you gave us from every quarter of the Empire during this unforgettable year now drawing to its end. We have promised to try and be worthy of your trust, and this is a pledge that we shall always keep.' Among the flood of congratulations and cards, he received one letter which he prized highly. It was from Dr Cosmo Lang, Archbishop of Canterbury: 'I find everywhere the same testimony to the impression which Your Majesty and the Queen have made upon Your people during the first year of Your reign. At first, the feeling was one of sympathy and hope. It has now become a feeling of admiration and confidence . . . I *know* this to be true. I have noticed, all who have in any way come into contact with Your Majesty have noticed, how remarkably and steadily, if I may presume to say so, You have *grown into* Your high office. Thus the courage with which a year ago You accepted the burden of a great responsibility suddenly thrust upon You, has been amply vindicated.'[14]

The opening months of 1938 demonstrated clearly that Hitler and Mussolini were moving towards a confrontation with those who stood in their way. On the personal side, there was impending tragedy for the Queen: her seventy-five-year-old mother's health was failing and it was apparent that she had not long to live. The Countess of Strathmore was a remarkable woman and had been Elizabeth's guide and example, mentor and companion, since childhood. Her illness could not have come at a more unfortunate moment, for on 28 June the King and Queen were due to make a State Visit to France, their debut of foreign travel as monarchs. The visit, in fact, proved even more vital and important than had been anticipated when the invitation came from President Lebrun.

In May there was severe criticism, from Mr Winston Churchill and others, of the lack of Britain's progress in aerial rearmament, this leading to the replacement of Lord Swinton as Secretary of State for Air by Sir Kingsley Wood. In Europe Hitler threatened attack upon Czechoslovakia to gain political autonomy for the Sudeten German minority there. In the face of strong opposition from Britain, France and Russia he held his hand but, in secret, on 28 May he decided that Czechoslovakia must be 'smashed' and settled on a deadline of 1 October that year. Mr Neville Chamberlain, who had succeeded Mr Baldwin as Prime Minister, sensed the danger and sent a mission to hurry a settlement between the Czech Government and the Sudeten minority. The French did not fully agree with this direct intervention, so the visit of the King and Queen, it was hoped, might give an opportunity to solve the problem by personal contact.

British Queens had conquered Paris three times in the previous century. Victoria, the first British Sovereign to enter the French capital since the infant Henry VI was taken there for his crowning in 1422, had been loath to go at first, considering Emperor Napoleon III somewhat of an upstart. But the reception that he staged in 1855 won for her an ovation that Paris never forgot. She fell in love with him just a little bit, and the effect of the visit would have lived on, and might have changed the face of Europe, had Albert not shown signs of jealousy and plugged his eternal pro-German, anti-France theme. In 1907 Alexandra took Paris by storm, her beauty and her clothes cementing the Entente Cordiale initiated by her husband. In April 1914, on the previous State Visit to France, Queen Mary achieved one of the greatest personal successes of her life, but the memory of it had been dimmed by the war that followed four months later.

From January 1938 onwards Mr Hartnell was busy preparing the Queen's wardrobe. When Duchess, Elizabeth's own comment about her clothes had been 'Some clothes suit me and some do not.' But when she became Queen the time had arrived when they had to suit her all the time. Mr Hartnell saw to that and the dresses that she wore in Paris in 1938 created a sensation. Having settled to her own satisfaction one of the two groups of image-makers, Elizabeth still felt the projection of her particular image was not satisfactory; she became worried that she was not photographing well. This was odd, for she knew her drill. She knew how to place herself before the right background; she knew how to smile; she knew how to draw the right people into the picture with her; and she knew how to please the camera-men, for she has always been their favourite. Yet she felt she was not coming out right – somehow the image of her was blurred and the life of her, and the force of her personality, were not coming through. A professional photographer said of her: 'That little lady has grounds for a libel suit every time her picture is taken.' So she sent for Mr Cecil Beaton and told him her problem.

To date the time limit allowed to royal photographers had been twenty minutes. Cecil Beaton spent three hours at the Palace. The Queen was photographed in 'spangled tulle like a fairy doll', in a crinoline gown, and in a garden party dress of champagne set off by a parasol. She posed by pillar and painted panel, in doorways and by priceless desks, on sofas and tapestried chairs. Beaton fell a little bit in love. He found one of her handkerchiefs behind a cushion in a chair; surreptitiously, he slipped it into his pocket and carried it away with him.[15] As for Elizabeth, her worry faded clean away, for no woman could have resisted the pictures that were taken of her that day even if, deep down, there remained a preference for wearing tweeds and an old felt hat; she once laughingly referred to the Hartnell creations as 'my props'.

For the French visit there were to be thirty dresses in all, dresses for banquets and balls, fêtes and garden parties, State drives and military occasions, the opera and the ballet, luncheons and receptions. Then, on 23 June, Lady Strathmore died. The Court went into mourning and President Lebrun called a halt to the preparations for the welcome. It was at first thought that the visit would be cancelled but, despite her sadness, the Queen was too wedded to duty to cause such an upset; she suggested a postponement. The President suggested 19 July as the departure date and this was agreed. The big problem now concerned the Queen's clothes: all black would be depressing indeed in the sparkle and sunshine of Paris and Mr Hartnell was consulted. He said: 'Is not white a royal prerogative of mourning, Your Majesty?'[16] So it was settled, and in a fortnight the designer's magic wand, and a great deal of hard work by his seamstresses, transformed the whole rainbow collection into white. On the appointed day HMS *Enchantress*, escorted by eight destroyers, took the King and Queen to France.

The next three days were ever to be remembered by George, as he watched a nation take his wife to its heart. He rejoiced at her success, a success which made his baptism of State Visits so much the easier. In the streets of Paris she received a welcome of unrestrained delight that was reported throughout the world. Her smile, her simple dignity, her pleasure at being among the French, the dresses which framed her in the style of a century before, fused into a picture which would remain fresh and loved throughout the weary years which lay ahead. The sunshine of her erased the sombre threat of the aircraft which droned in the sky and the tanks which squatted in the Place de la Concorde. In the splendour of the Elysée Palace and the gardens of the Quai d'Orsay, the charm of her brought smiles to the faces of politicians and generals, faces which before she came had been set and grim with worry over the threat of war. Revellers stayed in the streets to cheer her home to bed, and were still there, dancing and laughing, until the dawn and the first editions of the newspapers were on sale. 'Today France is a Monarchy again,' ran the headlines. 'We have taken the Queen to our hearts. She rules over two nations.' Norman Hartnell remembered:

> Paris never looked so beautiful to me as in those few days of July 1938 . . . The five all-white dresses for the principal occasions stand out in my memory. One for the evening reception at the Elysée Palace had its bodice and billowing skirt composed of hundreds of yards of narrow Valenciennes lace, sprinkled with silver. For the Gala at the Opera Her Majesty wore a spreading gown of thick white satin, the skirt draped with festoons of satin, held by clusters of white camellias. The Queen wore a dress that trailed on the green grass of the lawns at the Garden Party at Bagatelle. It was of the finest cobweb lace and tulle and with it was worn a sweeping hat delicately bordered with white osprey. It was while watching the ballet, performed by the lakeside on Ile Enchanté, that the Queen opened a parasol of transparent lace and tulle and delighted all

> the onlookers. At a stroke, she resuscitated the art of the parasol makers of Paris and London. A magnificent luncheon was held in the Galeries des Glaces at the Palace of Versailles where the Queen appeared in a spreading dress, again of ground length, in white organdie, embroidered all over in openwork design of *broderie anglaise*. The white leghorn hat was softly trimmed with a ribbon of dense black velvet.[17]

The last appointment was a visit to Villers-Bretonneux, where the King unveiled a memorial to the eleven thousand Australians who died in France during the First World War and have no known graves. The Queen scattered a bunch of red poppies, given to her by a child, on the open ground. Watching in Berlin, Adolf Hitler labelled HM Queen Elizabeth of Britain as the most dangerous woman in Europe.

The royal family left for Balmoral by sea at the end of the month, calling off at Southwold in Suffolk on the way to visit the Boys' Camp which was being held there. After a busy summer, George and Elizabeth were hoping for peace and relaxation, but this was not to be. Mr Chamberlain visited Deeside but had little cheerful news. Hitler's deadline for upset in Czechoslovakia was approaching; threat after threat came from the Führer; on 12 September he spoke at Nuremberg and spat out his vilification of President Benes. The Czechs waited for the German hordes to submerge them; there was hand-to-hand fighting in the Sudetenland. Mr Chamberlain flew to Berchtesgaden and the King journeyed to London. On his return, empty-handed, the Prime Minister lunched at the Palace. He was visibly depressed and told of Hitler's determination to occupy the Sudetenland before a plebiscite was held.

On the 25th Air Raid Precautions went on to a war footing. Cellars and basements throughout London were transformed into shelters; trenches slit the grass of the parks and the gardens in the squares, volunteers digging through the night by the light of flares. Anti-aircraft guns appeared and fighter planes patrolled the skies. School children were evacuated to the country and hospital wards were cleared, in preparation for an influx of casualties. Londoners were registered and gas-masks were issued.

On the 27th the King and Queen were due to launch the new,

85,000 thousand ton Cunard liner on the Clyde, but George considered the crisis was too grave for him to leave London, so Elizabeth went alone, the Princesses, who were still at Balmoral, joining her in Glasgow. As the giant vessel slipped into the water, she said: 'I name this ship *Queen Elizabeth* and wish success to her and all who sail in her.'

The next day became known as 'Black Wednesday'. It was to be 'the last day', many thought. In Paris crowds fought for seats on the trains and the roads leading out of the capital were blocked with traffic. That afternoon in London, as the Prime Minister told the House of the grim situation, he was handed a message. It was from Hitler inviting him to a talk at Munich. Mr Chamberlain returned on the 30th. He stepped from the plane waving a piece of paper – 'Peace in our time' was his joyful message. By command of the King he went straight to the Palace and came out on to the balcony there, to be greeted by the roars of a crowd who knew that they could sleep in peace that night. Before he returned to Scotland on 2 October, the King issued a message: 'The time of anxiety is past, and we have been able today to offer our thanks to the Almighty for His Mercy in sparing us the horrors of war . . . After the magnificent efforts of the Prime Minister in the cause of peace, it is my fervent hope that a new era of friendship and prosperity may be dawning among the peoples of the world.'

11

Across the Atlantic

In the spring of 1939 Arthur Bryant wrote: 'Much of the present English anger at the German Führer arises from the feeling that there was so wide a discrepancy between his words last September and his action in March as to constitute him a proved liar. That, in the English view, is an almost unforgivable thing to be.'[1] Despite his message at Munich, Hitler had continued to plot and plan for the smashing of Czechoslovakia. His efforts were so successful that in March the automonist Sudeten leaders there fled the country and begged him to authorize their independence. The independence of their areas was proclaimed on the 14th and on the next day the Czech President, summoned to Berlin, agreed, in the face of unspeakable bullying, to place the rest of his country under the protection of Germany. That evening Hitler entered Prague and issued the proclamation that Czechoslovakia had ceased to exist.

Adolf Hitler naturally chose to bring off his coups at moments most awkward to those in opposition to them. This was an outstanding example of his method. Ever since September Britain had been sipping the wine of peace, bottled in Munich, and the King had taken the opportunity to plan a trip to Canada and the United States in the early summer of 1939. Now the international situation prompted him to believe that the visit should be cancelled, for he was a man who liked to be at his desk at time of crisis. Fortunately other advice prevailed and it was decided that the arrangements should go forward.

The idea had originated with Mr Mackenzie King, Prime Minister of Canada, when he visited London for the Coronation. On hearing about it, President Franklin D. Roosevelt of the

United States suggested that the journey be extended to include Washington and New York. Mr Roosevelt's invitation included a weekend at his country home of Hyde Park. He wrote informally:

> I need not assure you that it would give my wife and me the greatest pleasure to see you and, frankly, I think it would be an excellent thing for Anglo-American relations if you could visit the United States . . . If you could bring either or both of the children with you they will also be very welcome, and I shall try to have one or two Roosevelts of approximately the same age to play with them![2]

However, it was decided that the tour would be too tiring and unsettling for the Princesses. George insisted upon one amendment to the programme. The plan had been that the royal party should travel in the battle-cruiser *Repulse* but he considered that the absence of this powerful warship from home waters for so long would convey the impression that Britain did not 'mean business' in her dealings with the dictators; so the Canadian Pacific liner *Empress of Australia* was substituted, being rated as a Royal Yacht. Hitler was by now the bogey man and the possibility was considered of his forces swooping upon the *Empress* in mid-Atlantic to spirit George and Elizabeth away. It would have been a fantastic plan, even for Hitler, but, to be on the safe side, *Repulse* was detailed to act as escort to the half-way stage.

Londoners gave the King and Queen a boisterous and impressive farewell as they drove to Waterloo Station on the morning of 5 May. With them to Portsmouth went a family gathering – Queen Mary, the Princess Royal and the Earl of Harewood, the Duke and Duchess of Gloucester, the Duke and Duchess of Kent and, of course, Lilibet and Margaret.* Queen Mary inspected the quarters on the *Empress* and found them to her satisfaction. Lilibet informed her sister that the handkerchiefs provided were for waving and not for crying into. As the white ship swung into the

* Their Majesties' suite consisted of: Lady Nunburnholme and Lady Katherine Seymour, Ladies-in-Waiting; the Earl of Eldon, Lord-in-Waiting; the Earl of Airlie, Lord Chamberlain to the Queen; Mr Alan Lascelles, Acting Private Secretary to the King; Captain Michael Adeane, Assistant Private Secretary; Lieut.-Col. the Hon. Piers Legh, and Commander E. M. C. Abel Smith, Equerries; Surgeon-Captain H. White, Medical Officer; and Mr G. F. Steward, Chief Press Liaison Officer.

Solent there came from shore to shore the sound of a hundred thousand people cheering, and of every craft in the area hooting its salute. Out beyond the Isle of Wight seventeen warships edged a wide sea-lane and a squadron of the Royal Air Force dived in salute from the clear evening sky.

George and Elizabeth could now relax. Back on his beloved sea, there came to him a peace such as he had not known since his father died. Elizabeth moved about the decks, talking and getting to know everybody. One of the crew said: 'The only difficulty there is in talking to the Queen is that she makes you feel so completely at ease that you keep forgetting that you are talking to the Queen.'[3] All went well until the fourth day out when a great gale struck them. A journalist on board reported: 'The *Empress* rode the storm magnificently, but it was heavy going. Sometimes she would sweep upwards, hover for a moment in the air, and come down into the sea again with a crash. The next moment another great wave would seem to knock her sideways. After each battering she would lie still in the sea for a few moments, as though recovering from the shock. Then up she would go again and come crashing down.'[4] During the night waves were breaking on the high bridge, a sight which the crew had never witnessed before. Of Hitler there was no sign, but there was enough trouble without him. After the gale came the icebergs.

The smell of ice came to the keen senses of the seamen on Wednesday night. The ocean flattened and the fog came down. When small bergs, known as 'growlers', were spotted, the *Empress* came to a halt, her siren blaring. Sight was lost of the escorting cruisers, *Southampton* and *Glasgow*. Between Thursday morning and Sunday afternoon only 172 miles were covered, heading south. The captain, Captain Meikle, never left the bridge. On Saturday a big iceberg showed as the fog lifted. 'Why, it looks just like Windsor Castle,' said the Queen's dresser. To add to the confusion, one of the crew of the cruiser *Glasgow* developed appendicitis and the two royal doctors went over the *Empress*'s side and into a small boat to be taken over to operate. On the lighter side the news ran round the ship that the First Officer's canary had laid an egg. As it was thought to be a cock, this was considered a good omen.

The Queen sent a description of the voyage to Queen Mary:

> For three and a half days we only moved a few miles. The fog was so thick that it was like a white cloud round the ship, and the foghorn blew incessantly. Its melancholy blasts were echoed back by the icebergs like the twang of a piece of wire. Incredibly eerie, and really very alarming, knowing that we were surrounded by ice and unable to see a foot either way. We very nearly hit a berg the day before yesterday, and the poor Captain was nearly demented because some kind, cheerful people kept on reminding him that it was just about here that *Titanic* was struck, and *just* about the same date!'[5]

And if anyone required details of that disaster, they were to be found near at hand. A member of the crew, Steward William Lucas, of Southampton was a survivor of the *Titanic*.

At midday on Sunday they ran into a field of ice. The *Empress* barged her way through at five knots: she was due at Quebec on Monday morning. The pack-ice was so thick it would have been possible to get off and walk on it. Three hours later the sea and weather cleared, and the liner made at full speed for Canada; by Monday evening she was holding a steady nineteen knots up the St Lawrence river. There was an air of the last day of term about Tuesday. Baggage stood outside cabin doors and the *Empress* was bright with bunting. When darkness came, cars on the shore flashed their headlamps and bonfires twinkled on the hills. The music of the ship's band drifted across the water – tunes like 'Lily of Laguna'. The dining-room was gay with balloons and coloured paper streamers, and the King and Queen handed out their presents to the crew. Just before midnight anchor was dropped.

There has been a vast change in relationship of Britain to the city of Quebec between then and now. Even so, the welcome handed out to King George VI and Queen Elizabeth amazed the local authorities in its enthusiasm; the police and red-coated Mounties had a formidable task in controlling crowds the like of which had never been seen. It was half past ten on the morning of 17 May when they landed at Wolfe's Cove, twenty-one guns fired a salute from the Citadel and the crowds loosed their first fusillade of cheering. After the official welcome in the Provincial Parliament, there was a luncheon in the great Château Frontenac Hotel. There were three hundred guests and, as the *Montreal Daily Star* reported, 'they gained a new impression of the everyday likeableness of this fine couple.' Speeches were short and to the point and, to everyone's delight, the King spoke in French as well as English, happiness and confidence overcoming his impediment. He gained the star spot when the wife of the Minister of Justice, who was sitting next to him, lost her handbag underneath the table: he went below to find it for her. The Queen harvested in the hearts. Comments on her varied from *'vraiment charmante'* to the plain, 'She's gorgeous.'

Mr Hartnell had been once more summoned to the Palace, to face probably the most difficult task ever for a royal designer. 'Dresses had to be suitable for every extreme of climate, from the sultry streets of New York in a heat wave, through the damp heat of a garden party at the White House, right up to the icy heights of the Rocky Mountains.'[6] Overcoats had to be designed to harmonize with gum boots. One innovation was the introduction of a 'hostess dress', to be worn to meet those who gathered at halts at small railway stations at any time of day or night.

They drove high to the Plains of Abraham where forty thousand children, each armed with a flag, were waiting for them. Thirty-nine thousand of them were Catholic. They sang the national anthem in French:

> Dieu protege le Roi!
> En lui nous avons foi,
> Vive le Roi!
> Qu'il soit victorieux,
> Et que son peuple heureux,
> Le comble de ses voeux,
> Vive le Roi!

There was a banquet that evening in the Château Frontenac – no speeches, champagne and a hidden band playing Scottish airs in honour of Elizabeth. The tour had got away to a memorable start.

Next morning the King and Queen boarded the train which was to be their home for the next few weeks. Twenty-four coaches, in blue and aluminium, had been built for the long haul to the Pacific coast and these were divided into two units – the Royal Train and the Pilot Train, carrying reporters, technicians and police and travelling thirty minutes ahead of the King and Queen. The outward leg was over Canadian Pacific Rail Road track, the return over Canadian National. Of the engines, CN 6057 was the largest in the Empire, being ninety-four feet long. CPR 2850 was driven by Eugene Leclerc, who had been fireman on the Royal Train in 1901 when George V (then the Duke of Cornwall and York) had visited the Dominion.

The coaches were all air-conditioned and fitted with radio and telephones – the charge for a call to London was about £4. A 'mileometer' in one of the sitting-rooms showed the exact distance which had been covered. If the King and Queen wished to check on any detail of the journey, all they had to do was to pull down wall maps which ran up and down like blinds. The trains were self-sufficient down to the last detail – even the milk was specially pasteurized and labelled 'Royal Train'. There were a barber's shop and a post office – the mail service was most efficient, and in great demand, for commemorative stamps were used and one of them carried the pictures of Lilibet and Margaret. Envelopes bearing the cancellation mark, 'Royal Train – Canada', were keenly sought after, and the demand came not only from the travellers: at stops on the way crowds waiting there to see the King and Queen carried packets of addressed envelopes, which they begged those in the royal caravan to post for them. In one day alone a quarter of a million letters passed through this mobile post office.

The King and Queen travelled in Cars 1 and 2, which were at the rear of the Royal Train. Car 1 contained two main bedrooms with dressing-rooms and private baths, a sitting-room for the King and Queen and two bedrooms for members of the staff. Car 2 contained a large sitting-room, an office, a dining-room with seating for twelve, and additional bedrooms. The Queen's suite was as charming as could be found in a country cottage. Both bedroom and dressing-room were decorated in blue-grey, with dusk-pink damask chair covers and curtains to match. The King's office was panelled in oak.

The first day's run was via Three Rivers to Montreal. People had travelled from many miles away, in cars and horse-buggies, to watch the train go by. Every wooden house and log cabin flew the Union Jack and the letters 'G' and 'E' were spelled out in stones upon the fields.

Montreal. The King and Queen stepped out on to Park Avenue

Station, he in an Admiral's uniform, she in her favourite powder blue, to begin a momentous twenty-four-mile drive. The crowds were thirty deep, including fifty thousand schoolchildren. They visited the City Hall and had tea at the chalet on Mount Royal.* In the evening, as they dined with Parliamentary members and civic officials in the Windsor Hotel, a crowd of a hundred thousand jammed themselves into Dominion Square, chanting 'We want the King, we want the Queen.' The steady chorus filled the banqueting-room and could not be denied. As the King and Queen came out on to the balcony, a spotlight picked them up, silhouetting them against the darkness. The chanting changed to a great roar of welcome, and swung into the strains of the National Anthem. These were some of the most precious seconds in the times of George and Elizabeth together.

Ottawa. The Governor-General of Canada, Lord Tweedsmuir – none other than John Buchan, the famous author – wrote home: 'Our Monarchs are most remarkable people. I have always been deeply attached to the King, and I realize now more than ever what a wonderful mixture he is of shrewdness, kindliness and humour. As for the Queen, she has a perfect genius for the right kind of publicity. The unrehearsed episodes here were marvellous. For example, when she laid the foundation stone at the new Judicative Building I heard the masons talking and realized that some of them were Scots, and she made me take her and the King up to them, and they spent ten minutes in Scottish reminiscences, in full view of seventy thousand people, who went mad! Then at the unveiling of the War Memorial, where we had some ten thousand veterans, she asked me if it was not possible to get a little closer to them. I suggested that we went right down among them, if they were prepared to take the risk, which they gladly did. It was an amazing sight, for we were simply swallowed up. The faces of the Scotland Yard detectives were things I shall never forget! But the veterans made a perfect bodyguard . . . The American correspondents were simply staggered. They said that no American President would ever have dared to do that.'[7]

So began the walkabout. It brought a new dimension to royal contact with the crowds and greatly increased everyone's interest

* Mount Royal, from which the city derives its name, rises to a height of 753 feet above sea level.

during engagements. Nevertheless it called for courage on the part of the stars repeatedly to venture into the mêlées.

On into the west and there was the same enthusiastic reception awaiting them at every station. Toronto, White River, Port Arthur to Winnipeg, where George delivered the longest radio speech he had ever made – over eight hundred words – and it was relayed throughout the world. He began:

> Today is Queen Victoria's birthday, as well as Empire Day: and I am glad that I can speak to you on this day amid surroundings eloquent of the Empire's achievement since Queen Victoria was born. Winnipeg was no more than a fort and hamlet upon the open prairie when Queen Victoria began to rule. Today it is a monument to the faith and energy which have created and upheld the world-wide Empire of our time. The journey which the Queen and I are making in Canada has been a deeply moving experience . . .

These words told clearly of his attachment to the Empire. His interest stemmed from the experiences on his East African tour; returning from that he had thrown himself with zest and energy into the task of being President of the British Empire Exhibition which opened at Wembley Stadium in May 1925. He had persuaded his father to open the Exhibition and, in a public appeal for support, the then Duke said: 'The task of showing fresh aspects of our great heritage has been taken up with vigour and enthusiasm, and the new picture of the Empire will be even more vivid than the old.'

After Winnipeg they travelled on into the wheat country. During the night watchers at the wayside stations kept their silence, to allow the travellers to rest, but with the dawn they were rewarded by the sight of the King and Queen waving from their car; she wore Norman Hartnell's 'hostess' dress. On through Brandon, Regina, Moosejaw, Medicine Hat to Calgary, then up to the mountains. There was a halt for two nights at the luxurious Banff Springs Hotel, then on they went across the Great Divide, through Kicking Horse Pass and down to the Pacific.

From Vancouver George and Elizabeth went by steamer to Victoria, on Vancouver Island, then once again they boarded their train, this time on the Canadian National track, and the giant locomotives snorted their way into the Rockies – through the canyon of Hell Gate and now high above the Fraser river, boiling, leaping, on its way to the sea, the tumult of its rushing so loud that it drowned the rumble of the wheels. Through Boston Bar, where the Americans known as 'Boston Men' had swarmed at the time of the great gold rush. Into ice-cold tunnels; over bridges which seemed to span depths of nothingness; under peaks so high they hid the light of the moon. Mile after mile and not a sign of habitation; yet every four hundred yards there were watchers with lanterns, by the track, waiting for the searchlight on the locomotive's head to pierce the darkness. The train stopped at a wayside halt for water. A group of about a hundred people was gathered by the tanks, curious, somewhat shy, not enough of them to make much noise. They saw the King and Queen come out on to the platform of the observation car. A man began singing 'When the moon comes over the mountain' and the others joined in.

In the morning the train breasted Mount Robson, at 12,972 feet the highest point in the Rockies. At Jasper the King and Queen stepped off for a day and a half of relaxation. They drove to 'Outlook Cabin' reserved for them at the summer resort of Jasper Park Lodge. Melville, Sudbury and so to Toronto again. At Windsor Elizabeth had her first glimpse of an American city skyline – George had seen it before, when he was a naval cadet in 1913. The lights of Detroit showed across the river, one electric sign flashing, 'Detroit Welcomes Their Majesties the King and Queen.' At St Catherine's the royal party left the train and went by car through the orchard country to Niagara Falls. Looking at the racing waters, the King recalled that eighty years before Charles Blondin, the tightrope-walker, had offered to wheel his grandfather, later Edward VII, across them in a wheelbarrow. No such invitation came to George.

After a short railway journey across the border, for the first time a reigning Sovereign entered the United States of America, to be met by Mr Cordell Hull, Secretary of State; he had a bouquet of orchids for the Queen. The *New York Times* said of her: 'Fresh as a debutante before her first big party, Queen Elizabeth wound up a strenuous day with her costume as crisp and her manner as gracious as if she were beginning – instead of entering the final phase of her tour.' At 10.58 on that night of 9 June 1939, as guns boomed out a salute, the Royal Train pulled out for Washington.

Washington sweltered. It was ninety-seven degrees in the shade and collars of men waiting to receive the King and Queen wilted round their necks. At eleven o'clock Mr and Mrs Roosevelt greeted their guests at Union Station. The President's welcome was informal and typical of the man: 'Well, at last I greet you. How are you? I am glad to see you.' The handshake with the King which followed was described by Ambassador Kennedy, father of a future President, as 'perhaps the most important handclasp of modern times'. Events were to prove him right, for from that moment the tide of American affection turned towards Britain.

Three-quarters of a million people lined the streets for the procession to the White House. Thirty tanks rumbled ahead and Flying Fortresses roared in the sky. A hundred and fifty tons of ticker-tape fluttered from windows upon the cavalcade below. By the time they had reached the White House George and Elizabeth were chatting animatedly with Franklin and Eleanor, and they got to know one another well over a private lunch. The meeting was an eye-opener for the President. He had been expecting an inexperienced couple, playing substitute for Edward VIII to the best of their ability. Instead he met a King who was assured, straightforward and shrewd, who was at home on a wide diversity of subjects, and he took to him at once. As for the King's wife, her impact had immediately been felt. The eight-year-old daughter of Mr Harry Hopkins, the President's friend and adviser, dubbed her the Fairy Queen. A Senator slapped the King on the back and informed him that he was a 'great Queen-picker'. A negro servant pinned a pretty label on her when he called her 'that honeychile Mrs Queen'.[8] She had a presence and a smile and a taste in clothes that enslaved the city. That afternoon there was a garden party at the British Embassy. The sun blazed down. The Queen felt giddy. She put up a parasol – and set a fashion throughout Virginia. In the evening lightning streaked and the rain came down. The clash of thunder formed a dramatic background to the State Banquet, at which the King and President pledged their friendship and desire for world peace. American dishes were served – a clam cocktail, boned capon and ice cream.

After a concert arranged by Mrs Roosevelt to demonstrate the development of American song and dance, at which Marian Anderson sang, the guests departed and the President took the King to his study and they chatted until the early hours. They came to understand one another well, seeing eye to eye on matters of politics and democracy. Their friendship proved the most important of the reign and these talks proved vital, for they paved the way to the US providing naval and aid assistance in the early years of the war. George, being a man of method and never one to delay a task, put on paper the main points of the talks before he left for home, while his memory was still clear. He wrote:

> I had two good conversations with the President, besides many opportunities of informal talks on current matters in the car driving with him. He was very frank & friendly, & seemed genuinely glad that I had been able to pay him this visit. He gave me all the information in these notes either in answer to my questions, or he volunteered it.
>
> Mr Mackenzie King was present at the first conversation at Hyde Park. We talked of the firm & trusted friendship between Canada & the USA. FDR mentioned that he thought it was a waste of money to build a Canadian fleet as he had already laid his plans for the defence of the Pacific Coast of Canada, especially Vancouver Island. (Assembling plants for aeroplanes in Canada.) On mentioning the Neutrality Act the President gave us hopes that something could be done to make it less difficult for the USA to help us. Cordell Hull & others as well as himself were doing their best to lead public opinion on to the right tack. He gave us the following story to illustrate how he was tackling the subject in the Middle West & putting it in a way which they as farmers would understand!
>
> 'In the event of a war & say Germany & Italy were to win it, which means that the British Fleet & the French Army had been defeated, which at the moment are our first lines of defence, how would you like to lose one of your best customers, the United Kingdom? Then again Hitler could say to our great neighbours to the south, the Argentine & Brazil: You cannot sell your wheat or your beef or your coffee in Europe except through me &

> Germany. I am the Master of Europe & in return I will send you the articles I think you will require in return at my price.'
>
> I was alone with him for the 2nd conversation. We discussed Europe in a general way. He hoped France & Italy would try & get together.
>
> He was doing his best to get New York to loan money to Roumania. I told him how difficult it was for us to help the Balkans as there was the Mediterranean to convoy things through, & they would want all they had got in a War. I explained to him Roumania's position as to frontiers, having four to cope with. Because of the air we were only just becoming frontier-conscious ourselves. In the whole of N. America he has none. He was definitely anti-Russian. I told him so were we but if we could not have an understanding with her, Germany would probably make one.
>
> He showed me his naval patrols in greater detail about which he is terribly keen. If he saw a U-boat he would sink her at once & wait for the consequences.
>
> If London was bombed USA would come in. Offensive air warfare was better than defensive & he hoped we should do the same on Berlin.[9]

The day after these talks the King and Queen fulfilled ten engagements in eleven hours, the first of which was a press conference. One of the most important was the meeting with members of the House and Senate at the Capitol. Senator Borah announced that it was the first time his morning coat had been out of moth balls for thirty-five years; Representative Nat Patton of Texas greeted the King with a hearty handshake, remarking, 'How do you do, Cousin George?' A great deal of planning had gone into the preparations for this historic tour, for 'nice couple' as the King and Queen appeared, they were in truth Emperor and Empress of India and the inheritors of the imperial majesty woven around the Crown by King George V, King Edward VII and Queen Victoria. There had been no major royal visits between that of the Prince of Wales in 1860 and those of his grandson, also Prince of Wales, after the First World War, and both of those were young men whose arrival had been treated as a major roadshow. This occasion was very different; protocol might have clashed with the democratic creed of the New World. The President had laid down that 'There'll be no curtsies or low bows and so on'; but his wife had obtained from the State Department detailed instructions on how to deal with every angle of the tour; for instance, she had consulted the British Ambassador's wife, Lady Lindsay, and learned that the King must be served at meals exactly thirty seconds before the Queen.[10]

After the Capitol came a trip down the Potomac river in the Presidential yacht to Mount Vernon, home of George Washington, the first American President. Now George and Elizabeth were treading back over the pages of history, for in 1860 Albert Edward, Prince of Wales, had sailed that way in company with President Buchanan and his charming niece, Harriet Lane. The Prince had planted a chestnut tree by Washington's tomb and the man from *The Times* wrote: 'It seemed when the royal youth closed in the earth around the little germ that he was burying the last faint traces of discord between us and our great brethren in the West.' Within two years of that Britain and America were close to war. George and Elizabeth also visited the tomb. She thought the white mansion, in its Colonial style and packed with memorabilia of Washington, was 'one of the loveliest places she had ever seen'. They returned to the capital, visiting on the way the National Cemetery at Arlington, where the King laid wreaths on the Tomb of the Unknown Soldier and on the Canadian Cross.

The King and Queen ended their visit to Washington by entertaining Mr and Mrs Roosevelt to dinner at the British Embassy. It was an informal meal but the massive walnut table was brilliant with silver. Elizabeth, in a Victorian frock of rose tulle, with a diamond tiara and two diamond necklaces, looked every inch a Queen. At half past eleven the couple left for the station to entrain for the overnight journey to New York, one crowded programme switching to another.

The highlight of the New York visit was to be a reception at the World's Fair but nobody guessed just what a highlight it would prove. The King and Queen arrived at the Battery on board the United States destroyer *Warrington*, flying the Royal Standard for the first time in history. They found three million people waiting for them, along fifty-one miles of Manhattan streets: the roofs, windows and fire-escapes of every building were packed and the ticker-tape tumbled down. The Queen smiled with delight. She said to the Mayor, La Guardia, escorting them, 'There is nothing nicer in the world than friendship. Friendliness is about the nicest thing in the world, isn't it?'

They were half an hour late by the time they reached the Fair Site in Flushing Meadows and there so many people were waiting to be presented that the schedule slipped to an hour behind. George and Elizabeth went without coffee after lunch in order to catch up, and began the tour of the pavilions – Irish, Canadian, Rhodesian, Australian, New Zealand and British. The sun blistered down. Rockets exploded, bands played 'Land of Hope and Glory' and Red Indians whooped. It was half past four when the couple rejoined their car. Just one more engagement before they reached their weekend oasis, a call at the Columbia University, where they were received by the President, Dr Nicholas Murray Butler.

The night was to be spent at Hyde Park, the ancestral home of the Roosevelts in Dutchess County; the visit meant a great deal to the President. John Wheeler-Bennett wrote: 'Here on the steep bank of the Hudson River, beautiful in spring with dogwood, his family had lived for a hundred years. Of patroon ancestry, they came of that proud, solid Knickerbocker stock which even Ward McAllister, New York's social arbiter of the 'eighties, had found 'unsnubbable', and which formed the backbone of that curious organism of New York society depicted in the novels of Henry James and Edith Wharton. Here Mr Roosevelt had been born: from here he had made his early forays into the field of New York State politics, and had begun his fruitless campaign for the Vice-Presidency. Here, too, in the 'twenties, he came after his agonizing and gallant recovery from infantile paralysis; and hence he had gone forth in triumph as Governor of New York and as President of the United States.'[11]

The King and Queen were due at Hyde Park at six o'clock, about the time that they were leaving Columbia University, so their sixteen-limousine convoy made fast time on the eighty-mile journey, the parkways crowd-packed, flower-strewn. 'No American,' said a commentator, 'ever received such an ovation from his countrymen.'[12] Church bells were ringing as they drove up to Hyde Park.

As at the White House, the most careful planning had gone into the preparations for their visit, masterminded by the eighty-five-year-old mother of the President, Mrs Sarah Delano Roosevelt. She was somewhat of a tartar and a fastidious housekeeper. She it was who decreed that George and Elizabeth should be served with good old English tea when they arrived. The President considered eight o'clock too late for this and ordered cocktails. As the King entered the house, he said: 'My mother thinks that you should have a cup of tea. She doesn't approve of cocktails.' 'Neither does my mother,' George answered, and took a glass with gratitude.

There had been certain problems below stairs. The President had brought with him his coloured staff from Washington but the thought of his Sovereign being served by these intruders was too much for Mrs Sarah's English butler, and he went on holiday rather than be party to the humiliation. Maybe he had second sight, for catastrophe followed catastrophe. During dinner a side table collapsed and a part of the precious dinner service crashed on to the floor and broke into small pieces. Breaking the hush, a voice, that of one of the President's daughters-in-law, exclaimed in anguish: 'I hope none of my dishes was among them.' Everybody burst out laughing.[13] The party adjourned to the library for post-prandial drinks. There entered, down the steps which led to it, a coloured butler, on his backside. Ahead of him slid a tray, its load of bottles, decanters and glasses cascading across the floor, leaving a pool of alcohol and ice upon the carpet.

Once again King and President sat up late discussing international affairs. Mr Roosevelt was a good conversationalist, able to listen as well as to talk. He had already broken down the natural reserve in George and the result was that he spoke without a stammer. Both men talked completely frankly with one another and took it as an accepted fact that war in the near future was inevitable. One subject which was discussed in detail that night was the establishment of US bases in the North and South Atlantic, bases which would ensure the security of America. In her reminiscences Mrs Eleanor Roosevelt summed up her husband's *raison d'être* for the visit:

> My husband invited them [the King and Queen] to Washington largely because, believing that we all might soon be engaged in a life and death struggle, in

> which Great Britain would be our first line of defence, he hoped that the visit would create a bond of friendship between the people of the two countries. He knew that, though there is always in this country a certain amount of criticism and superficial ill-feeling towards the British, in time of danger something deeper comes to the surface, and the British and we stand firmly together, with confidence in our common heritage and ideas.[14]

Time passed quickly and, looking at his watch, the President saw that it was half past one. Realizing that the King had had a long, exciting and most tiring day, he put his hand on his guest's knee and said: 'Young man, it's time for you to go to bed.' But George didn't go to bed. Instead he called to his room Mr Mackenzie King, the Prime Minister of Canada, who was also staying in the house. He told the statesman how much this visit to Canada and the United States meant to him and expressed his deep gratitude. He also paid tribute to his host. He asked: 'Why don't my Ministers talk to me as the President did tonight?'

The President had said before the Hyde Park visit: 'They are coming away for a quiet weekend with me. I'll put the King into an old pair of flannels and just drive him about in my old Ford.' And that was the order of the day for Sunday. There was morning service at the parish church of St James's which, in a letter home to Queen Mary, Elizabeth described as being just like an English service, even including the prayers for the King and the royal family. Then the President fulfilled his promise and drove the King round the estate. Now the roles and the conversation of the two men switched. No longer were they two world leaders but the squire of Hyde Park, Dutchess County chatting to the squire of Sandringham, Norfolk, about crops and cows, woods and gardens.

Lunch was a picnic at a cottage on the estate. Water-melons, doughnuts and 'hot dogs' were served on paper plates. And out of this picnic emerged the most publicized incident of the American tour. Had the King and Queen really eaten hot dogs? This was news and the telephone lines buzzed. The royal staff seemed reluctant to admit that they had, and it wasn't until the evening that the reporters felt sufficiently confident to say that they had done so.[15] America loved that.

King and President took to the swimming bath, splashing in the sun while their ladies watched. After a convivial dinner came the time to say goodbye. The Queen turned to Mrs Roosevelt and said: 'Oh, I forgot to thank your chauffeur for driving the King so carefully.' And that was put to rights. Mrs Roosevelt recalled: 'Franklin and I went with them to the Hyde Park railroad station, where their special train was waiting. Nobody had arranged any ceremony but, of course, the public knew the time of their departure and crowds had gathered. The steep little banks rising on the side of the river were covered with spectators who waited, rather silently, until our goodbyes were said. But, as the train pulled out, somebody began singing 'Auld Lang Syne' and then everyone was singing, and it seemed to me that there was something of our friendship and our sadness and something of the uncertainty of our future in that song that could not have been said in any other words.'[16] The King and Queen stood on the rear platform of the train and waved goodbye. When they woke next morning they were in Canada and the Mounties were on guard. There was still a long way to go.

They ran along the southern bank of the St Lawrence, from Levis, opposite Quebec, to Rivière du Loup, so named as here Champlain first met the du Loup tribe of Indians. On 13 June the train crossed into the Maritime Provinces, the first stop there being at Newcastle, New Brunswick. Then on to Fredericton, the sleepy little capital. They passed their last night on the Royal Train near New Glasgow; thence to Halifax and the end of their eight thousand mile journey on Canadian track. There the forty-two-thousand-ton liner *Empress of Britain* was lying, waiting to take the travellers home. The bells of the locomotives were clanging as the blue and silver trains came to the dockside. Those who had travelled on them – crew and Mounties, cooks and stewards, reporters and barbers, post office officials, engineers – lined up by the coaches and the King and Queen bade them goodbye and shook each by the hand. It was the end of a chapter which none of them was likely ever to forget. Canada was making certain, in this final reception, that the King and Queen would never forget either. People had come from all over the Eastern side to say goodbye and all night long they walked the streets of Halifax, searching for a bed and even begging berths on the little ships which filled the harbour.

After the official welcome at Province House, there was a luncheon at the Nova Scotian Hotel, to be followed by a broadcast to the Empire by the King and Queen, the culmination of their tour. A key figure in its presentation was Richard Dimbleby, the BBC announcer, but it wasn't his day. It was Dimbleby's job to start the proceedings with an introductory commentary, a task at which he was unrivalled. He arrived at the Nova Scotian Hotel in good time and presented his credentials to the sergeant at the door. 'You can't come in here,' said the sergeant, 'only those who have invitations for lunch.' And Dimbleby, occupied with his preparations for the broadcast, had not been invited to the meal. He retreated, thought up a new line of approach, and tried again. Again the police refused him entry. He tried another door and failed once more. Time was running out and his customary phlegm deserted him. He charged. In the ensuing scuffle he lost his press armband but managed to gain entrance and contact those within who knew him. He reached the microphone just in time to make contact with London.[17]

The King spoke first, delighting French Canadians again by talking partly in French. He spoke well and sat down to great applause, clearly delighted with himself, as if to say, 'Well, Mr Logue, what do you think of that!' He adjusted his tie, took a drink and looked at his wife. 'Your turn now.' Those who were near to Elizabeth noticed that, for once in her life, there were signs of nervousness as she faced the three golden microphones. But she steadied, and mellow and sweet the words came through:

> This wonderful tour of ours has given me memories that the passage of time will never dim. To the people of Canada and to all the kind people in the United States who welcomed us so warmly last week – to one and all on this great friendly continent, I say Thank You. God be with you and God bless you. *Au revoir et Dieu vous benisse.*

That evening there was a party on the *Empress of Britain.* Canadian officials and the men and women of press and radio received mementoes and signed photographs of George and Elizabeth. Mr Mackenzie King was in ebullient form. So much were the guests enjoying themselves that they had to run to catch the red-carpeted gang-plank before it was pulled away. As the sirens screeched, the giant liner slipped out on the evening tide, George and Elizabeth waving from the bridge.

The *Empress of Britain* had a full-size tennis court, an enormous swimming pool and a Turkish bath. The ballroom and cinema had been designed by Sir John Lavery; the panelled dining-room seated over four hundred. One could walk for an hour about the decks without meeting a member of the royal party. When the King came out on to the promenade deck after dinner, he said: 'Where do we go from here?' A day of rest followed, a day with a touch of loneliness in the great ship sailing an empty sea. In the evening they reached Newfoundland, the *Empress* being the largest ship ever to enter Conception Bay. What a wonderful tour it had been, and so very necessary. Canada was waving the flag from coast to coast and Mr Mackenzie King had become a close friend of George and Elizabeth. Apart from the importance of bettering Anglo-American relations in view of the approaching war in Europe, some patching-up had been essential in America as a result of feelings engendered by the Abdication and the part played by Mrs Simpson. George V, a lover of protocol, had not been American-minded and contacts had been allowed to lapse. Now, and just in time, all had been put to rights. America had shown an enthusiasm beyond any expectation and the royal visitors had won the hearts of the President, his family and his advisers, forging a link which was to withstand the strain of the six years which lay ahead.

12

Strange Interlude

WHILE THE KING AND QUEEN were away on their seven-week tour of Canada and the United States, an uneasy calm had rested over Europe. There had been no marked deterioration of the position, although the Pact of Steel, made between Italy and Germany in May, had been an indication of how the powers were lining up. Britain and France had been negotiating with Turkey for the provision of mutual aid should war break out, and Anglo-French talks had opened in Moscow, aiming at a guarantee against aggression. But, deep in the public mind, tension was building and received both some relief and some expression in the great reception given to the King and Queen when they arrived home.

On 22 June Princesses Lilibet and Meg boarded the destroyer *Kempenfelt* and were taken out to the Solent to meet the *Empress of Britain*. They excitedly greeted their parents, from whom they had never been parted for so long. They were welcomed by the captain and presented with nightdress cases in the form of giant pandas, which had been subscribed for by the crew of the liner. Then came the landing and it was immediately apparent that something strange had happened in the hearts of the British public while the King and Queen had been absent. At Southampton, reporters described their welcome as 'fantastic' and 'unbelievable'. It was confirmed beyond doubt when the royal train pulled into Waterloo at 5.25 that evening. For the two-mile journey to Buckingham Palace the streets were packed as tightly as they had been for the Coronation; but now the crowds were more enthusiastic, more exhilarated. Harold Nicholson summed up the aura of the day when he described in his diary how MPs, gathered in Parliament Square, viewed the procession:

> We lost all dignity and yelled and yelled. The King wore a happy schoolboy grin. The Queen was superb. She really does manage to convey to each individual in the crowd that he or she has had a personal greeting. It is due, I think, to the brilliance of her eyes . . . We returned to the House with lumps in our throats.[1]

When the royal family came out on to the balcony at the Palace, the tumult grew. The vast crowd had no intention of going away and stood there, singing 'Under the Spreading Chestnut Tree' and 'The Lambeth Walk', while George and Elizabeth dined. At 8.40 they gave in and came out on to the balcony again; there was no alternative. It was near midnight before the Mall emptied.

At this time of crisis, as Europe moved inexorably towards war, the British people needed a hero and a heroine. They wanted figureheads and leaders to match the pulling power of Hitler and Mussolini. There had been a void: the benign and stately George V was dead; Edward VIII, royalty's biggest star and the legendary darling of millions, had departed into the night. In their place had stepped a simple, quiet man who many had considered unfit to fill the role of King, a man whose very selection had been in doubt. He had progressed but by no manner of means could he be said to have reached the heights before he left the shores of England. What, then, had been responsible for this miracle of change? In the main, the answer must be the press, radio and news-reels of Canada and America. The King knew it, and said so.[2] The Prime Minister, Mr Chamberlain, knew it, and he said so in the House.[3]

The truth was that the coverage had been so wide and so sustained that the British public had become jealous. The feeling was summed up by a cartoon in the *New York Daily Mirror*. A squat John Bull stands beside Mr Chamberlain on a tiny island labelled 'Great Britain'. Across the waters are seen the skyscrapers of New York, lines rising above them into the sky whereon is written, 'Hail to Their Majesties'. John Bull says to the Prime Minister: 'I say, just whose King *is* he?' The British people were determined to put the balance right, and they did so, very clearly and at short notice. They claimed their Sovereign back. Yet, behind the change, there was something of far greater import and value than the acclamation of written and spoken words. The King and

Queen had benefitted beyond all measure from the wide experience gained and by the fillip of success. They summed it up themselves in four words, and both said them. The words were: 'This has made us.' The change in the King was assessed by his biographer, John Wheeler-Bennett:

> The North American tour had taken him out of himself, had opened up for him wider horizons and introduced him to new ideas. It marked the end of his apprenticeship as a monarch, and gave him self-confidence and assurance. No longer was he overawed by the magnitude of his responsibility, the greatness of his office and the burden of its traditions. Now at last, he felt, he could stand on his own feet and trust his own judgment. It had, moreover, provided him with a further means of implementing his old ideal of identifying the royal family with the people . . . He had given to the Americans and the Canadians – and indirectly to the world at large – a first glimpse of his new concept of kingship – the concept that the King must have a first-hand knowledge of his peoples and of their affairs, that he must have the common touch.[4]

While in Canada George had said to one of his advisers: 'There must be no more high-hat business, the sort of thing my father and those of his day regarded as essential . . .'[5] That typified his new approach, and it had proved resoundingly successful.

There was a surprise in store for the distinguished audience at the Guildhall where he went with the Queen, through crowded streets, on the day after his arrival home. The delivery and content of his speech were a revelation. Sir Alan Lascelles commented that he had seldom heard anyone speak so effectively or movingly. His words were hailed in Europe and America and Canada as a précis of Britain's beliefs and determination. He put feeling into his message and some of those who listened thought he was so stirred he might break down. That day he proved himself to be a first-rate public speaker and even that brilliant orator, Winston Churchill, was impressed. On being congratulated afterwards, George admitted that speaking used to be 'Hell', but now it was not so any more.

As for his wife, she was thrilled beyond words by the King's success, on tour and at home; it mattered more to her than the star part she had played, which resulted in her being voted *Woman of the Year* in America. She was ever to regard the royal task as team-work, the degree of achievement something attained jointly. The King knew her powers and delighted in them: whenever the cheers broke out, he would automatically draw back, as if to let her have the accolade – in New Zealand in 1927 he had jumped from the train as it entered a station and ran with the crowd as they cheered his wife standing at a window. This tickled his dry sense of humour. In any case he knew, and she knew, that only he could have conducted the vital talks which took place in Canada and America with Mr Mackenzie King and Mr Roosevelt.

In that summer the grind of kingship and war began for George, a grind which was to continue for six long years. Although he had been kept in touch with international affairs while away, there was much work to catch up on and a great number of people to see and talk to. He had to learn from the Prime Minister and the Foreign Secretary all the details of their first-hand information. To them, he had to impart the impressions which he had gained in the United States and Canada. He had to consider what he could do, as King, to better relations. He thought of making a personal appeal to Hitler but, after much discussion, this was rejected. He had to keep in touch with the heads of the three services and discuss plans with them. There was a long list of measures to be taken in case of war that had to be carefully considered and approved. In addition he had to cope with the backlog of routine work of kingship – appointments and honours and the like – which had piled up while he was away, and it was late each evening before he could join his family. There was a short weekend break at the Royal Lodge, then back to another week of grind. Although he had worked hard indeed in the United States and Canada, this was not comparable to the strain to which he was now subjected. His big task was to ensure that Hitler knew Britain and the Empire were in earnest and that there would be no more Munichs. He made this quite clear when he spoke to twenty thousand members of the Civil Defence Forces in Hyde Park on 2 July but, in his megalomania, the German Führer remained convinced that he could fool the British whenever he wished.

At the end of July the King took a well earned rest. He visited

Dartmouth Naval College, accompanied by his wife and children, to see how the Navy was preparing for emergency. They travelled on the Royal Yacht and with them went Lord Louis Mountbatten, who had a little scheme up his sleeve: he was playing at boy-meets-girl. The visit could have been better timed. It was pouring with rain and the cadets were suffering from the joint scourge of mumps and chicken-pox, although they managed to make cheerful noises from the windows in greeting. The fear of infection greatly interfered with the sightseeing programme of the two Princesses and they were consigned to the care of the Captain's Messenger of the day, who happened to be eighteen-year-old Prince Philip of Greece, an appointment which suited Lord Louis Mountbatten admirably.

Elizabeth and Philip were both great-great-grandchildren of Victoria, but they had never met officially – owing to wars and revolutions, the two family lines had drifted apart. There was no Greek blood in Philip; his great-grandmother, Alice, had married a German, who became Grand Duke of Hesse. Their daughter, Victoria, married Louis, one of the gay Battenberg Princes, soldiers of fortune who upset ladies' hearts at the end of the nineteenth century. Their daughter, Alice, married Prince Andrew of Greece, son of King George I of Hellenes, a Dane and brother of Queen Alexandra. Their only son was Philip, born in 1921.

Elizabeth, at thirteen, was only a year junior in age to Queen Victoria's eldest daughter, 'Vicky', Princess Royal, when she had become engaged to Prince Frederick William of Prussia in 1855. But 'Vicky' had been precocious; in 1939 Elizabeth was a shy, retiring child but, like Queen Victoria, she could look, and steadily, and see what she wanted. The male gender at eighteen doesn't mix easily with the opposite sex of thirteen. Philip found it hard going with Lilibet. Eight-year-old Meg was easy: she was full of fun and he teased her, winning her approbation when he swallowed a gargantuan pile of shrimps at tea. Elizabeth was watching him. Her governess, Miss Crawford, recalled: 'She never took her eyes off him the whole time. At the tennis courts I thought that he showed off a good deal, but the little girls were much impressed. Lilibet said, "How good he is, Crawfie! How high he can jump!" He was quite polite to her, but didn't pay any special attention. He spent a lot of time teasing plump little Margaret.'[6]

When the visit was over a very mixed flotilla followed the Royal Yacht out to sea. Those who were fit among the boys had commandeered anything that floated and raced to keep close to the stern. The King became worried for their safety and ordered that they be signalled to turn back. All did bar one. In a small rowing boat a lone oarsman bent to his task unheedingly. It was Philip of Greece. Against the rail of *Victoria and Albert* leaned Lilibet. She was watching him through a giant pair of binoculars. And so did she until he turned, waved, and made for the shore.

In August the King and his family went, according to custom, to Balmoral. This year there were special guests on Deeside, for the King had arranged that his Camp – still known as the Duke of York's Camp – should be sited in the grounds of Abergeldie Castle. Two hundred boys attended and George was Camp Chief. He had never before played so active and personal a part.

These weeks were a source of happiness for the King. He was forty-four, he was fit, had never been in better health. The days passed in the tradition of Queen Victoria, the emphasis being on expeditions into the hills and along the loch shores. He knew every inch of the terrain and the habits of every animal and bird. Each day he took out a party of selected boys, pointing out to them the sparrow hawk hovering in the sky, the tracks of deer and the identity of the birds which broke from the heather. And he found that he could out-walk the posse of youth which followed him. There was a unique, personal touch for these boys from the industrial areas; they were asked to tea at Balmoral Castle; the Queen and the Princesses came to supper with them and they sang popular songs round the camp fire.

On the last evening the King lit the traditional bonfire which marked the camp's ending. The Balmoral pipers circled it, playing Scottish tunes and the National Anthem. Then the boys entered the motor coaches which were to take them to Aberdeen. The King would meet some of them again – this time in uniform; he never forgot a face. As he waved them goodbye, the lights began to go out in Europe. Then he was summoned to London and on Sunday, 3 September 1939, the Second World War began. On that evening King George broadcast to the people:

In this grave hour, perhaps the most fateful in our history, I send to every household of my peoples, both at home and overseas, this message, spoken with the same depth of feeling for each one of you as if I were able to cross your threshold and speak to you myself.

For the second time in the lives of most of us we are at war. Over and over again we have tried to find a peaceful way out of the differences between ourselves and those who are now our enemies. But it has been in vain. We have been forced into a conflict. For we are called, with our allies, to meet the challenge of a principle which, if it were to prevail, would be fatal to any civilized order in the world.

It is the principle which permits a State, in the selfish pursuit of power, to disregard its treaties and its solemn pledges; which sanctions the use of force, or threat of force, against the Sovereignty and independence of other States. Such a principle, stripped of all disguise, is surely the mere primitive doctrine that Might is Right. And if this principle were established throughout the world, the freedom of our own country and of the whole British Commonwealth of Nations would be in danger. But far more than this – the peoples of the world would be kept in the bondage of fear, and all hopes of settled peace and of the security of justice and liberty among nations would be ended.

This is the ultimate issue which confronts us. For the sake of all that we ourselves hold dear, and of the world's order and peace, it is unthinkable that we should refuse to meet the challenge.

It is to this high purpose that I now call my people at home and my peoples across the Seas, who will make our cause their own. I ask them to stand calm and firm and united in this time of trial. The task will be hard. There may be dark days ahead, and war can no longer be confined to the battlefield. But we can only do the right as we see the right, and reverently commit our cause to God. If one and all we keep resolutely faithful to it, ready for whatever service or sacrifice it may demand, then, with God's help, we shall prevail.

May He bless and keep us all.

13

The First Years of War

WARS BRING WITH THEM an increase in the speed of the rate of change of time. During the Second World War the changes were phenomenal. Bi-planes gave rise to pure jets; bombs of 1918 design progressed to atom bombs. Primitive range-finding equipment was replaced by radar instruments which could locate a flying bomb at sixty-five miles' distance and which were so accurate that a court of enquiry was held if a bomb escaped the guns. In 1939 the Lieutenant-Colonels were men who had served between 1914 and 1918; by 1945 youngsters who had been at school at the outbreak of war had taken over. George had been trained by men who learned the sea under sail, before submarines became a reality. Their thinking, and their way of life, went down with the warships *Repulse* and *Prince of Wales* in December 1941. Few men in their forties could keep pace with these revolutions. Had the King been twenty years younger, he could well have done; had he been twenty years older, he would not have been expected to. As things were, it was taken for granted that he could, and this he struggled to do.

He had just got into the sway of kingship, after a shaky start. The triumphs in France, Canada and America had built him up, for he needed acclamation and a measure of fun to offset his mostly serious nature. He was a man who, when given a job to do, gave his all. He would tolerate no advantages from his position. He was ever striving to do more, ever attempting to be with the men in the firing line. If, in the early days of the drabness and severity of war, he did not always demonstrate the pulling power with the troops which had been the natural gift of his elder brother, his constant travels around the country, and his appearance wherever bombs had fallen, wove him into the hearts and love of his people and kept alive the image of monarchy. For the King, there were no leaves, no periods of rest. The best that he could manage was an occasional weekend in the garden at Royal Lodge or in the fields of Sandringham; often he put in a twelve-hour day.

In September 1939 his first task was to consolidate friendships and gain support for the Allied cause: as the leader of the nation, there was much that he could do. Besides this, there was a plethora of work to be done on the home front, approving wartime regulations such as security measures and rationing. Air-raid shelters for the public received his special attention. And then there was the safety and way of life of his family to settle.

Before joining her husband in London, the Queen moved the children to the seclusion of Birkhall, leaving them there in the care of Sir Basil Brooke, the Queen's Treasurer, and their governess. Queen Mary was at Sandringham, which was too near to the East Coast for the King's liking: the Norfolk estate had been bombed in the First World War. On 4 September she departed, in a cavalcade of sixty cars, for the safety of the Duke of Beaufort's home, Badminton in Gloucestershire, the Duchess being her niece. Ninety-year-old Princess Louise, Duchess of Argyll, a daughter of Queen Victoria, was deemed to be too old to be uprooted from Kensington Palace; she died there in December. Then there were the royal homes to be put on a war footing. Sandringham was closed, Appleton House, the former home of Queen Maud of Norway, the King's aunt, becoming the Norfolk residence when opportunities came for a visit. The dust sheets went over the furniture at Balmoral. As soon as war started, George became obsessed with rationing. Lines were painted round the baths to indicate the limit of water level. Bread served in the Palaces was the same as that supplied to the canteens. Expense on drink and clothing was cut to the bone.

The outlook of the King and Queen towards the war was one of aggression and spirited retaliation. They thus trod in the footsteps of Queen Victoria. After a black week in South Africa during the Boer War, she had laid down, and firmly, that there was to be no despondence or talk of defeat in her homes. Both Edward VII and George V had lacked the pugilistic tendency, neither showing any predilection to venture forth and kill the enemy – both George and Elizabeth would have proved dangerous opponents in any encounter. Firing ranges were constructed at Buckingham Palace and at Windsor, and on mornings when time would allow they would blaze away at the targets. George became most efficient with a tommy-gun and when he was on tour there was always one close to his hand. Elizabeth began with a revolver. She said: 'I shall not go down like the others,'[1] referring to European royal houses. This was an attitude which appealed to Mr Churchill and he sent her a particularly deadly American automatic weapon. She took no step backwards, showed no trace of fear. When kind friends suggested that she send her children to America, she replied: 'The children will not go without me. I won't leave the King. And of course the King will never leave.'[2] She said that personal patriotism was the motive power of her being and that, if for any reason she had to leave her country, she would die. The martial music of her thinking enthused her husband, and people noticed. Harold Nicolson met them both and later told his wife: 'I cannot tell you how superb she is . . . What astonished me is how the King is changed. He is now like his brother. He was so gay and she so calm. They did me all the good in the world. We shall win. I know that.'[3]

There was little thought on the part of the King and the Queen about their personal safety in air raids; they did not even have their own shelter in Buckingham Palace. When the sirens sounded, everyone made for the basement and the chance was equal. In the evenings at Buckingham Palace and Windsor, George would walk around outside to see that the black-out was complete. As the autumn turned to winter and the 'Phoney War' dragged on, it was deemed safe to bring the Princesses from Scotland to Windsor. There they joined a stirrup-pump squad, being referred to by number instead of by name. They learned how to extinguish incendiary bombs. They found it rather fun.

As 1939 drew towards its close a problem faced George, one which gave him grave doubts: pressure was put upon him to make a Christmas broadcast, and he did not wish to do so, in fact he dreaded the prospect. His father's Christmas broadcasts had become legendary and George was very doubtful whether he could measure up to the standard. But the importance of his so doing was stressed and at length he agreed. He need not have feared, for that first* Christmas message of his was an outstanding success, and part of it made historic impact. While he was working on its text he received a poem from a collection published in 1908 under the title of *The Desert*; the author was Miss Marie Louise Haskins, a woman with a distinguished career in public service and a lecturer at the London School of Economics. Certain lines from the poem preoccupied him and he chose them to end the broadcast:

> A new year is at hand. We cannot tell what it will bring. If it brings peace, how thankful we shall all be. If it brings us continued struggle we shall remain undaunted.
>
> In the meantime, I feel that we may all find a message of encouragement in the lines which, in my closing words, I would like to say to you: 'I said to the man who stood at the Gate of the Year, "Give me a light that I may tread safely into the unknown." And he replied, "Go out into the darkness, and put your hand into the Hand of God. That shall be to you better than light, and safer than a known way."'

Winter gave place to spring and, amid the sun and the flowers, the 'Phoney War' came to an abrupt end: on 9 April Germany invaded Denmark and Norway. The King went to the War Room of the Admiralty to see the disposition of the Fleet. He longed to be with it. That evening he wrote: 'I have spent a bad day. Everybody working at fever heat except me.' He was soon to be thrust to the forefront. A group of Tories revolted against Mr Chamberlain and Labour too wanted him out. Mr Amery's impassioned words rang through the House: 'You have sat here for too long for any good you have been doing. Depart, I say, and let us have done with you. In the name of God, go!' The King backed Chamberlain. He recorded: 'I told the PM that I did not like the way in which, with worries & responsibilities he had to bear in the conduct of the war, he was always subject to a stab in the back . . .'[4] The two men had great respect for each other; both were men of highest principle and integrity, though with a streak

* The King did not consider his radio message at the end of Coronation year to be the first of an annual event.

of obstinacy. Chamberlain still thought that he could lead a Government: he misjudged the temper of the House and of the people. There was a vote of confidence. Forty-four Conservatives voted against the Government. Mr Amery wrote of the sensational result:

> We strained our ears to hear David Margesson* read out the figures: 281 to 200. A gasp, and shouts of 'resign, resign.' The drop from the normal majority of over 200 was enough to show that the confidence was no longer there, that the Government, as it stood, was doomed. Chamberlain stood up, erect, unyielding, sardonic and walked out past the Speaker's Chair and over the feet of his colleagues, who then followed. The Government benches cheered, while the Socialists shouted: 'Go, in God's name, go!'[5]

To the King's grief, Chamberlain resigned. What should happen next? A. J. P. Taylor thus précised events:

> According to all the precedents, Attlee, leader of the second largest party, should have been asked to form a Government. Only when he failed – and he would have failed – could the net have been cast wider . . . Precedent was not followed in May 1940. George VI invited Chamberlain to name his successor. Chamberlain summoned (Lord) Halifax and Churchill. These three, sitting round a table, chose the next Prime Minister. They chose the right one. For two out of three, the only wise action in their lives. The King's advisers tried to save appearances. They gave out that Chamberlain was being consulted as Leader of the Conservative party, not as a Prime Minister who had resigned. The real defence is that, with the German attack in France, everyone was in too great a hurry to observe the rules. Besides the King's mistake (the break with precedent) worked out all for the best. Though the Labour Party certainly insisted on Churchill, the decision came from the Conservatives, and they could not repudiate it. Even so, for the first few weeks Churchill was received with cheers from the Labour benches and in cold, hostile silence on the Conservative side.[6]

* 1st Viscount; Chief Whip.

Churchill had also to overcome some misgivings on the part of the King – memories were revived of his spirited championship of Edward VIII's case prior to the Abdication. George wanted Lord Halifax as his Prime Minister. On 11 May he wrote in his diary: 'I cannot yet think of Winston as PM . . . I met Halifax in the garden [of Buckingham Palace] & I told him I was sorry not to have him as PM.'[7]

At first Churchill attended formal audiences weekly at the Palace. But soon the ice began to crack. The gravity of the situation, the statesman's vast knowledge of affairs and his respect for the monarchy, his personal charm and his spirit of aggression won the day. The formal audiences changed to informal lunches on Tuesdays; when air raid warnings were on, these were held in the basement. No servants were present, but the Queen often was. They helped themselves from a side-table. One day there were sandwiches for lunch. 'I don't know what's in them,' said the King, 'sawdust, I suppose.' Sometimes George and Winston became so involved in their talks that they forgot to eat. Then Elizabeth would act as parlour maid. 'This is like Marlborough and Queen Anne,' mused Churchill. Soon the King was writing, 'My dear Winston . . .' and using plain PM in conversation. By the end of the year he was saying, 'I could not have a better Prime Minister.' Thus a great friendship came into being.

On 10 May 1940 Germany invaded Holland. At five o'clock on the morning of the 13th the King was awakened by a telephone call. Queen Wilhelmina of the Netherlands was on the line, begging for British aircraft to defend Holland. Prince Bernhard, his wife, Princess Juliana and their two small girls reached London during the morning. Prince Bernhard returned to Holland. Then the telephone rang again: Queen Wilhelmina was at Harwich, having been brought over by a British destroyer. The intrepid lady wished to return to her country, but was eventually convinced that conditions there were such that return was impossible. So she travelled to London, where the King met her and installed her in Buckingham Palace. She had no luggage except a tin hat which had been given her by the captain of the destroyer. Soon she was joined by another royal exile – King Haakon of Norway.

Queen Wilhelmina and King Haakon had been subjected to

persistent attempts to capture them and they made abundantly clear their belief that it was Hitler's intention to 'put into the bag' the Sovereigns of any country which the Germans invaded. Both were appalled at the casual comings and goings of King George and Queen Elizabeth and the general lack of security measures. What would happen, they asked, if parachutists descended from the sky into the Palace garden? The King, confident that all eventualities had been guarded against, pressed the button that was the alarm signal and then, smiling, led the royal exiles out on to the lawn to watch the result. Nothing happened. An old gardener went on with his weeding. No scurry of running feet came from the corridors and no bayonets flashed in the sunlight. There was a look of 'I told you so' on the faces of Wilhelmina and Haakon; Queen Elizabeth burst out laughing. A fit of Teck temper swept over the King and away he raced to find out what had gone wrong. It appeared that the Guardsmen on duty had heard the alarm and consulted the police, who said they had received no information about a raid, so it must be a false alarm. Thus the peace of the summer's afternoon remained unbroken. After that matters changed rapidly in the field of security, urgency being added by the fall of France and a real fear of invasion. Dorothy L. Sayers wrote these words:

> Praise God, now, for an English war –
> The grey tide and the sullen coast,
> The menace of the urgent hour,
> The single island, like a tower,
> Ringed with an angry host.[8]

An air-raid shelter was constructed at the Palace and a house in the West Country was selected as a headquarters for the King and Queen if invasion took place. A picked body of soldiers, known as the Coates Mission, was detailed for their protection, made up of men of the brigade of Guards and the Household Cavalry; the Mission was on alert night and day, to guard against surprise attack. If parachutists were to attempt to capture the Sovereign in his car, the driver was given instructions to drive fast, while the King and those in attendance upon him shot it out. Should matters come to the point when the formation of a British Resistance Movement became necessary, George volunteered to be its leader.

Although the vast majority of Americans were pro-Ally, ninety-five per cent of them were opposed to active intervention. This was the outlook of Ambassador Kennedy, and the King's interview with him in September 1939 had been a disappointment: Kennedy, a believer in Chamberlain, did not consider that war was ever worth the while. Since Eastern Europe was of little use for finance and material, why not let the Germans occupy it? He did not appreciate Britain's deeper motives, though the King went to great trouble to explain these in a personal letter, worried as he was as to the kind of reports which were reaching Washington. It was clear that gaining active US support was going to be a struggle, and this was confirmed when President Roosevelt's special envoy, Mr Sumner Welles, visited London early in 1940. 'The fact is,' noted the King, 'the US is not coming in to help us, and nothing yet will make them, but they are pro-British in the main.'

George began to think that he had gained an over-optimistic view of the President's remarks made at Hyde Park about furthering aid for Britain. Yet those few sunny days were, in the end, to prove of outstanding value. Based on their friendship, King and President began a confidential correspondence. The first step was to explore what American aid would be forthcoming for Europe after the war was over and material and financial ruin reigned; this debate the Americans could conduct without danger of recrimination from Britain's enemies. In their letters there was frequent reference to memories of the visit of June 1939. President Roosevelt to King George, 1 May 1940:

> Last June seems years distant. You will remember that the Saturday night at Hyde Park when I kept you up, after a strenuous day, I may have seemed pessimistic in my belief in the probability of war. More than a month after that I found the Congress assured that there could be no war, and for a few weeks I had to accept the charge of being a 'calamity-howler'.
>
> I certainly do not rejoice in my prophecies but at least it has given me the opportunity to bring home the seriousness of the world situation to the type of American who has hitherto believed, in much too large numbers, that no matter what happens there will be little effect on this country . . .

> Always I want you and your family to know that you have very warm friends in my wife and myself over here, and you must not hesitate to call on me for any possible thing if I can help or lighten your load . . . My very warm regards – and may I add that I really hope you are taking care of your own health because your continued fitness is of real moment to the world.[9]

Then came Dunkirk. Mr Churchill appealed to America for help and the President authorized the sale of half a million rifles, nine hundred field guns and eight thousand machine guns. The tide was on the turn. The Prime Minister asked for destroyers, and the King backed him. He wrote to the President:

> The Queen and I often think of the delightful days which we spent with you and Mrs Roosevelt little more than a year ago. I remember very well our talk that night when you spoke of the probability of war . . . As you know, we are in urgent need of some of your older destroyers to tide us over the next few months. I well understand your difficulties, and I am certain that you will do your best to procure them for us before it is too late. Now that we have been deprived of the assistance of the French fleet . . .* the need is becoming greater every day if we are to carry on our solitary fight for freedom to a successful conclusion.

The period of the evacuation from Dunkirk was the most worrying of the King's life. He wrote in his diary on 23 May:

> I sent a message to Winston asking to come & see me after dinner . . . The Prime Minister came at 10.30 p.m. He told me that if the French plan made out by Weygand did not come off, he would have to order the BEF back to England. This operation would mean the loss of all guns, tanks, ammunition, & all stores in France. The question was whether we could get the troops back from Calais & Dunkirk.

Thereafter, every evening, he entered the numbers of men who had got back until, on 3 June, he was able to write: 'We have now

* France capitulated on 22 June. On 3 July the British attacked the French fleet at Oran. On 5 July Vichy France broke off relations with Britain.

evacuated 224,000 men of the BEF and 85,000 Frenchmen. The last of the BEF have been evacuated.'[10]

The bombs began to fall and 'the Few' twisted, turned, killed and died in the sky. The East End of London took the brunt and, in the mornings, the figures of the King and Queen were to be seen threading their way among the debris. A group of Cockney women were searching for possessions among the fallen bricks and tiles. One said, loud and clear; 'Oh, ain't she luverly! Ain't she *bloody* luverly!' On 9 September a bomb fell on the Palace, lying, unexploded, below the King's study. It was de-fused. Little notice was taken. A new study was found for the King and he went on working.

On the morning of Friday, 13 September, the King and Queen drove up from Windsor and prepared for a day's work at the Palace. The sirens were sounding and it was raining. A German bomber slipped out through the clouds over Admiralty Arch and roared above the Mall towards Buckingham Palace. The King described what happened next:

> We were both upstairs with Alex Hardinge* talking in my little sitting room . . . All of a sudden we heard an aircraft making a zooming noise above us, saw 2 bombs falling past the opposite side of the Palace, & then heard 2 resounding crashes as the bombs fell in the quadrangle about 30 yards away. We looked at each other, & then we were out into the passage as fast as we could get there. The whole thing happened in a matter of seconds. We all wondered why we weren't dead.

But for the fact that the window was open, they would have been lacerated by broken glass. Six bombs were dropped. The Chapel was wrecked. Four men in the flattened plumber's workshop were wounded. There were two great craters in the forecourt and all the windows facing it were smashed.

George and Elizabeth went down to the basement and checked that the staff who had sheltered there were safe. The Queen joked with a policeman: 'I'm glad we've been bombed. Now I can look the East End in the face.' The raid was made light of, hushed up. Even Winston Churchill did not appreciate how serious it had been. After the war was over he wrote:

* 2nd Baron of Penshurst; Private Secretary to the King.

> I must confess that at the time neither I nor any of my colleagues were aware of the peril of this particular incident. Had the windows been closed instead of open the whole of the glass would have splintered into the faces of the King and Queen, causing terrible injuries. So little did they make of it that even I, who saw them and their entourage so frequently, only realized long afterwards . . . what had actually happened.[11]

Now, like the rest of London, George and Elizabeth paid the price. When the whine of the aircraft was heard in the sky, there followed the moments of separation from the world about them, the tensing of the body, the racing of the heart. A week later the shock was still upon the King. He admitted that he disliked working in his room, found difficulty in reading and was for ever glancing out of the window. For the Queen, tears came more readily to her eyes when she listened to the tragedies of others. She received this poem from an admirer in Chicago:

> Be it said to your renown
> That you wore your gayest gown,
> Your bravest smile, and stayed in Town
> When London Bridge was burning down,
> My fair lady

In September 1940 fifty re-conditioned First World War US destroyers were transferred to the Royal Navy. The King sent a letter of appreciation and the Queen added her good wishes in a postscript. But the supply of ships, like that of weapons after Dunkirk, was clearly an un-neutral act and there was speculation about Hitler's reactions. The bombing of London caused a wave of sympathy to sweep through America, but nevertheless the feeling there was still – all aid short of war. Understandably, the British were half-hoping Germany would leave the United States no chance of staying neutral.

That autumn came the Presidential elections; Mr Roosevelt was running for the third time. The King awaited the result in trepidation for, although Mr Wendell Wilkie, the Republican candidate, was personally in favour of continuing aid, his party was traditionally isolationist. Much therefore depended on the result. Mr Roosevelt won. He wrote to the King on 22 November:

> I think and hope that there will be definite benefit to your Nation and to this by a continuity of existing policies . . . In regard to materials from here, I am, as you know, doing everything possible in the way of acceleration and in the way of additional release of literally everything we can spare . . . May I also tell you that you, personally, and the Queen have deepened the respect and affectionate regard in which you are held in this country by the great majority of Americans.

By this time Britain's dollar assets in America were running out. 'Lend-Lease' was introduced, which meant Britain was allowed to receive necessary supplies, and pay later. 'The American Lease and Lend Bill' was signed on 11 March 1941 and arrangements were made for American forces to escort the supplies across the Atlantic. The King wrote to the President:

> After so many years of anxiety, when what we wanted to happen seemed so far from realization, it is wonderful to feel that at last our two great countries are getting together for the future betterment of the world. I do thank God that it was possible for the Queen & me to come to America in those few months before the war broke out in Europe, a visit which gave us the chance to meet you & so many Americans . . . My Prime Minister, Mr Churchill, is indefatigable at his work, with his many & great responsibilities. He is a great man, & has at last come into his own as leader of his country . . .

This opened the way for further personal contact. On the morning of 9 August 1941 Mr Churchill, on board the new British battleship *Prince of Wales*, sailed into Placentia Bay, Newfoundland, where the President was waiting for him on the USS *Augusta*. Roosevelt, in a letter to the King reporting the favourable outcome of the talks, wrote: 'I wish that you could have been with us at Divine Service yesterday on the quarterdeck of your latest battleship. I shall never forget it. Your officers and men were mingled with about three hundred of ours, spread over the turrets and superstructure – I hope you will see a movie of it.' Before they parted the President and Prime Minister issued a joint declaration, laying down certain principles and defining the aims of the two nations. It was called the Atlantic Charter.

1941 ended in a cannonade of historic events. On 7 December the Japanese, without warning, bombed the US Fleet base of Pearl Harbour in Honolulu, leaving only two effective American ships in the Pacific. The next day Britain and the USA declared war on Japan, who occupied Siam and attacked the Philippines and Malaya. On the 10th the British battleship *Prince of Wales* and the battle-cruiser *Repulse* were sunk by Japanese action. The King was touring South Wales; the news broke his heart. He wrote to Mr Churchill: 'I thought I was getting immune to hearing bad news, but this has affected me deeply . . . There is something particularly "alive" about a big ship, which gives one a feeling of personal loss . . .' On the 11th Germany and Italy declared war on the United States. On Christmas Day, as the King broadcast to the nation, the Japanese took Hong Kong.

American troops began to arrive in Britain, filling the camps and transforming the life of the villages. The President wanted to know how they were settling in and how their training was progressing. He would dearly have liked to see for himself, and the way was open, as he and his wife had a standing invitation to visit the King and Queen whenever they wanted to. But for obvious reasons he couldn't leave Washington at such a crucial time. He decided that Eleanor should take his place. 'Are you willing to go, Babs?' he asked. She jumped at the chance. For security reasons she had to travel under a code name; the label given to her was 'Rover'. Her husband hooted with laughter.[12]

Mrs Roosevelt landed in Bristol in October 1942. The US Ambassador met her and outlined the manner in which she was to be received. Shaking her head, she exclaimed: 'I can never get used to being treated as an important person . . . What makes all this fuss harder is that, thanks to the regulations about luggage on a plane, I can't even dress the part!'[13] As her train pulled into Paddington station, she spotted the red carpet being rolled out along the platform. Then she saw the King and Queen waiting to greet her and her fears evaporated. She wondered, as she drove with them to the Palace, at the lack of fuss and security in the streets. The King said to her: 'I hope that you will not find your rooms unbearably cold. We can only give you a small fire and two years ago the blitz knocked us about a bit.'

Eleanor was given the Queen's own bedroom on the first floor.

Its windows had been blown out by a bomb and in their place were wooden frames covered with isinglass. The Queen came in to see that she was comfortable and herself pulled the blackout curtains. Eleanor wrote in her diary: 'Buckingham Palace is an enormous place, and without heat. I do not see how they keep the dampness out. The rooms were cold except for the smaller sitting-room with an open fire.'[14] Mr Roosevelt's son, Elliott, came later to see her. When he saw her apartments, he exclaimed: 'Good heavens, mother! What mammoth rooms! After this you'll never be satisfied at the White House unless you use the whole second floor for your bedroom.'[15]

Guests at dinner that first night included Mr and Mrs Churchill, General Smuts and his son, and Lord and Lady Mountbatten. General Montgomery had just begun his historic advance from the Egyptian frontier towards El Alamein; Mr Churchill was silent and distrait. At last he could stand the strain no longer and hurried off to telephone 10 Downing Street for the latest news. When he returned he was smiling like a cherub and singing 'Roll out the barrel.'

14

The War's Ending

THE LONG TRAIN stood silent in the Norfolk siding, its engine's smoke lending a tang to the summer air. Darkness fell and the silhouette of sentries showed on the embankment. No chink of light escaped the dark blinds at the windows. Alongside the track walked a man and a woman; he was in uniform. King George and Queen Elizabeth were taking an evening stroll, beside the coal bunkers and the still goods wagons, before they retired to bed and prepared for another arduous day.

The royal couple travelled tens of thousands of miles in this train between 1939 and 1945, from the West Country to Tyneside, from Lakenheath to Ayr. In it they visited RAF stations and naval dockyards, factories and bombed cities, reviews of armoured divisions and Home Guard parades. It was a ten-coach train, built in the last days of Queen Victoria. A highly practical mobile home, it was connected with Buckingham Palace by telephone. The King and Queen, should they have wished it, could have spent the nights in some stately home near to their stopping-place but they preferred this way, without distractions to their preparation for the work of the morrow, ever ready to move should emergency come. MPs were enthusiastic about these constant journeys around the country. Mr Morrison,* Home Secretary and Minister of Home Security, was convinced they did more to keep up the spirits of the public than any other factor. After the bombing raids on Coventry and Southampton, Bristol and Birmingham, the sight of the King walking among the debris gave new heart to many who were dazed with shock and sadness. Always he was in uniform, always his identity card was ready for inspection by an

* Afterwards Lord Morrison of Lambeth.

enquiring sentry, an experience which made him smile. He decorated all ranks himself, the first King to do so; on his visits to factories he surprised workers and managers by his knowledge of engineering.

He did not falter. That was what his daughter said when she became Queen Elizabeth II: 'Much was asked of my father in personal sacrifice and endeavour, often in the face of illness; his courage in overcoming it endeared him to everybody. He shirked no task, however difficult, and to the end he never faltered in his duty.'[1] A. J. P. Taylor said the same – he did not falter. Of his attitude in 1940 Taylor wrote: 'Probably only the united resolve of King and Prime Minister prevented a wholesale scuttle of Court, Government and Parliament into the country. Such plans had been made by the previous Government. George VI and Churchill tore them up.'[2]

By 1942 George was a tired man, his health was cracking and he was often in pain. After shaving he would apply a tan 'make-up'[3] so that he went out into the world looking the picture of open-air health. He was determined to go on like that until he fell.

He had his share of sadness to bear. In August 1942 he was at Balmoral, snatching a few days' rest. During dinner he was called to the telephone; he was told that his brother, George, Duke of Kent, had been killed in an air crash. The Duke had had a busy war. In 1939 he was Governor-General Designate of Australia but withdrew from the post, wishing to help the war effort at home. Although his royal status entitled him to the rank of Air Marshal in the Royal Air Force, he accepted that of Air Commodore and carried out regular routine duties. His chief interest lay in furthering the welfare of the flying men and his ideas led to many welcome steps being taken. In 1941 he visited Canada, studying the Empire Training Scheme, and then went on to the United States where he met, and made friends with, President Roosevelt.

At one o'clock on the afternoon of 25 August he had taken off from Cromarty Firth in a Sunderland flying boat, bound for Iceland to inspect RAF establishments there. The weather was vile, with mist, rain and an east wind. After half an hour's flying time the giant plane crashed into a mountain at Morven. It hit the topmost slope, turned over in the air and slid down the other side on its back. The flames of its burning made a scar two hundred yards long by a hundred wide. There was no skeleton of its frame left – just a scattering of unrecognizable pieces. There was one survivor – the rear gunner, Flight-Sergeant Andrew Jack.* His arms were burned and a hand was broken. He saw the scorched uniform of an Air Commodore and realized the Duke was dead. He staggered off along a shepherd's path and, when darkness came, fell into the ferns and slept. At dawn he struggled on and reached a cottage. Particular poignancy lay behind the Duke's death, for seven weeks earlier he had become the father of a second son. The baby was christened Michael George Charles Franklin; the last name was after the President of the United States, who was a godfather.

The funeral was at St George's Chapel, Windsor. The King wrote: 'I have attended very many family funerals in the Chapel, but none of which has moved me in the same way . . . Everybody there I knew well but I did not dare to look at any of them for fear of breaking down.'

George had never had a 'set' of friends, as had Edward VII and Edward VIII. He was not an imaginative man and was ill at ease with brightly amusing, clever people, nervous of engaging in conversations where he might get lost. The closest of his friends came into the category of cronies. Christopher Hibbert said: 'He preferred the company of sailors whose experiences he had shared, of men in positions of high responsibility whom he could question about their work, of men like gardeners, whose interests were his interests.'[4] One of George's closest friends was Lord Louis Mountbatten, afterwards Earl Mountbatten of Burma; they shared the bond of relationship and the Navy. In addition, though Mountbatten was five years his junior, George trusted his judgement and advice. As his friendship with Roosevelt had been deepened by shared private interests, so that with men holding high royal position, men like the Dukes of Beaufort and Norfolk, was founded on a love of the land, of husbanding estates, of country sports.

He was fortunate, too, in his relationships with succeeding statesmen and politicians, where necessity of encounter so often became willing exchange and sometimes close friendship, the particular example being Sir Winston Churchill. At first George

* Afterwards Flight-Lieutenant.

found Anthony Eden 'difficult to talk to' but, with the passing years, confidence between them grew and the King came to rely strongly on Mr Eden's unique knowledge of foreign affairs. On the Labour side, George also had initial difficulty with Clement Attlee, both men being shy. But the liking for detail and exactness was shared and soon a rapport developed, allowing of straight talking. Bevin, too, became a favourite of the King. Still, rewarding though such friendships were and though an understanding of and with the men themselves was of such importance to George, he was essentially a man for family and the closeness of old-established bonds. He had come very close to his brother in the past five years, admiring the effort he put into his work. He wrote to Louis Greig: 'I shall miss him and his help terribly.' Winston Churchill noted that the loss had affected the King 'most poignantly'.

Elizabeth's youngest brother, David, was at the heart of the intimate circle of herself and her husband. The Hon. David Bowes-Lyon and his wife, a niece of Lord Astor, lived at St Paul's Waldenbury, the Queen's childhood home. Her love for it lay in every tree and flower-bed, barn and hedge, and she and George were frequent visitors. They shared with their host an absorbing hobby, that of gardening. To David it was perhaps more than a hobby – it was a way of life. He was renowned for his knowledge and is well remembered as the President of the Royal Horticultural Society. Attempts to get him on the telephone at weekends always met with the same reply: 'Mr Bowes-Lyon is in the garden. You might catch him at lunch-time – or tea-time . . .' The King learned much from David Bowes-Lyon and the result may be seen in the gardens of Windsor, Sandringham and Balmoral.

The Queen also had her personal sorrows. One nephew, John Patrick, Master of Glamis, was killed in action in 1941; another, Andrew Elphinstone, was a prisoner. And there were real fears as well as sorrows: one evening at Windsor, when she was in her bedroom dressing for dinner, a man's hand came out from low down behind a curtain and gripped her by the ankle. Later she said 'For a moment my heart stood absolutely still.' She reached a bell and a page came in. It transpired that the intruder was a deserter, all of whose family had been killed in an air raid. He had obtained a job with a building firm working in the Castle and reached the Queen's room on the pretext of renewing a light bulb. He meant no harm – he wanted help. But the realization came that if one man could reach the Queen's room, so might another with, in time of war, a very different intention.

After the death of the Duke of Kent Elizabeth had another worry to face, and that was when the King was flying. The testing time came in June 1943, when the King visited the armies in North Africa. The York aircraft in which he travelled was due to re-fuel at Gibraltar; the Queen was kept in touch with the journey's progress and it was reported that the plane would soon be landing there. Then silence. Elizabeth sent a message to Queen Mary:

> I have had an anxious few hours, because at 8.15 I heard that the plane had been heard near Gibraltar, and that it would soon be landing. Then after an hour & a half I heard that there was thick fog at Gib. & that they were going on to Africa. Then complete silence till a few minutes ago, when a message came that they had landed in Africa, & taken off again. Of course I imagined every sort of horror, & walked up & down my room staring at the telephone.[5]

George's relief at that journey's ending was tempered by the development of 'Desert tummy', a virulent form of today's 'tourist' variety, and common among troops in Africa. Sanitary arrangements in the villa he occupied at Algiers didn't help matters. He commented in his diary: 'Like all French houses, its plumbing was defective & erratic.'

The King entertained the Commander-in-Chief. Mr Harold Macmillan* wrote:

> He was very good with Eisenhower, who was himself in excellent shape – interesting, amusing, not too shy or too much at ease – in fact, the real natural simple gentleman which he is. After dinner, in the chief sitting-room of the villa, the little ceremony took place to which Eisenhower had looked forward with great and genuine pleasure. The King took the General a little apart . . . and presented him with the GCB with a few very well chosen phrases.[6]

There was also an historic lunch with the French leaders, at which

* Minister at Allied Force Headquarters.

the King sat between General de Gaulle and General Giraud, 'as a result of which, it is said, both withdrew the resignation which they had tendered that same morning'.[7]

The King inspected the men of the First and Eighth Armies and of the US Fifth Army, and the British and American naval units at Algiers. Unannounced, he went to a beach where five hundred soldiers were bathing. They mobbed him, singing, 'For he's a jolly good fellow.' He decided to go to Malta, the George Cross island. The question then arose – should he go by air or by sea? The Air Force wanted him to fly; the Navy was equally determined on the sea, despite the risk involved. The King was faithful to his first love and went in the cruiser *Aurora*, waving aside the menace of mines, submarines and air attack. It was a nice piece of flagwaving, for Mussolini had dubbed the Mediterranean 'Mare Nostrum'. He was to learn otherwise, although British naval officers had no sleep throughout the King's time at sea.

Early on the morning of Trinity Sunday, 20 June, in glorious sunshine, *Aurora* reached Malta. Mr Macmillan was travelling with the King:

> At 8.15 the King came on the bridge; a special little platform had been constructed for him . . . Here he stood alone, in white naval uniform. As we steamed into the Grand Harbour . . . all the cliffs and forts, filled with troops, sailors, airmen and civilians, thundered out a tremendous welcome. It was really a most moving sight. On the old castle of St Angelo were rows of sailors and marines. On all the other vantage points were infantry, gunners, airmen, Boy Scouts, Girl Guides and the dense eager crowds of the civilian population. Whenever possible, there was a choir or a band.[8]

It was a day of moving reception everywhere, a day when tears of emotion fused with the cheers. The King returned to Tripoli that night and a very tired crew sought their rest. Four days later the York touched down at Northolt and George's nearly seven thousand-mile journey was over. A member of his entourage wrote: 'Thus ended a Royal Tour unique in history, and one which will, without doubt, be remembered long after this generation, and the next, have passed away.'[9] He was greeted by a greatly relieved wife and two exuberant daughters.

A gnawing worry for the King during the war years was that he was not able to spend as much time as he would have liked with his children. It was a worry he shared with many serving men, but his case was special as Lilibet was heir to the throne: a great deal depended on her training during her teenage years. Margaret was in a different category – only nine when war began, she was under governess rule; precocious, ever trying to bridge the four-year gap between them, she bounced through life. But Lilibet was serious, apt to remain inside herself, and Windsor in wartime was hardly a cheerful place – under-heated and dimly lit, edged in by coils of barbed wire and the barrels of Bofors guns, in the dark hours the drone of German bombers echoing in the gun turrets as the planes made for Coventry and the Midlands. Sometimes the castle would shake with the force of the bombs falling on London, and the two sisters would often sing duets to drown out the sounds. Air raid warnings were a commonplace, but Windsor took a little time to adjust itself. On one occasion, as the siren wailed and there was a scuttle for the cellars, it was found that the Princesses were absent. A search revealed that they were still in their rooms: Nanny ('Alla'), who took over from the Governess at six o'clock, had decided that her charges must be properly dressed before taking shelter. She was considered a dragon by some – even the Master of the Household had to summon up courage before telling Nanny that, when the siren sounded, the Princesses must descend immediately, regardless of what they were wearing.

Lilibet made her public debut at the age of fourteen when, in 1940, having been well coached by her mother, she broadcast on the BBC to evacuated children. Her education widened; Canon Crawley, a member of the Chapter of St George's Chapel, gave her religious instruction and Sir Henry Kennett Marten, Vice-Provost of Eton, taught her history. In 1942 she was prepared for confirmation. Queen Mary motored up from Badminton for the occasion and commented that her granddaughter 'looked so nice in white with a small veil & was quite composed'.[10] She was appointed Colonel of the Grenadier Guards and on her sixteenth birthday inspected them with an aplomb and efficiency outstanding in a girl of her age. She registered for National Service and began to plague her father to let her join the Forces. He said 'No.' She increased the pressure and had her way. She put on ATS uniform, being entered in the records as 'No. 230873 Second Subaltern Elizabeth Alexandra Mary Windsor. Age 18. Eyes, blue. Hair, brown. Height, 5 ft 3 in.' She went to a training centre near Camberley to learn about lorries, getting smeared with grease in the process. Like her father, whatever she had to do she did it with all her might. It proved somewhat overpowering for mother. The Queen commented: 'Last night we had sparking plugs all through dinner.'

Lilibet liked an authority to quote. At the war's beginning it was the views of her groom which were expounded as fact. On occasions her father, fresh from an interview with the Prime Minister, would raise his eyes to heaven when he learned the stable interpretation of international affairs. Then the source of all wisdom switched from the saddle to the sea. Lilibet would announce, as a settlement of all argument, 'Philip says . . .' The Prince of Greece and Denmark had progressed from being a cadet at Dartmouth to a very active naval officer. He wrote to Lilibet; his photograph was in her room. When he was on leave they danced together at a party given by Marina, Duchess of Kent, and he was a guest at Windsor for Christmas 1943.

Spring of 1944 found the King and Prime Minister wrapped in the detailed planning for D-Day – the invasion of Europe, code-named 'Overlord'. Co-operation was complete except on one point: both men had a secret – they each planned to be in on the landing, but they didn't tell one another so. The King didn't even tell the Queen. The cat came out of the bag on 30 May when Churchill glibly announced that he would be watching the initial attack from one of the bombarding ships. George, taken by surprise, said, 'So shall I.' That evening he told Elizabeth. She was, he wrote, 'wonderful as always', and encouraged him.

Sir Alan Lascelles, the King's Private Secretary, was appalled. He told the King he presumed that Princess Elizabeth would be fully briefed regarding her succession, and that arrangements would be made to appoint a new Prime Minister in the event of both her father and Churchill being killed. He added that he did not envy the lot of the naval commander who carried both the Sovereign and the Prime Minister into battle. The King slept on it and regretfully came to the conclusion that he should not go. He was of the same opinion about Churchill and told him so. Churchill replied that he had flown to America, the Middle East and Russia, that he had crossed the Atlantic by sea, and that the D-Day trip 'was nothing'. He was obviously going to be awkward. Admiral Ramsay, the naval C.-in-C., was in violent opposition to either man going. Churchill agreed that the King should not go, but said nothing about himself. On 2 June the King wrote to him:

> I am a younger man than you, I am a sailor, & as King I am the head of all three Services. There is nothing I would like better than to go to sea but I have agreed to stop at home; is it fair that you should then do exactly what I should have liked to do myself? You said yesterday afternoon that it would be a fine thing for the King to lead his troops into battle, as in old days; if the King cannot do this, it does not seem to me right that his Prime Minister should take his place . . .[11]

Churchill received this letter just before he left Downing Street for General Eisenhower's headquarters near Portsmouth. He did not reply. George became thoroughly upset and made plans to leave Windsor at dawn next morning by car and drive to Portsmouth to ensure personally that Churchill did not embark with the invasion fleet. Fortunately Sir Alan Lascelles managed to contact the Prime Minister by telephone; it was only then that the militant statesman surrendered.

The King had not long to wait before his wish for action was granted. On the night of 15 June he crossed to France:

> When we reached the other side I got a very good view of the mass of shipping which is there stretching for miles in both directions . . . The cruiser *Hawkins* was actually firing in support of an attack as we came in. I went ashore in a M.L. & changed into a 'Duck', the amphibious craft, & drove ashore over the beach where the Canadians landed & was met by Gen. Montgomery at Courcelles beach. We drove to his tactical H.Q. & had lunch . . . In his caravan he explained to me how the battle was going on . . . The position at Caen is the most delicate.

On the same night that the King crossed to France a new menace reached London – the V1 bombers began to fall. These pilotless, explosive-packed planes made a deep mark on public morale;

there was a measure of uncanniness about them, in the nerve-shattering seconds between the cutting-out of the engine and the explosion. As the Queen said: 'There is something very inhuman about death-dealing missiles being launched in such an indiscriminate manner.' The windows of Buckingham Palace were blasted out as soon as they were repaired. Seventy-five yards of garden wall were laid low. Then came the destruction of the Guards Chapel at Wellington Barracks, where many of the worshippers were friends of the King and Queen. George and Elizabeth determined to see for themselves how the flying bombs were being dealt with. They visited Light and Heavy Anti-Aircraft Batteries in Sussex:

> We went to East Grinstead where a FB had just fallen & we talked to the people & on to a HAA Battery site. From here we lunched at Lingfield in the mess of a Mixed Battery of HAA. The ATS girls work all instruments. After lunch the alarm went & we watched the 3·7″ guns go into action against the FBs. Six of them came over at very short intervals at a rate of not less than 400 m.p.h. at 3000 ft. The shooting was very level but a bit 'behind'. This is due to a 'time lag' in the Radar Automatic instruments but it will be got over by practice. This battery shot two down out of five fired at yesterday. I hoped it was not because we were there which had made them nervous. They think they hit one later, but a fighter was on its tail as well. We saw 2 fighters 'standing' by a FB at one time.

A victory sign was needed and George gave it, in the way that he liked best. At the end of July he was visiting the armies abroad again. He spent eleven days in Italy, under the guidance of General Alexander, visiting American, French, Polish and Brazilian units as well as British and Imperial. George had now made his own reputation with the troops and the sight of him was a fillip to men feeling rather 'out of it' by the emphasis that was being placed on Normandy. The King treasured an incident which happened in Naples. He was quartered at the Villa Emma, where Lady Hamilton had met Nelson. The sea around it was patrolled throughout the night by a picket boat. At 5.30 in the morning George was awakened by an altercation without. He put his head out of the window and demanded what the blazes was going on. He saw a young naval officer guarding a man and a woman.

'Says he's the King, sir,' said the officer.

'What King?' asked the King.

'King of Italy, sir.'[12]

And it was. Without asking anybody's leave, King Victor Emmanuel and Queen Elena had arrived in Naples ten days earlier. They decided to go out fishing in a small boat. Busy with their tackle, they glanced up at a hail and, to their consternation and indignation, found themselves looking into the business end of a Lewis gun. The Queen was most noisy in her remonstration. At length she produced a huge visiting card, with 'Queen of Italy' written on it. The King of Great Britain, highly amused, took the card from the officer and kept it as a souvenir. In October King George was off again, this time visiting 21st Army Group as the guest of General Montgomery.

The long winter began for a tired nation. Abroad news see-sawed from good to bad. At home the V1 bombers were conquered but their place was taken by V2 rockets, ballistic missiles which crashed, without warning, from the stratosphere upon London and the South-east. Between September and December 1944, 1425 people were killed and 3134 injured by the 'V' weapons. But the King and indeed the country could look forward to the spring and a demonstration of the bond between Britain and America – it was in the spring that the King planned to have Mr and Mrs Roosevelt to stay with him at Buckingham Palace.

In November the President had been elected for the fourth time and by an impressive majority, but there were signs that his health was cracking. This was noticed by many when he attended the Yalta Conference with Stalin and Churchill in February 1945. On 12 March the King wrote to him:

> I am very glad to hear that it may be possible for you to make your long promised visit to my country . . . You may be sure that you will get a very warm welcome from the people of Great Britain, & I send you and Mrs Roosevelt a very cordial invitation to be our guests at Buckingham Palace. We are still under daily bombardment at the moment but we hope & trust the situation

> will be better in a few months' time. We shall do our best to make you comfortable here & it would be a real pleasure to the Queen & myself to have you with us & to continue that friendship which started so happily in Washington & at Hyde Park in 1939.[13]

At the end of the month the President went for a rest to Warm Springs, Georgia. He died there from a brain haemorrhage on 12 April. Those about him – family, staff, doctors, nurses – had the look of people for whom the sun had gone down for ever. He was buried in the rose garden at Hyde Park. King George ordered a week's Court mourning and attended the Memorial Service at St Paul's.

The royal family was at Appleton House, Sandringham, in the first week of May. A telephone call came from Winston Churchill: his message was that the war in Europe was nearing its close.

Evening, 8 May 1945 – VE-Day. The Palace was floodlit. A searchlight picked out Nelson on the top of his column in Trafalgar Square and a cone of them came to a head, like a maypole, high above a quarter of a million people. Earlier the two Princesses had slipped out to join the throng. 'It was absolutely wonderful,' in Margaret's view. 'Everybody was knocking everybody's hats off, so we knocked off a few too.' Now bombers were dropping flares and coloured lights; there was the tang of bonfires in the air. The crowd was shouting, 'We want the King, we want the Queen.' They came out on to the balcony, Churchill with them, and the Princesses, Elizabeth in uniform. Eight times the call was answered. There he stood, a slight figure in the brilliance, grinning and waving, the man whom many had said could not play the part of King. Now his people were calling for him, from Constitution Hill and along the length of The Mall. King George VI and Queen Elizabeth were being accorded the greatest victory reception since Napoleon came back from Austerlitz.

15

A Time of Change

WARS, AND THE RUMOURS OF WARS, have taken heavy toll of recent British Sovereigns and their consorts. Prince Albert's last illness was exacerbated by the threat of war with America; strain and worry over the Boer War contributed to the collapse of Queen Victoria. The sabre-rattling of Emperor William of Germany hastened Edward VII into his grave; George V was a youngish man in 1914 and had aged almost beyond belief by Armistice Day. But it was George VI who paid the biggest price. He was tired out, as was his Prime Minister, who was so fatigued that he had to be carried by Marines up the stairs of the Cabinet Office. And the end of the war in Europe brought no lightening of the workload. The King's programme was sharply divided. On the one, and brighter, side, he was coping with the acclamation and the triumph; on the other, he was occupied with the fate of Germany, relations with Russia, the re-birth of France, the continuing war with Japan and, at home, the quickly approaching General Election.

On 9 and 10 May the King and Queen made State Drives through East and South London. In preceding years they had been there to inspect the war damage. Now the people let them know of their gratitude in no uncertain fashion; their reception was tumultuous. The King couldn't understand how the carriage horses, which had been doing farm work since 1939, behaved so impeccably. He discovered they had been subjected to a course of listening to the Forces' Programme on the BBC emitted at full blast.

Each night of that Victory Week George and Elizabeth were called out on to the balcony of the Palace. On the 13th they drove to St Paul's for a National Service of Thanksgiving, and on the 16th they were in Edinburgh for a similar Service in St Giles' Cathedral. Then:

> The two Houses of Parliament assembled in the royal gallery. The King, attired in naval uniform, came accompanied by the Queen and the two Princesses. The Lord Chancellor read an address of congratulation from the House of Lords, and the Speaker one from the House of Commons. The King answered in a prepared speech of thanks. This ceremony was without precedent. The two Houses had addressed monarchs for centuries. And Kings had replied. But always by messenger. Never in this intimate fashion, met together in one place. As the King rose to leave there came something still more surprising. Winston Churchill waved his top-hat in the air and cried: 'Three cheers for his Majesty.' Lords and Commons responded with full-throated acclaim. Solemn formality turned into a family party . . . No other King of Britain has received this simple, heartfelt tribute.[1]

The royal family retired for a short rest at Windsor and the King wrote in his diary:

> We have spent a very busy fortnight since VE Day & feel rather jaded from it all. We have been overwhelmed by the kind things people have said over our part in the War. We have only tried to do our duty during these 5½ years. I have found it difficult to rejoice or relax as there is still so much hard work ahead to deal with.[2]

The Queen showed less sign of the strain, but then she was younger and blessed with resilient health. She knew that change was coming to Britain and went with the tide. Yet, although ever beside her husband and ever ready with advice, the ultimate decisions rested with him, and, in the field of politics, the weight of these decisions was becoming hard to bear.

George had been in agreement with the decision of the two main Parties, made in autumn of 1944, that a General Election should be held as soon as possible after the end of the war in Europe. Then came the completion of a startling new weapon –

the atomic bomb. Very few people were let into the secret. The King and Mr Churchill knew, but even Mr Attlee, the Labour leader, did not. The invention meant that the war with Japan was now likely to be brought to an end much sooner than anticipated – it had been thought it would drag on for another eighteen months. Consequently the King and Mr Churchill changed their minds and wished the existing Government to continue until all hostilities were concluded but they could not say so without suspicions of their motives piercing the veil of secrecy. So Britain went to the Polls. On 26 July the count of votes was made. The final state of the Parties was Labour, 392; Conservatives, 189; Liberal Nationals and Liberals, 25 between them. Sadly, Mr Churchill went to the Palace to say goodbye. Afterwards the King wrote to him:

> My dear Winston
>
> I am writing to tell how very sad I am that you are no longer my Prime Minister . . . Your breadth of vision & your grasp of the essential things were a great comfort to me in the darkest days of War, & I like to think that we have never disagreed on any really important matter. For all those things I thank you most sincerely . . . I feel that your conduct as Prime Minister & Minister of Defence has never been surpassed . . . Your relations with the Chiefs of Staff have always been most cordial & they have served you with a real devotion. They I know will regret your leaving the helm at this moment. For myself personally, I regret what has happened more than perhaps anyone else. I shall miss your counsel to me more than I can say . . .
>
> Believe me
> I am,
> Yours very sincerely & gratefully,
> GRI[3]

Mr Attlee became Prime Minister and, as such, returned to the Potsdam Conference in Berlin, taking with him Mr Bevin as Foreign Secretary.

A great loneliness filled King George. There were no more informal lunches with Winston; a considerable number of politicians, whom he had seen often and worked with in amity, had lost their seats. Now there were new men he must come to know, whose ways he must learn. There was another friend whom the King sorely missed – Franklin D. Roosevelt. No longer was it possible for him to drop a hint to, or ask a favour of, the President of the United States. However, he was determined to establish a like rapport with Roosevelt's successor, Mr Truman, and went to much trouble to arrange a meeting. It took place on 2 August in Plymouth Sound and proved successful.

> I arrived at Milbay Station, Plymouth, & went on board the *Renown* which was lying at anchor in the Sound. The USS *Augusta* was at anchor nearby. President Truman, Secy of State Mr Byrnes and Fleet Adl Leahy came on board to call on me at 12.30 p.m. I welcomed him to this country & we had half hrs. talk before lunch . . . I liked him. Attractive, of Irish origin & a great talker . . .

The regard was returned, Mr Truman commenting: 'I was impressed by the King as a good man.' He was delighted when George asked for his autograph – 'for my wife and daughters'. That established him as a 'human being'.[4] A week later the atomic bombs were dropped on Japan. Then came the jubilation of VJ Day, with George and Elizabeth called out on to the Palace balcony six times by the delirious crowd. The King's one regret was that Mr Churchill could not be accorded the reception he so richly deserved.

New challenges were now to be met, new efforts made. For six years the King and those about him had had but one aim – the good of the country and its survival. Now the old order had changed and Party took precedence, the goal of self-advancement showing where before, when the bombs were dropping and the guns firing, the only thought had been the common weal. There could be no going back, as there had been under George V, to the gay times of King Edward and the imperial splendour of Victoria. A new feeling was spreading through Britain, a feeling that wealth should be distributed more evenly, that class distinction should fade, that opportunity should be for all. Even while appreciating this, some of the new ways were not the King's ways. He was shocked when a Cabinet Minister, Mr Aneurin Bevan, refused to wear evening dress on the ground that it was 'upper class uniform'. He was irritated when he saw decorations worn in the wrong place at the wrong time. He was hurt when the Palace staffs formed a union and demanded higher wages. George VI, as Duke of York, had been out of tune with the thirties, but kingship and war had put him back on course and back in fashion. Now, in the autumn of 1945, it was as though he had been tossed by a wave and left stranded on a new beach, unfamiliar and empty of his beliefs and ideals.

He rested at Balmoral; he went to the ploughed lands of Sandringham. He would dearly have liked to tarry at either place, breeding his Southdown sheep and Red Poll cattle, shooting in the wide fields and over the hills. But that was not to be. He may have felt outmoded but in fact he was wanted now – he was an authority. His knowledge of America and his links with the Dominions were invaluable; he was on friendly terms with the leaders of the world, in particular, those of France; he had been hand-in-glove with Chamberlain and Churchill; he was most popular with the armed forces. Lord Mountbatten summed it up in a letter to him: 'You will find that your position will be greatly strengthened, since you are now the old experienced campaigner on whom a new and partly inexperienced Government will lean for advice and guidance.'[5] Certainly George VI played a role, and held a responsibility, far in excess of anything which was to be asked of his daughter, Queen Elizabeth II.

And so the strain built up. At Christmas George wrote to his brother Henry, Duke of Gloucester, from Sandringham:

> I have been suffering from an awful reaction from the strain of war I suppose & have felt very tired, especially down here but I hope I shall soon start to feel well again. Medicine, not even Weir's,* is of any use as I really want a rest, away from people and papers, but that of course is impossible. I am perfectly well really but feel that I cannot cope competently with all the varied & many questions which come up. My new Government is not too easy & the people are rather difficult to talk to. Bevin is very good & tells me every-

* The King had absorbed from his physician, Sir J. Weir, a belief in homoeopathy, the system which aims at curing diseases by administering small doses of medicines which produce in healthy persons symptoms similar to those they are designed to remove.

> thing that is going on. The others are still learning how to run their departments, & their efforts have not made life any easier so far.[6]

He ate little, seldom relaxing and clearly finding even light conversation a strain. A clear picture of the change in the way of life of the royal family came from the pen of Mabell, Countess of Airlie, for fifty years lady-in-waiting to Queen Mary and her lifelong friend. In January 1946 she went to Sandringham. Many memories were awakened for her; the train journey was much the same as it had been in the old days, she travelling in the little compartment reserved for ladies-in-waiting. But the 'Big House' was in startling contrast with the times of George V. In the entrance hall there now stood a baize covered table on which jig-saw puzzles were set out. The younger members of the party . . . congregated round them from morning till night. The radio, worked by Princess Elizabeth, blared incessantly. 'No medals or orders were worn at dinner time; it was much more like ordinary family life than it had been in the old days. It was in the way in which the King said, "You must ask Mummy," when his daughters wanted to do something . . . in Princess Margaret's pout when the Queen sent her back to the house to put on a thicker coat . . . in the way both sisters teased, and were teased by, the young Guardsmen.' These Queen Mary referred to as 'The Body Guard'. Of the whole house it seemed that only her room remained unchanged.

'At dinner on the first evening I sat next to the King. His face was tired and strained and he ate practically nothing. I knew that he was forcing himself to talk and entertain me. He had worked on his Boxes right up to dinner time and afterwards went back to them again. It was obvious how hard he was driving himself.' Dancing began at 11.30 and Queen Mary and the Countess, both nearing eighty, took part in the old country numbers, outshining the Princesses and their guests. Lady Airlie was watching Lilibet closely. 'I thought that no two sisters could have been less alike, the elder with her quiet simplicity, the younger with her puckish expression and irrepressible high spirit. In that family setting Elizabeth seemed to me one of the most unselfish girls I had ever met, always the first to give way in any of the small issues that arise in every home.' When Lady Airlie congratulated the King on his Christmas broadcast he smiled across at Elizabeth and said: 'She helps me.'[7]

As the years passed, George and Elizabeth leaned more and more for interest and relaxation on the gardens of their various homes. During the war years of natural course these had deteriorated, for reasons of expense and shortage of labour. The couple could do little themselves but basic maintenance in their few, free hours. In the post-war years there came a fundamental change in outlook towards gardens, with the emphasis on informality and, even more important, on privacy. This was best illustrated at Sandringham. There, in 1947, the King asked Sir Geoffrey Jellicoe to design a garden extending away from the north front of the house. As a first step the course of the drive was altered and a belt of shrubs planted, blocking out the view of the house from the Norwich Gates to give a 'personal, intimate garden in the midst of the sweeping lawns and stately trees . . . The garden which emerged is a long rectangle filled with a formal pattern of intricately connected enclosures, each surrounded with hedges of box. In most of the enclosures mixed flower-beds containing, in particular, many roses for the benefit of Queen Elizabeth, are divided by trim grass and gravel paths; and in the middle of the garden, on either side of the long central grass path, are two secluded patches of box-enclosed lawn, designed for the royal family's tea parties in the summer.'[8] All around were the favourite plants of George and Elizabeth – rhododendrons, azaleas, magnolias and camellias. The two of them took the greatest interest in the making of this garden and it remains a place of remembrance of the days when King George VI and Queen Elizabeth were the master and mistress of the royal homes.

The gardens of Balmoral, a very special place to George, did not feel the touch of the royal gardeners' hands until 1937, leaving but a short and busy time before the war came. At Balmoral the emphasis is more on the estate than the gardens, and special attention was paid to vistas, showing the windings of the silver river Dee. A favourite area of the King was the pansy garden, which lay below the ballroom terrace; another treasure was the sunken garden made by Queen Mary. Mr Shewell-Cooper thus described it:

> There are six steps down to the formal rose beds with grass verges around, planted up, in the main, with the 'Else Poulsen' roses edged with that lovely frilled-edge crimson Polyantha, 'Mrs Strathan van Ness'. All around the top of this sunken garden there is a path, and around the edge in a narrow border is planted very attractively what one may call a 'cottage garden' mixed border. Here one finds verbenas jostling antirrhinums; petunias nestling up to penstemons; asters vying with salpiglossis, to see which can make the best show; godetias and annual scabious, the everlasting helichrysum, the lovely blue of the 'Clive Greaves' scabious next to the featheriness of the nepeta, or catmint; nemesia and alonzoa with the 'Jubilee Gem' cornflower in front; annual chrysanthemums sprinkled here and there, and planted throughout the border as 'dot' plants, tall, plumy gladioli used to break up any idea of flatness. Here is a riot of colour indeed! Some may argue that it is not 'correct,' but no one could deny that it is very beautiful for a perfect mass of bloom.[9]

The imprint of George and Elizabeth upon Birkhall was stronger. It was the favourite holiday home when they were Duke and Duchess of York, and particularly so after the birth of their daughters. Birkhall has the advantage of being only six hundred feet above sea-level, against Balmoral's thousand, and accordingly is much warmer. George and Elizabeth planted apple trees and enlarged the vegetable garden, some of it being on steep banks. It was Elizabeth's love of colour which provided the most striking change, borders thick with Michaelmas daisies and heather. Autumn plants crowded two herbaceous borders. Everywhere there was a mass of bloom, a feature to be found wherever the couple worked. Elizabeth referred to it as 'a delicious garden'. One of the delights, particularly for the young Princesses, were the three summer houses, one high on a mound, one by the river and the third hidden in a clump of trees. Here Lilibet and Meg would take turn to act as hostess at tea-time. Birkhall was little changed, and full of memories, when Elizabeth returned there alone in 1952. She made it into a lovely home as, in the near future, she was to do with the Castle of Mey.

Scotland provided one other great source of pleasure and

much-needed relaxation for the royal couple – fishing. George had been an enthusiast and an expert from his cadet days, and Elizabeth certainly wasn't far behind. That great enthusiast, Mr Neville Chamberlain, was most impressed with her skill and the two exchanged books on the subject. Seeing her standing in the waters of the rivers Thurso or Dee, the non-angler might mistake her for a vendor of clothes-pegs or a teller of fortunes, but those who know the difference between a Jock Scott and a Hairy Mary stand around to watch a real craftsman in action.

For George, there was special pleasure, too, in the discovery that Lilibet was a natural fisherwoman. The elder girl was her father's shadow, ever wanting to be with him, to walk with him and to shoot with him. Her fear was that she would be outshone and it was a very real fear, for Meg was dynamic and could be, as she admitted, a 'holy terror' if she chose it that way, which was when she was crossed. Queen Mary described her as *espiégle* – 'so outrageously amusing that one can't help encouraging her.'[10] In fact only Queen Mary's brother Frank had ever equalled her for mischief. On being informed that she was too young to attend the races, she waited until her parents' car was clear of the palace, then ordered another and followed it. When she was told to go steady with the sherry, she threatened to refuse to launch any ships unless her glass were re-filled. She used slang expressions; asked where she had picked them, she answered. 'At my mother's knee, or some such low joint.' Having read in a magazine that her eyes were beautiful, she learned early to turn their rays on men. The question which intrigued her father was, where did she get the *espiègle* quality from? It wasn't in the stamp of her mother who, although she had got up to rural escapades as a child, had ever been sedate in the drawing-room, a poise which had earned for her the nickname 'Princess'. It certainly couldn't be traced back to Albert, who was a studious little prig as a boy. So it had to be Victoria. George did his best to control Meg and Mrs Roosevelt, on a visit to Windsor, noted that he told her firmly to turn down the volume of the dance music she was playing on her gramophone. But he was too tired, and perhaps too intrigued, to act the stern parent: she could reduce him to giggles.

The two Princesses were far apart in character. Meg, it seemed, was a throwback to Princess Louise, Duchess of Argyll, the vivacious and talented daughter of Queen Victoria, while there was much of Queen Mary in Lilibet, the seriousness and the determination. Her father was sad at the thought of losing her in marriage; he had misgivings about the future and the heavy duties that would one day be hers. As part of her training she was appointed Counsellor of State while he was in Italy in 1944, and she launched the battleship *Vanguard* in December of that year. George saw in her many traits of himself, her determination to master subjects, her common sense, her devotion to public service and her love of sport.

Lilibet was always with her father when he sought relaxation in his favourite sport – shooting. He was a very good shot, taking after his father, one of the finest in the country and better than *his* father. In Edward VII's days the guns ruled Sandringham, regardless of the needs of agriculture, so the love, and the lore, of guns had been bred in George and stayed with him until the last day of his life. His game book was meticulously kept. The first entry was in 1907: 'Papa, David & myself. My first day's shooting. I used a single barrel muzzle loader, with which Grandpapa, Uncle Eddy* and Papa all started shooting. I shot three rabbits.' This book was a well-worn track leading back through time and George was a lover of the past. He could look at some brief entry, listing with whom he had shot, the bag and the weather, and a distant afternoon would return clear before his eyes. 'We were out for two hours. Had to get a grouse for dinner.' 'Plenty of birds and perfect day. They flew very well.' Then there were the milestone outings; 'My first woodcock.' 'I shot my first pheasant.'[11]

George was in a very different category from his grandfather, who assessed the success of a shoot in terms of the size of the bag and the grandeur of the lunch. He was not battue-minded and liked a varied bag. Aubrey Buxton wrote:

> In George VI we had a new sort of sporting monarch – a king who was not just an observer, nor a casual participant, but who was himself a significant factor in the recreation he so greatly enjoyed. In due time he became, as it were the author, the producer, the stage manager, and the leading man all at once.[12]

* Duke of Clarence.

His powers of intense concentration helped him to become the expert shot that he was and when he had a gun in his hands he was able to forget the worries of his job and this was very necessary for him. Satisfaction flowed through him, not only as a result of the sport but because he was fascinated by the country around him, deeply imbued as he was with the love of nature. There was another point. When he was out in the fields and on the hills and marshes, he knew everyone with whom he came in contact – every tenant, farmer and beater at Sandringham and Balmoral and the members of the staff on the estates which he visited. Best he loved wildfowling in Norfolk, particularly in the immediate post-war years. He would rise in the dark, sip a cup of tea and shout for Lilibet. Together they made towards the Babingley river and Cat's Bottom and then, crouched low together by Pooley's Pond, in the last of the darkness before the dawn, wait for the duck to come in.

Though he never became the addict that Edward VII had been for horse-racing – he was more in the category of that other sailor king, William IV who, when asked what horses he wished to run in the Goodwood Cup replied, 'Start the whole fleet' – George had headed the list of winning owners in 1942. He did not experience the thrill of seeing one of his horses first past the post until 1945 when he watched Rising Light win by a head over a mile and a half at Ascot. He won £37,000 between 1946 and 1949, but his 'horsey' daughters were not impressed and would tease him about his racing activities.

For Elizabeth, the love of racing was rich on both sides of her family. She brought back to the paddock, after half a century, the famous Strathmore colours of her grandfather, the black cap with the gold tassel, and the blue and the buff. Through her mother she is related to Lord George Bentinck, the son of the Duke of Portland, who dominated English racing in the early Victorian days. In 1949 Lord Mildmay of Fleet was a guest at Windsor. Anthony Mildmay, known to the racing crowds as 'Lordie', had headed the list of amateur riders in the 1946–7 season. He had ridden Cromwell into third place in the Grand National when he was suffering from a slipped disc and could not move his neck. The Queen listened to Mildmay's story of his blind ride around Aintree and the magic of it enthralled her. She decided to see the

Strathmore colours again and, in partnership with Lilibet, she bought Monaveen, a nine-year-old which cost them £1000. Monaveen ran in the Grand National, won some £3000 in prizes and then, to the great sadness of the owners, was killed at Hurst Park; the horse's memory was kept alive in the Monaveen Chase.

Two subjects dominated the King's thoughts in 1946–7 – the end of the British in India and the engagement of his elder daughter. He had known of the moves about India for a long time. He had written in his diary in July 1942:

> The Prime Minister amazed me by saying that his colleagues & both, or all 3, parties in Parliament were quite prepared to give up India to the Indians after the war. He felt they had already been talked into giving up India. Cripps,* the Press & USA public opinion have all contributed to make their minds up that our rule in India is wrong & and has always been wrong for India. I disagree . . .[13]

But it had to be and in December 1946 Mr Attlee put forward the name of Lord Mountbatten as the man who should handle a mission the object of which was nothing less than the liquidation of the Indian Empire. At first Mountbatten refused the appointment. He said that he would be out of his mind to tackle 'an insoluble problem', and that in any case he wished to continue in his naval career. It was the intervention of his cousin, the King, who had come to terms with the idea of India's independence which caused him to change his mind, and within a year came the partition of the sub-continent of India. Seventy years before Disraeli had presented to Queen Victoria the 'bright jewel' which was the glory of the British Empire. She began to sign herself 'VR & I' – *Victoria Regina et Imperatrix*. On 15 August 1947, when the British flags came down, King George VI underwent a change in style and title. *Imperator* no longer applied. Three days later Queen Mary commented: 'the first time Bertie wrote me a letter with the I for Emperor of India left out. Very sad.'[14] Sad indeed it was for her, for she adored the country and forecast that when she died the word India would be found written across her heart. Sad also for George. He had much wished to travel east and see the splendours of Simla and Delhi, but circumstances had prevented

* Sir Stafford Cripps.

him. Now he had one last wish. He asked that the last of the Union Jacks, which had flown over the residency at Lucknow night and day since the siege of 1857, should come to Windsor and there hang with other flags which were part of history. His wish was granted.

And so to Lilibet. She and Philip had fallen in love at the Christmas party at Windsor in 1943. They became engaged at Balmoral in August 1946. Her parents agreed, but stipulated that their daughter must wait for marriage until she was twenty-one. There were snags. Firstly came Philip's Greek connection: fighting was taking place in Greece. The Labour Party backed the People's Liberation Army, which had been supplied with arms to resist the Germans. Many Conservatives considered that these guerilla bands, under Communist leadership, were set on bringing chaos to the country so it was obviously unwise to exacerbate matters at this moment by involvement between the Royal Houses of Britain and Greece. Secondly came Philip's German ancestry, and it was forecast that the British public would never accept a member of the House of Glucksburg as husband to the Heir. It was considered politic to move slowly and it was not until March 1947 that he became plain Lieutenant Philip Mountbatten, RN. Somewhat conveniently, a royal tour took Princess Elizabeth away from Britain for a while, thus allowing the young couple time to ponder on the step which they intended to take and subjecting them to a testing time of absence. Both the King and Queen liked Philip, but they felt that it was coincidence indeed that Lilibet should fall irrevocably in love with the first eligible man she met. They wanted to make sure.

George and Elizabeth, with their happy memories of New Zealand, Australia and Canada, were looking forward to being able to make another Commonwealth tour. In addition, the King was very much in need of the tonic of winter sunshine. Field-Marshal Smuts had suggested the royal family should visit South Africa and that the King should open Parliament in Cape Town. On 1 February 1947 the King and Queen and the Princesses left Portsmouth on board the battleship *Vanguard* which Lilibet had launched in 1944.

The Arctic cold of that never-to-be-forgotten winter closed over Britain. Lumps of coal became precious as jewels, the lights were low, and pangs of conscience pierced the King. There he was, basking in the sunshine while his people shivered and struggled with burst pipes. He was a man who ever thought it his duty to share the hardships of others. He telegraphed the Prime Minister, suggesting that he return. Mr Attlee was adamant that he should not. He commented, in his dry way, that he could not see what even a King could do about the weather.

The South African tour was a repeat of previous successes. The tumultuous reception in Cape Town, where the King decorated Field-Marshal Smuts with the Order of Merit on opening the Union Parliament, was repeated over and over again wherever the 'White Train' halted. This travelling home of the royal family, dressed in ivory and gold, was one third of a mile long, the longest train ever to travel the South African tracks. It was made up of fourteen coaches, eight of which had been shipped from England and six borrowed from the Johannesburg-Cape Town express. It was preceded by a Pilot Train, carrying railway officials and reporters, and followed by a 'Ghost Train', laden with railway spares and equipment.

Port Elizabeth, East London, Bloemfontein, Pietermaritzburg, Durban, Pretoria, Johannesburg, and on to Salisbury, Southern Rhodesia. There again the great event was the State opening of Parliament.

> Every punctilio of Westminster that can be adapted was scrupulously observed. Sir Alan Welsh, the Speaker, wore the same black and gold state robe as his elder brother at St Stephen's; the Sergeant-at-Arms led in the procession of members in English court dress with a mace copied from that of the House of Commons; and when all were assembled came the familiar simple cortége, the King handing the Queen to her throne with the same forms of courtesy as in every Parliament, large or small, in which he had had the opportunity to preside.[15]

At Bulawayo the royal party entered cars and drove out to Matabeleland. They clambered up a rough path in the Matopo Hills to the summit and stood by the granite slab beneath which Cecil Rhodes had been laid in 1902. Rhodes had named this lonely spot in the bush country, 'World's View'. Princess

Elizabeth wandered away on her own, standing, a still slight figure, looking out over the emptiness. The King's eyes followed her. Turning to his wife and the few who stood about him, he said: 'Poor Elizabeth. Already she is realizing that she will be alone and lonely all her life; that no matter who she has by her side, only she can make the final decisions.'[16]

From the Matopo Hills across the Kalahari Desert to Mafeking, steeped in the legend of its siege. Their arrival was a very special occasion for the little town, and a very boisterous one. The bars opened early, resulting in another 'Mafeking Night', just as rowdy as that which had enriched London half a century before. On 20 April the White Train returned to Cape Town. The next day was Princess Elizabeth's twenty-first birthday. There was a march past and a youth rally, and she broadcast to the Commonwealth. At a ball at Government House, she was the star; the King and Queen retired at midnight, leaving Lilibet to dance on towards the dawn.

The 22nd belonged to the Queen. Field-Marshal Smuts, Chancellor of the University of Cape Town, conferred upon her the honorary degree of Doctor of Law. The Queen then made an address. It was the only formal speech she made on the tour, but it was to prove one of the most eloquent that South Africa had ever heard from a member of the Royal Family. She defined the four cardinal virtues of the academic faith – honesty, courage, justice and resolve. But, she added, religious faith was the indispensable foundation. On 24 April *Vanguard* eased out into Table Bay. The guns fired, the bands played and across the sea came the music of the thousands on the waterfront singing 'Auld Lang Syne'.

On 10 July 1947 the Court Circular bore a typewritten addition. It read: 'It is with the greatest pleasure that the King and Queen announce the betrothal of their dearly beloved daughter The Princess Elizabeth to Lieutenant Philip Mountbatten, RN, son of the Late Prince Andrew of Greece and Princess Alice (Princess Alice of Battenberg), to which union the King has gladly given his consent.' On 19 November Philip was created a Royal Highness and Baron Greenwich, Earl of Merioneth and Duke of Edinburgh, and a Knight of the Garter. The next day the couple were married.

George had learned from experience that things can go wrong

at Westminster. He took every precaution but on this occasion the first – and only – mishap came before he reached the Abbey. Except for one dresser, George and Lilibet were alone in the Palace: the Queen had already driven off down the Mall and the staff was gathered in the forecourt to cheer the bride on her way. After one last glance in the mirror, she turned to pick up her bridal bouquet. It was nowhere to be seen. A quick check revealed no clue – it had completely disappeared. Father was called in to help. He too failed to find it and fired off some naval expressions unfitting to a wedding day. As the Teck temper built towards explosion point, the bouquet was discovered in a cupboard where some thoughtful soul had put it to keep cool. The bride was sixty seconds late at Westminster where the Queen waited with some concern. She was, in the interval before the star arrived, the focus of all eyes, particularly for those of the congregation who had seen her come to the Abbey as a bride twenty-four years before. Little had they realized then that she would become Queen. Now, in a proud and precious moment, she was to watch her daughter also marry a descendant of Queen Victoria. Anne Edwards wrote these telling lines about her:

> Not every mother who makes her daughter a star can see the star shine so brightly . . . You could detect the imprint of her personality everywhere. It was the Queen's personality which had shaped the entire wedding. She was the one, it seems, on whom everyone relied to make the tedious decisions. She was the one who knew just where to stop the list of invitations, knew how to welcome delightedly people she did not know very well and had not seen for years. It was the Queen who (present at every fitting) finally decided the details of the wedding gown, who asked also for the details of the clothes to be kept a secret because she meant this to be her daughter's day. How like each other the two are! Their voices are almost the same; their mannerisms, as they wave from the royal cars, their knack of perking up interest at the right thing; most of all, perhaps, their clothes . . .[17]

In the evening crowds packed the streets to cheer Elizabeth and Philip on their way to honeymoon at Broadlands, the Hampshire home of Lord and Lady Mountbatten. The next time the people gathered in strength for a royal occasion it was for one which belonged exclusively to King George VI and his Queen.

26 April 1948 was their Silver Wedding Day. In the morning, in the brilliant sunshine, they drove with a Sovereign's Escort of the Household Cavalry to St Paul's for the Thanksgiving Service. In the afternoon they drove through twenty-two miles of London's streets. In the evening they were called out so many times on to the balcony of Buckingham Palace that an observer remarked they must have been dizzy. George wrote to Queen Mary that he and Elizabeth were both dumbfounded by their reception and also by the flood of congratulatory letters which had reached them from all over the world.

Perhaps they may not have realized how successful they had been in their tasks, but for many the Archbishop of Canterbury's words in the Cathedral that morning said it all: 'The Nation and the Empire bless God that He has set such a family at the seat of our Royalty.'

16

Curtainfall

George was exasperated by illness and a bad patient. He was energetic by nature, a stubborn worker who pushed his strength and stamina far harder than they could withstand. Neither the frailty nor the strength of will in him were perhaps fully appreciated by Edward VIII at the time of his abdication. When, in January 1948, he began to suffer from cramp in the legs, he made light of it, though he kept a private check on the symptoms. On holiday at Balmoral in August, relaxing, picnicking in the hills, there was an improvement; but by October his left leg was numb all day, then the pain shifted to the right.

The relapse couldn't have come at a worse time, on three counts. Firstly, the royal programme was packed: the King and Queen of Denmark arrived on a visit; Parliament was to be opened in state for the first time since the war; there was a full scale review of the Territorial Army in Hyde Park; and on 7 November there was the Remembrance Service at the Cenotaph. Secondly, preparations were in full swing for a visit in 1949 by the King, the Queen and Princess Margaret to Australia and New Zealand. Thirdly, and of the closest personal interest to George, Princess Elizabeth was expecting her first baby.

It wasn't until the end of October that the King found time to consult Sir Morton Smart, his manipulative surgeon. Sir Morton was appalled at what he discovered. He called in other specialists, including Professor Learmouth, a leading authority on vascular complaints, whose diagnosis specified an early state of arteriosclerosis. There was a danger of gangrene setting in, which would necessitate amputation of the right leg. All doctors agreed that the tour of Australia and New Zealand must be postponed. This upset

George exceedingly. He wanted very much to go; he hated the thought of letting people down and rebelled at what he considered to be 'giving in', something foreign to his nature. He proved just as obdurate as had been his grandfather, Edward VII, when told in June 1902 that he had peritonitis and would have to postpone his Coronation. The doctors talked with the Queen, the Queen talked with her husband and, very reluctantly, he gave in. The following bulletin was issued:

> The King is suffering from an obstruction to the circulation through the arteries of the legs, which has only recently become acute; the defective blood supply to the right foot causes anxiety. Complete rest has been advised and treatment to improve the circulation in the legs has been initiated and must be maintained for an immediate and prolonged period. Though His Majesty's general health, including the condition of his heart, gives no reason for concern, there is no doubt that the strain of the last twelve years has appreciably affected his resistance to physical fatigue.

At least he had the consolation of knowing that he would not be parted from Lilibet and her child.

November proved a dramatic month for the Queen. In one wing of the Palace Princess Elizabeth awaited her baby, in another the King lay, still under the threat of amputation. It was vital that neither should be worried about the other though George did fret about Lilibet, natural enough with a first child but a worry exacerbated by his own state of health. Fortunately there were no complications but there might well have been had Lilibet known the full and sombre truth about her father. So the Queen moved, smiling, from room to room, comforting and encouraging each. Undoubtedly for her there were memories of Bruton Street in 1926: in the new nursery was the cot in which Lilibet had been placed when she was born; beside it was the wickerwork Moses basket in which she had been carried back and forth from her mother's room. But for the spectre of gangrene, these would have been roseate days. On 10 November Lilibet went to the cinema. At a quarter past nine on the evening of the 14th her baby was born.* Prince Philip was

* On 15 December the baby Prince was christened Charles Philip Arthur George, in the Music Room at Buckingham Palace.

playing squash; he rushed upstairs and was in time with a big bouquet of roses and carnations before she closed her eyes to rest.[1]

Becoming a grandfather had a profound and, to those about him, a most satisfactory effect upon George. He began to relax, to be an excellent patient and to do exactly what he was told. He hated being confined to bed, but now put up with it with a grin. On 18 January he was able to shoot for a short while at Sandringham; he believed himself well on the road to complete recovery. He was due for a shock. In March his doctors told him that if his existing improvement were to be maintained, he would have to live the life of an invalid. They recommended, as an alternative, that he underwent an operation to relieve the thrombosis.

George's temper flared. 'So all our treatment has been a waste of time,' he thundered. It had to be pointed out to him that but for the treatment and the convalescence, he might have had to face the amputation of his right leg. The doctors knew the King could never play the role of invalid. He knew it himself. And there was another point to consider: would the public, in its entirety, accept a King who could do but half his task? He remembered clearly the prophecies of 1936 that he would be only a 'rubber-stamp' monarch. He had proved otherwise, but he could not have faced the same questions again at fifty-three. A lumbar sympathectomy was accordingly performed. Crowds gathered outside the Palace; there was heart-felt relief when the newspaper sellers ran among them, their placards bearing the words: 'He's all right!'

In April 1949 the Conference of Commonwealth Prime Ministers opened in London. On the 27 May they made the following declaration:

> The Governments of the United Kingdom, Canada, Australia, New Zealand, South Africa, India, Pakistan and Ceylon, whose countries are united as Members of the British Commonwealth of Nations and owe a common allegiance to the Crown, which is also their symbol of their free association, have considered the impending constitutional changes in India.
>
> The Government of India have informed the other Governments of the Commonwealth of the intention of the Indian people that under the new constitution which is about to be adopted India shall become a

> sovereign independent Republic. The Government of India have, however, declared and affirmed India's desire to continue her full membership of the Commonwealth of Nations and her acceptance of the King as the symbol of the free association of its independent member nations and as such the Head of the Commonwealth.
>
> The Governments of the other countries of the Commonwealth, the basis of whose membership of the Commonwealth is not hereby changed, accept and recognize India's continuing membership in accordance with the terms of the declaration.
>
> Accordingly the United Kingdom, Canada, Australia, New Zealand, South Africa, India, Pakistan and Ceylon hereby declare that they remain united as free and equal members of the Commonwealth of Nations, freely co-operating in the pursuit of peace, liberty and progress.

It was some boost to the King's morale that he had been acknowledged Head of the Commonwealth of Nations; it was a personal tribute to him and a wider tribute to British leadership. Beneath that awareness, however, there was a kind of resistance, a reluctance for change to come too fast, too soon. It had been drummed into him since boyhood that tradition and leadership were all, and in 1936 with the Crown he had assumed the mantle of Queen Victoria, of Edward VII and George V. He had already survived periods of great change, both personally on becoming King, and as King with Britain's altered society and the independence of India. As he weakened physically it seemed to him that a parallel diminution of his role had been accomplished which he was powerless to prevent, and which robbed him of a large part of his meaning. At times it appeared as though changes, great and small, were being made almost for change's sake. The old order had to go, whether it be private ownership of services and industry, the colour of railway carriages or the design of stamps; and at some of this George baulked.

Despite the barometer reactions of his mood to such events, his health overall picked up. In June he was able to watch the Trooping of the Colour from an open carriage and he attended Ascot races. A holiday at Balmoral speeded his recovery. For hill-climbing he used a long trace, one end of which was fastened round his waist and the other attached to a pony. To offset the risk of the pony bolting, a quick-release mechanism was incorporated in the trace.

That year saw rapid deterioration in Britain's economic state; a repeat of the 1931 crisis was feared in most quarters, and by the King. The Chancellor of the Exchequer, Sir Stafford Cripps, had talks in Washington and returned with some relief for the country's problems, the United States having realized that Great Britain must not be allowed to go to the wall. American investments were increased and the terms of Britain's eligibility for Marshall Aid widened. In his Christmas broadcast the King said:

> We are deeply grateful to our good friends in the United States for the imagination and sympathy with which they first realized our problems and then to work to help us over them. Without this understanding help we could not have made the progress towards recovery that has already been achieved.

In January 1950 Mr Attlee requested a dissolution of Parliament. At the ensuing General Election Labour won 315 seats, Conservatives and National Liberals 298 and Liberals 9. The small overall majority led to increased strain on both the Prime Minister and the King. In the last century no greater burden had been placed upon a government, and this was increased in June when the North Korean War broke out.

'Naked aggression and it must be checked,' was the comment of Mr Attlee. On the acceptance of the proposal of the United States that the United Nations should give support, a brigade was despatched from Britain. It became part of the Commonwealth Division. At home opinion was sharply divided as to how far, in terms of territory and in terms of men, the support should go. Many saw in the conflict the beginnings of a Third World War, and the split between Labour and Conservatives widened still further. Finance was a major problem, defence spending having been drastically cut. In July Mr Shinwell, Minister of Defence, announced that a further £100 million should be allotted to armaments, though Mr Churchill was of the opinion that his proposals were 'few and far between'. Once more, on a personal front, relations between the United States and Britain were eased by the rapport between the King and Queen and Mr Lewis Douglas, US Ambassador to Britain from 1947 to 1950. It was from Mr and Mrs Douglas that they learned even more about American ways and slant of thinking. It was a close friendship, strengthened by their delightful daughter, Sharman, who became an intimate friend of the Princesses. Now Americans were seen more frequently at Royal functions, and the Queen in particular became deeply interested in the English Speaking Union, and the exchange of school-teachers between the two countries.

During the summer of 1950 her interest, and that of her husband, was focussed on the birth of Princess Elizabeth's second child. The Queen, remembering the tension which the King had undergone on the previous occasion, packed him off to Balmoral, knowing that otherwise he would be constantly on the telephone to Clarence House, into which the Princess and her husband had moved in 1949. It was fortunate that she did so, for Princess Anne arrived late, on 15 August. Her father was out in the hills, and it was an hour before a gillie found him and told him the news.

George looked an old man now. There were streaks of silver in his thinning hair and the strain of life showed in the lines on his face. It was noticed that, whenever possible, he sat down. He still held firm to his resolve to visit New Zealand and Australia in 1952 but before that he had to weather 1951, the year of the Festival of Britain.

The Festival marked the hundredth anniversary of the Great International Exhibition at the Crystal Palace in Hyde Park in 1851. Master-minded by Prince Albert, that had been a gigantic success and a milestone in the nineteenth century; now Mr Herbert Morrison slipped in to the Prince's shoes and was nicknamed 'Lord Festival'. A more immediate intention of the 1951 Festival was to demonstrate the strength of recovery of the British people, although the country's financial position was still precarious and the news from Korea depressing. London prepared its Exhibition on the South Bank and its Fun Fair in Battersea Park, and celebratory programmes were staged throughout the country. The King was very much in demand; he visited the Midlands and Cambridge in April. On 3 May he and the Queen drove to St Paul's to attend the service which initiated the Festival. Queen Mary was with them. She wrote: 'A hundred years ago today, my mother was present at the Opening of the 1851 – when she was 17 – & now I, her daughter, was present at this opening at the age of nearly 84 – Lovely service – most impressive, Bertie's speech on the steps of St Paul's was very good.' The old Queen was in the royal party which toured the South Bank Exhibition the following day. She considered it 'really extraordinary & very ugly'.[2] It was noted that the King was not in the best of humours and that he was very impatient.

On the morning of the 24th he went in state to Westminster Abbey for the installation of the Duke of Gloucester as Great Master of the Order of the Bath. In the afternoon he visited the Imperial Institute in South Kensington. That evening he retired to bed with influenza. A visit to Northern Ireland, where a busy programme awaited him, in June was cancelled. The curtain had fallen on his public life. The Queen went to Belfast alone and each evening rang up to find how her husband was progressing. She was due to go on to Scotland to fulfil engagements there, but the news she received on the telephone caused her to return direct to London. Throughout June and July the King rested at Buckingham Palace and in his beloved garden at the Royal Lodge. On 3 August the royal family travelled to Balmoral.

One of the reasons for the purchase of the Deeside residence by Queen Victoria and Prince Albert had been the bracing quality of the air. It most certainly is bracing but, over the years, it had proved deceptive too: it had allowed people in poor physical shape to consider themselves fitter than they really were. It had happened to Prince Albert; now it happened to his great-grandson. George always perked up when he reached Balmoral and this August was no exception. Finding that he could manage a full day's shooting without undue fatigue, he overstretched the mark. When the weather turned cold and wet, he still went out with the guns and developed a chill and sore throat.

It was the Queen who suspected that the cold was indicative of a state beyond a minor ailment, and it was she who insisted that specialists should be summoned from London. Dr George Cordiner, radiologist, and Dr Geoffrey Marshall, chest specialist, duly arrived. They wanted to examine more closely and on 7 September the King travelled to London to attend Dr Cordiner's consulting room in Upper Wimpole Street. X-rays were taken.

The King flew back to Balmoral and on arrival announced, disgustedly: 'Now they say there's something wrong with me blowers!'[3]

Two days later came the verdict. A sample of tissue had to be removed on the 16th for examination and this confirmed previous suspicions: the King was suffering from a malignant growth. At a medical conference the doctors agreed that the whole of the left lung should be removed. The King was informed of this, and agreed, but he wasn't told that he had cancer – he never knew, although his wife did. There were two major risks in the operation, which was performed by Mr Price Thomas on the 23rd. The first was that a coronary thrombosis might occur, bringing about the patient's death. The second was that, as certain nerves of the larynx would have to be sacrificed, he might never speak above a whisper again. Neither of these dangers materialized and in fact the King made satisfactory recovery progress. But the doctors had found that the other lung was affected. Sir Harold Graham Hodgson, royal radiologist for many years, gave his private opinion: 'The King is not likely to live more than eighteen months. The end will probably come suddenly. The operation was six months too late.'[4] Still the King was kept in ignorance. He wrote to Queen Mary:

> At least I am feeling a bit better after all I have been through in the last 3 weeks. I do seem to go through the most serious operations anybody can do, but thank goodness there were no complications & everything has gone according to plan. I have been most beautifully looked after from the surgeon to the nurses & doctors . . . I have been sitting up in a chair for the last week & have had my meals up as well. So I am getting strong & can walk to the bathroom.[5]

Meanwhile the Government was staggering along on its tiny majority, members even being brought from hospitals if necessary so that they might vote and stave off defeat. The King had been in touch with the Prime Minister about the unstable position since June: Mr Attlee said that he would ask for a Dissolution in the autumn, but he did not give a date. The King took action on his own account. On 18 September he saw Mr Attlee to inform him of the forthcoming operation. They talked of the political situation.

The King, bearing in mind the possibility that the operation might not prove successful and wishing to make sure that there would be a stable Government should his daughter have to succeed, proposed that a General Election should be held without delay. He asked the Prime Minister if he would agree. Mr Attlee jumped at the suggestion. This was 'a striking illustration that the Crown still plays an active part in the workings of British politics'.[6]

The Conservatives won, but had a majority of only seventeen. On 26 October seventy-six-year-old Mr Churchill drove to Buckingham Palace and once again became Prime Minister.

These were crowded days for the Queen. As a Counsellor of State she was doing much of a Sovereign's work. She was a nurse to her husband; often, during his bad days, he would call for her and, on being told, she would hurry to his room and hold his hand. She was also keeping up with her own public programme, which included the opening of an extension to the Royal Free Hospital School of Medicine of the University of London, when she paid tribute to the care which her husband had received. In addition she was a part-time 'Nanny', for she had the care of Prince Charles and Princess Anne while their parents were in Canada and America. Princess Elizabeth and Prince Philip proved an overwhelming success in Canada, where they visited every province of the Dominion. It was 1939 all over again. The same can be said of the United States, where they were guests of the President. King George received the following letter from Mr Truman: 'We've just had a visit from a lovely young lady and her personable husband . . . As one father to another, we can be very proud of our daughters. You have the better of me – because you have two!'[7]

The King came from the sickroom on 30 November and motored to Windsor to weekend at the Royal Lodge. As well as the Lodge being a loved and familiar home, there were other attractions near at hand. He was particularly proud of the paintings at Windsor; he was a traditionalist in art as in most things and loved the historical associations in these pictures. He took an active part in the restoration of the Royal Collection, watching with attention as his favourite paintings were cleaned, among them Gainsborough's group of the three eldest daughters of George III.

He had joined with Elizabeth in commissioning some new works, and John Piper was asked to make water-colours and drawings of Windsor. On 10 December he revoked the mandate of the Counsellors of State and took up his burden once again. He celebrated his fifty-sixth birthday at Buckingham Palace and pre-recorded his Christmas message, a sentence at a time. The task took two days. He wrote to Mr Lionel Logue about this, saying he had had trouble with his throat but that the disability was passing. He added that the doctors had assured him he had completely recovered from his operation in September, and that he was looking forward to leading a normal, healthy life.[8]

On the 21st the royal family left for Sandringham. The King told his doctors: 'You have had your fun. Now I am going to have mine.'[9] And by fun, he meant shooting. There were lighted Christmas trees on the platform of Wolferton Station to greet the largest royal gathering since before the war. Queen Mary lent tradition and memory, but in the main it was a children's festival. Princess Elizabeth and Prince Philip were there with Charles and Anne, the Duke and Duchess of Gloucester with William and Richard, and the Duchess of Kent with Edward, Alexandra and Michael. Prince Charles was now of an age when he could appreciate the thrill of Christmas and gave endless delight to his grandparents.

George went out shooting and, to his relief, found that his skill had not been impaired. He wore an electrically heated waistcoat and boots, and used special ammunition designed to lessen the force of recoil on the shoulder. On 29 January 1952 he saw his doctors at Buckingham Palace. They were well pleased with him and, to celebrate the good news, next evening the King took his family to see *South Pacific* at Drury Lane. It was also a farewell party, for Lilibet and Philip were leaving next day for East Africa, on the first leg of their journey to Australia, the tour which the King and Queen had much looked forward to making themselves.

George and Elizabeth stood on the tarmac at London Airport and watched the Argonaut climb into the south-eastern sky. It was early afternoon and the wind blew cold across the flatness. The King wore no hat and the thinning hair frisked about his forehead. On his face, behind the half-smiling mask, was the imprint of deep sadness. His eyes were fixed on the speck in the sky, and his right hand was held high in farewell. He was a ghost figure, detached from the crowded scene about him. Elizabeth touched his arm, telling him that it was time to go. They had tea with Queen Mary and returned to Sandringham. Soon, they consoled themselves, they would be in the sunshine themselves, for they had accepted the offer of Dr Malan, Prime Minister of South Africa, to holiday in a private house near Durban; they planned to leave in the second week of March.

On Tuesday, 5 February, the Queen and Princess Margaret went out to lunch. The King was shooting, for it was a 'Keepers' Day'. There were twenty guns in the party – tenants, police and gamekeepers – and the weather was perfect – dry, sunny and cold. The ground was hard underfoot and the mating partridges called their song of spring across the fields. The hares ran fast. Almost an echo of his first-ever bag, with his last three shots of the afternoon, George killed.[10] He said to his friends: 'A good day's sport, gentlemen. I will expect you here at nine o'clock on Thursday.'[11]

Meanwhile Elizabeth and Meg had lunched with Mr Edward Seago, the artist, at his riverside home at Ludham. Afterwards they boarded the motor cruiser *Sandra* and went with him to Barton Broad, taking tea at Barton Hall. They were late back, bringing with them the pictures which Seago had been commissioned to make of Sandringham. Elizabeth went straight to the King's room, as she always did, to say that she was back and to see how he was. She found him well and in good spirits. They went together to the hall where the pictures had been set out and had a happy time looking at them.[12] There was much fun and laughter over dinner and George was like his old self. They looked at the pictures again and Meg played the piano. Then George walked to the kennels: the paw of his golden retriever had been cut by a thorn and he wished to check that the wound was clean. He came back through the gardens. They listened to the BBC news and heard that all was well with Lilibet and Philip. Picking up a countryman's magazine George went early to rest. 'I'll see you in the morning,' he said, leaving Elizabeth sitting by the fireside.

But for him there was no morning.

17

Postscript

THE SIXTH OF FEBRUARY 1982 . . . for many the ghost of King George VI stalked the day, yet only those who have reached middle age can really remember him now. But for those many never has thirty years appeared so short a space, partly for the reason that the woman who was his wife and helpmate marched on as assuredly as she had done in 1952. She has changed so little, the same smile, the same stamp on her dress, fulfilling much the same programme of royal engagements – as, in fact, she has been doing since 1923. She said, in her message to the British people when George died, 'My only wish is now that I may be allowed to continue the work we sought to do together.'

Elizabeth stood foursquare to the tragedy of early widowhood. On the evening of the day of her husband's death she came downstairs to play with Charles and Ann. She said: 'I've got to start some time and it might as well be now.' She went with George as the wagon carried his coffin across the park to the little church of St Mary Magdalene, where the people of his beloved Sandringham said their special goodbye. She was with him, in the darkness, as the procession wove its stately way from Westminster Hall to Paddington and on to Windsor. As the strong shoulders carried his coffin into St George's Chapel where fifty-one years before, he had watched the funeral of Queen Victoria, he was still the star, Elizabeth still his leading lady. When she came out, alone, into the blaze of flowers which covered the turf and the cold stones, the leading lady had switched her role, and was now the mother of the Queen. By the springtime she was back in harness, helping Queen Elizabeth II as she settled into her reign, helping to prepare for the Coronation. She suffered the loss of another link with her husband on 24 March 1953, when Queen Mary died and the flag above Marlborough House came fluttering down at the close of the long story of 'May' of Teck. Between then and now she has established herself as a world figure in her own right. She has travelled widely in Australia, Canada and Africa; she was the first member of the royal family to circumnavigate the globe by air. She is a frequent, and most welcome, visitor to Europe; she has had audience of the Pope in the Vatican. In 1954 she travelled to America: Mr Lewis Douglas had launched a fund to commemorate King George VI, a plan backed by President and Mrs Eisenhower, and now his widow was to be presented with the result. The substantial sum raised was devoted to the technical training in America of young people from the Commonwealth. She triumphed in New York as she had done in 1939. The *World-Telegram* described her as 'the royal lady with peaches-and-cream complexion and twinkling orbs'. She chatted again with Mrs Eleanor Roosevelt; she was entertained by President Eisenhower in Washington. She came back from the United States with a new title: the American people had christened her 'The Queen Mum'.

At home she has most amply fulfilled the wish that she should be able to continue the work begun by her husband and herself. She is committed to the welfare of hospitals, charities and institutions caring for the good of the young and the handicapped. She has occupied prominent posts, such as the Chancellor of London University and Lord Warden of the Cinque Ports. She has been the darling of the Services. She has given her brilliant support, and her love, to the arts. She has become a leading figure in the sport of steeplechasing, continuing to race her husband's horses, then becoming a leading owner in her own right. She has retained her interest in horticulture and put her gifted touch to the gardens of Birkhall and Castle of Mey. Day after day, through all the years, she has fulfilled the programme of inspections, dinners, receptions, State functions.

Above all, in both her public and her private life, she has set an example which is unrivalled in the history of public figures. Never, since she went to Westminster as a bride in April 1923 until the Diamond Jubilee of that day, has there been criticism of her word or deed. Sadness may be mixed with a sense of achievement but looking back to the beginning of it all Her Majesty the Queen Mother can say, as once she said: memories are the second happiness.

NOTES

CHAPTER 1

1. 21 December 1895
2. In the *London Gazette*
3. Wheeler-Bennett, p. 6
4. Nicolson, p. 55
5. Marquess of Carisbrooke
6. Pope-Hennessy, p. 35
7. *Ibid.*, p. 62
8. *Ibid.*, p. 222
9. *Eugenie and Napoleon III*, p. 276
10. *Ibid.*
11. *Queen Victoria's Letters*
12. Pope-Hennessy, p. 302
13. Gould Lee, p. 297
14. Gore, p. 137

CHAPTER 2

1. Wheeler-Bennett, p. 18
2. Pope-Hennessy, p. 366
3. *Ibid.*, p. 367
4. *Kings, Commoners and Me*
5. *Ibid.*
6. Pope-Hennessy, p. 372
7. Windsor, Duke of, pp. 18–30
8. Villiers, p. 317
9. Wheeler-Bennett, Chapter II (II)
10. Private information

CHAPTER 3

1. In the *Illustrated London News*
2. *Ibid.*
3. *Daily Telegraph*, 26 May 1980
4. Asquith, p. 53
5. *The Sphere*, 28 April 1923
6. *Ibid.*
7. *Illustrated London News*, 28 April 1923
8. Private information
9. 27 May 1865
10. *Live Wires*
11. Wentworth Day, p. 15

CHAPTER 4

1. Hatch, p. 71
2. Lee, Vol. II, p. 331
3. *Ibid.*, p. 332
4. *Sunday Express*, 15 September 1957
5. Verney, p. 37
6. Wheeler-Bennett, p. 32
7. Frankland, p. 4
8. Windsor, Duke of, p. 59ff.
9. *Sunday Express*, 15 September 1957
10. Wheeler-Bennett, p. 57
11. Verney, p. 48
12. Nicolson, p. 14
13. Pope-Hennessy, p. 480

CHAPTER 5

1. Asquith, p. 83
2. Bolitho: *George VI*, p. 58
3. R.A. G.V. Q. 832/366
4. Eye-witness report, quoted in Stuart, p. 45
5. Bolitho: *George VI*, p. 68
6. Despatch from HMS *Collingwood*
7. D. M. Stuart, p. 47
8. Wheeler-Bennett, p. 97
9. Bolitho: *George VI*, p. 70
10. In a letter to his father

CHAPTER 6

1. *Daily Mirror*, 17 January 1923
2. Bolitho: *George VI*, p. 112
3. Wheeler-Bennett, p. 135
4. *Ibid.*, p. 131
5. Hatch, p. 186
6. Airlie, p. 166
7. *Ibid.*
8. *Ibid.*, p. 167

CHAPTER 7

1. *Daily Mirror*
2. Wheeler-Bennett, p. 153
3. Chatwyn, p. 74
4. *The Light of Common Day*
5. Wentworth Day, p. 98
6. *Ibid.*, p. 101
7. Wheeler-Bennett, p. 193
8. Wakeford, p. 79
9. *Elizabeth of Glamis*, p. 89
10. Wheeler-Bennett, p. 203

CHAPTER 8

1. Wheeler-Bennett, p. 213
2. Battiscombe, p. 136
3. Bryan and Murphy, p. 58
4. Marie Louise, p. 303
5. Colville, p. 128
6. Airlie, p. 202
7. Lacey, p. 122
8. Windsor, Duke of, p. 193
9. Private information
10. Hatch, p. 124
11. Bolitho: *Edward VIII*, p. 205
12. Wheeler-Bennett, p. 232
13. *Elizabeth of Glamis*, p. 114
14. Gore, p. 388
15. *Diana Cooper*
16. Christopher of Greece, p. 164
17. Airlie, p. 197
18. *Elizabeth of Glamis*, p. 154
19. Quoted in Wheeler-Bennett, pp. 260–2
20. Gore, p. 430
21. Watson, p. 279

CHAPTER 9

1. Pope-Hennessy, p. 559
2. In the *Daily Express*
3. Windsor, Duchess of, p. 225
4. Windsor, Duke of, p. 311
5. Pope-Hennessy, p. 568
6. Wheeler-Bennett, p. 273
7. Pope-Hennessy, p. 574
8. Wheeler-Bennett, p. 277
9. *Ibid.*, p. 280
10. Windsor, Duke of, p. 335
11. *Elizabeth of Glamis*, p. 173
12. Wheeler-Bennett, p. 285
13. Pope-Hennessy, p. 578
14. Wheeler-Bennett, p. 285
15. Lacey, p. 75

16. Windsor, Duke of, p. 400
17. Bryan and Murphy, p. 272
18. Wheeler-Bennett, p. 286
19. *Ibid.*, pp. 286–287
20. Pope-Hennessy, p. 581

CHAPTER 10

1. Pope-Hennessy, p. 583
2. Wheeler-Bennett, p. 309
3. *Ibid.*
4. *Ibid.*, p. 296
5. *Ibid.*, p. 744
6. Pope-Hennessy, p. 583
7. 22 May 1937
8. Quoted in Wheeler-Bennett, pp. 312–13
9. *Ibid.*
10. *The Sphere*, 22 May 1937
11. *Thatched with Gold*
12. Wheeler-Bennett, p. 737
13. Hartnell, p. 94
14. Wheeler-Bennett, p. 316
15. *The Candid Eye of Cecil Beaton*
16. Hartnell, p. 96
17. *Ibid.*, p. 97

CHAPTER 11

1. *The Sphere*, 13 May 1939
2. Quoted in Wheeler-Bennett, p. 372
3. Young, p. 23
4. *Ibid.*, p. 41
5. Quoted in Wheeler-Bennett, p. 378
6. Hartnell, p. 99
7. Wheeler-Bennett, p. 380
8. Wakeford, p. 177
9. Royal Archives
10. Eaton, p. 143
11. *Ibid.*, p. 385
12. Wheeler-Bennett, p. 387
13. *Ibid.*
14. *Ibid.*, pp. 183–4
15. Young, p. 257
16. *This I Remember*
17. Young, p. 273

CHAPTER 12

1. Nicolson: *Diaries and Letters, 1930–39*
2. Young, p. 314
3. *Ibid.*, p. 308
4. Wheeler-Bennett, pp. 392–3
5. *Ibid.*
6. Crawford, p. 59ff.

CHAPTER 13

1. Nicolson: *Diaries and Letters, 1939–1945*, p. 97
2. *Elizabeth of Glamis*, p. 243
3. Nicolson: *Diaries and Letters, 1939–1945*, p. 97
4. Wheeler-Bennett, p. 439
5. Amery, Vol. III, pp. 368–9
6. A. J. P. Taylor. *Sunday Express*, 29 September 1957
7. Wheeler-Bennett, p. 446
8. *The English War*
9. Letters from George VI to Mr Roosevelt and Mr Roosevelt to George VI, are quoted in Wheeler-Bennett
10. *Ibid.*, p. 458
11. Churchill, Vol. II
12. Eaton, p. 167

13. *Ibid.*, p. 168
14. *This I Remember*
15. Eaton, p. 169

CHAPTER 14

1. At the unveiling of King George VI's Memorial in the Mall on 21 October 1955
2. *Sunday Express*, 22 September 1957
3. *Ibid.*
4. Hibbert, p. 280
5. Quoted in Wheeler-Bennett, p. 568
6. Macmillan, p. 345
7. Wheeler-Bennett, p. 569
8. Macmillan, pp. 349–50
9. Wheeler-Bennett, p. 570
10. Pope-Hennessy, p. 607
11. Quoted in Wheeler-Bennett, p. 605
12. Macmillan, p. 525
13. Quoted in Wheeler-Bennett, p. 619

CHAPTER 15

1. A. J. P. Taylor in the *Sunday Express*, 22 September 1957
2. Quoted in Wheeler-Bennett, p. 627
3. *Ibid.*, p. 637
4. *Ibid.*, pp. 643–44
5. Royal Archives, 28 July 1945
6. Wheeler-Bennett, p. 654
7. Airlie, pp. 224–8
8. Plumptre, p. 29
9. Shewell-Cooper, p. 21
10. Airlie, p. 225
11. Quoted in Buxton
12. *Ibid.*, p. 8
13. Quoted in Wheeler-Bennett, p. 703
14. *Ibid.*, p. 716
15. *The Royal Family in Africa*
16. *Elizabeth of Glamis*, p. 281
17. In the *Daily Express*

CHAPTER 16

1. Lacey, p. 168
2. Pope-Hennessy, p. 617
3. *Elizabeth of Glamis*p. 302
4. *Sunday Express*, 6 February 1972
5. Wheeler-Bennett, p. 790
6. A. J. P. Taylor in the *Sunday Express*, 29 September 1957
7. Quoted in Wheeler-Bennett, p. 799
8. *Sunday Express*, 6 February 1972
9. A. J. P. Taylor in the *Sunday Express*, 29 September 1957
10. Buxton, pp. 137–8
11. A. J. P. Taylor, *Ibid.*
12. Goodman, p. 213

BIBLIOGRAPHY

Airlie, Mabell, Countess of *Thatched with Gold* 1962
Alice, HRH Princess, of Athlone *For My Grandchildren* 1966
Amery, Leo *My Political Life* (3 vols.) 1953–5
Anon *Our King and Queen* 1937
Arthur, Sir George *King George V* 1934
Asquith, Lady Cynthia *The Married Life of the Duchess of York* 1933
Asquith, Lady Cynthia *Queen Elizabeth* 1937

Battiscombe, Georgina *Queen Alexandra* 1969
Beaton, Cecil *The Candid Eye of Cecil Beaton* 1961
Benson, E. F. *King Edward VII* 1933
Bolitho, Hector *Edward VIII* 1937
Bolitho, Hector *George VI* 1937
Broad, Lewis *The Abdication* 1961
Bryan, J. and Murphy, C. J. V. *The Windsor Story* 1979
Bryant, Arthur *George V* 1936
Buchan, John *The King's Grace* 1935
Buckle, G. E. (ed.) *Letters of Queen Victoria*, 2nd and 3rd series
Buxton, Aubrey *The King in His Country* 1955

Carey, M. C. *Princess Mary* 1922
Channon, Sir Henry *Chips: The Diaries of Sir Henry Channon* 1967
Chatwyn, Alys *The Duchess of York* 1927
Christopher, Prince, of Greece *Memoirs* 1938
Churchill, Sir Winston *The Second World War* (6 vols.) 1948–54
Colville, Lady Cynthia *Crowded Life* 1963
Connell, Brian *Manifest Destiny* 1953
Cookridge, E. H. *From Battenberg to Mountbatten* 1966
Crawford, Marion *The Little Princesses* 1950
Cresswell, Mrs G. *Eighteen Years on Sandringham Estate* 1887
Curzon, Marchioness of Kedleston *Reminiscences* 1955

Darbyshire, Taylor *King George VI* 1937
Dennis, Geoffrey *Coronation Commentary* 1937
Dent, H. C. *Milestones to the Silver Jubilee* 1935
Domville-Fife, Charles W. *King George VI and His Empire* 1937
Donaldson, Frances *Edward VIII* 1974
Duff, David *Alexandra: Princess and Queen* 1980
Duff, David *Elizabeth of Glamis* 1973

Eaton, Jeanette *The Story of Eleanor Roosevelt* 1956
Ellis, Jennifer *The Royal Mother* 1954
Emden, Paul H. *Behind the Throne* 1934

Frankland, Noble *Prince Henry, Duke of Gloucester* 1980
Fulford, Roger *Dearest Child* 1964

Goldsmith, Barbara *Little Gloria . . . Happy at Last* 1980
Goodman, Jean *Edward Seago* 1978
Gore, John *King George V: A Personal Memoir* 1941
Gorman, Major J. T. *George VI: King and Emperor* 1937
Gould Lee, A. (ed.) *The Empress Frederick writes to Sophie* 1955
Graham, Evelyn *Edward P.* 1929
Gunther, John *Roosevelt in Retrospect* 1950

Hartnell, Norman *Silver and Gold* 1955
Hatch, Alden *The Mountbattens* 1965
Hibbert, Christopher *The Court at Windsor* 1964

Judd, Denis *George VI* 1982

Kinloch Cooke, C. *HRH Princess Mary Adelaide, Duchess of Teck* 1900

Lacey, Robert *Majesty* 1977
Laird, Dorothy *Queen Elizabeth the Queen Mother* 1966
Lee, Sir Sidney *King Edward VII* 1925
Longford, Elizabeth *Victoria R. I.* 1964

Macmillan, Harold *The Blast of War* 1967
Magnus, Philip *King Edward the Seventh* 1964
Maine, Basil *Edward VIII: Duke of Windsor* n.d.
Makin, W. J. *The Life of King George the Fifth* 1936
Marie Louise, H. H. Princess *My Memories of Six Reigns* 1956
Massey, Gertrude *Kings, Commoners and Me* 1934
Masson, Madeleine *Edwina* 1958
McGill, A. and Thomson, K. *Live Wires* 1982
Morrah, Dermot *The Royal Family in Africa* 1947

Nicolson, Harold *Diaries and Letters 1930–1939* 1966
Nicolson, Harold *Diaries and Letters 1939–1945* 1967
Nicolson, Harold *King George the Fifth* 1952
Norwich, Viscount *Old Men Forget* 1953

Petrie, Sir Charles *Monarchy in the Twentieth Century* 1952
Plumptre, George *Royal Gardens* 1981
Ponsonby, Sir Frederick *Recollections of Three Reigns* 1951
Pope-Hennessy, James *Queen Mary: 1867–1953* 1959

Roosevelt, Eleanor *This I Remember* 1949

St Aubyn, Giles *Edward VII, Prince and King* 1979
St Aubyn, Giles *The Royal George* 1963
Salusbury, F. G. H. *King Emperor's Jubilee* 1935
Sayers, Dorothy L. *The English War* 1942
Sheppard, Edgar (ed.) *George, Duke of Cambridge* 1907
Shewell-Cooper, W. E. *The Royal Gardeners* 1962
Stuart, James (Viscount Stuart of Findhorn) *Within the Fringe* 1967
Stuart, Dorothy Margaret *King George the Sixth* 1937

Tschumi, Gabriel *Royal Chef* 1954

Verney, Major F. E. *HRH* 1926
Villiers, George *A Vanished Victorian* 1938

Wakeford, Geoffrey *Thirty Years a Queen* 1968
Watson, Francis *Dawson of Penn* 1951
Wentworth Day, James *The Queen Mother's Family Story* 1967
Wheeler-Bennett, John W. *King George VI* 1958
Windsor, Duchess of *The Heart has its Reasons* 1956
Windsor, HRH, Duke of *A King's Story* 1951
Woodward, Kathleen *Queen Mary* n.d.

Young, Gordon *Voyage of State* 1939

Ziegler, Philip *Diana Cooper* 1981

INDEX